W9-BVU-432

THE ANATOMY OF DRAMA

THE ANATOMY OF DRAMA

Alan Reynolds Thompson

Second Edition

Essay Index Reprint Series

BOOKS FOR LIBRARIES PRESS, INC.
FREEPORT, NEW YORK

Second Edition First Published: 1946

Reprinted, 1968, By Arrangement With
The University of California Press

LIBRARY OF CONGRESS CATALOG NUMBER:
68-14911

PRINTED IN THE UNITED STATES OF AMERICA

Preface to the Second Edition

If I had the gift of prophecy and had wanted to choose a really bad year to publish a serious study of dramatic theory, I could not have chosen a worse one than 1942. Under the circumstances I am naturally gratified that the first edition has been exhausted.

It is also gratifying to have a chance at revision. Some faults, of course, hid themselves throughout the whole process of publication but became conspicuous as soon as it was too late to correct them. Others have since been pointed out by reviewers, friends, and students, to all of whom I am grateful. (I wish particularly to thank my friends Rudolph and Julia Altrocchi, Arnold Rowbotham, and Henry Schnitzler.)

I have added some fresh material, particularly on irony, and made one important change—a qualification of my explanation of the "tragic lift" (chapter vii). Few new plays have claimed a place in the discussion, unfortunately. The times have not encouraged that kind of dramatic effort.

Now that the war is over, are they going to be more encouraging? Broadway is practically limited to money-makers: even more than before the war, for its producers, it is the "smash hit" or nothing. But sincere dramatic writing is apt to have a special appeal, take time to win its audience, be unappreciated at first. The more original and deeply conceived it is, the more is all this true. Broadway can't risk it. Neither, to any great degree, can community theaters, for they too must consider the box office first. It is only the departments of drama in our universities that are free, to any generous extent, to consider new plays on their merits. If the professional theater wants new dramatists with anything vital to say and any knowledge of how to say it, where can it look for them but in the universities?

The growth of university dramatics in recent years has been great, and in the near future promises to be enormous. Some university theater buildings, built before the war, surpass all but a few of the surviving commercial theaters as physical plants. Some departments carry on extremely ambitious production programs. This work is amateur, but in the best sense. It is for love, not money; it is not "amateurish." The professional theater could well afford to take an interest in it.

Let us hope, however, that professionalism will never influence the work of these departments so much that they will lose sight of their proper function as parts of liberal arts colleges. This is a real danger already in some institutions. Students of dramatics are first of all human beings and citizens, and need liberal education to live well in society. They also need it to do their best in their own specialties. The whole of my book is in one sense an effort to show why this is so. It cannot be repeated too often: the drama is not just a "script," but, at its best, literature. It is always, whether good or bad, a message to society and an influence upon civilization. Its potential influence is enormous. What it will actually do depends on all who work with it.

Its future depends on us. But will we have increasing coöperation, or continuing isolation and specialization? Will the fences grow higher that now separate the professional theater, the community theater, the educational theater, the students of dramatic literature?

There is one fact about the atomic age we are entering, one fact new in the history of mankind: we *must* coöperate, or perish. And if those concerned with drama should feel that their contribution to good will among men is small, they should be mindful that no form of human communication has such concentrated power to move the heart and stir the mind as the drama. But it cannot attain that power if those who work with it are merely specialists.

A. R. T.

Berkeley, March, 1946

Preface to the First Edition

IN TIMES OF PEACE it is hard enough to get a serious hearing for a serious study of an art, and this is an era of world-wide revolution and war. Most people regard art as mere recreation, to be disregarded in times of public danger except as it may entertain soldiers on leave. Yet the quality of a civilization is judged and preserved mainly by its art; and if, as we constantly hear asserted, the main task of men of good will today is to preserve civilization against the attacks of the new barbarians, they should have special reason to cherish its art in our time.

Much that goes by the name of art, to be sure, is not worth preserving, still less cherishing. It is either mere sterile imitation of what was vital in other times or places, or the product of introverted cults in metropolitan Bohemias, or commercialized public entertainment. But genuine art deserves our best efforts on its behalf. The conviction that great drama deserves them underlies the writing of this book.

My title indicates that I wish to analyze the drama and speculate on its powers. My book is therefore addressed primarily to the serious student. It attempts to approach a philosophy of drama on the basis of which more specialized activities such as playwriting, directing, or the criticism of particular dramatists may be prosecuted with improved effectiveness and understanding. I have tried to speak plainly and clearly, and much that I say will be familiar to the practiced scholar. But the book is not merely for a beginner. I have tried to reach the bottom of my subject, the foundations of which go deep into psychology and philosophy; and some of the theoretical suggestions made here may prove unfamiliar even to the specialist.

A belief underlying this work is that the study of technique apart from the circumstances of life under which dramatists have written is likely to be an unfruitful occupation, academic in the bad sense. In any genuine creation the writer's subject matter determines the particular form that he chooses. He gets his subject matter from the life around him; and his audiences respond to his work in proportion as it reminds them of life itself.

Thus the student cannot afford to limit his study of a play to what may be found in the limits of its text alone, or of the theater that produced it; he must also try to understand the personality of the man who wrote the play, and the dominant forces in the man's environment. A proper study of plays thus becomes also a study of civilizations. Nothing really significant in a social order can be wholly unimportant to the understanding of one of its products.

It is possible, to be sure, that a student might stray from his proper job by becoming immersed wholly in social history. But that is an extreme less likely to afflict him than the opposite one of concerning himself too narrowly in the affairs of the theater, or in the structure of particular dramas. It is also possible to define too narrowly the important forces in a social environment. Thus in recent years Marxist critics have insisted on interpreting all art with reference to economic forces. Though they have done a useful service in reminding us of much that is genuinely significant and that we had tended to overlook, their emphasis is one-sided because strongly materialistic.

It is not the things a civilization possesses that determine its fate and shape its character, but the dreams that fill its members' heads, the ideals they seek, the faiths they live by; in short, their religion.

I use the word religion in its widest sense, to include all basic beliefs that shape men's lives, whether formalized in a creed or not. In this sense, it is religion that ultimately informs the dramatist's work as well as other men's, and gives it whatever human significance it has. If his religion is mean and barbarous his plays will be so, too, no matter how skillful and clever. Technique is necessary to make a play effective, but out of a high religion alone can the substance of a great play come.

The need for knowing the dramatist's religion is clear enough when the Greek and medieval plays are the subjects of inquiry, since these works grew out of the activities of formal religion. It is less clear when modern dramatists are studied, because their faiths have been diverse and often vague, and the theaters they wrote for have been wholly secular. But if we keep the broad meaning of religion in mind we shall see that the need is nevertheless great. To understand Ibsen, for example, it is of the first importance to understand Ibsen's Protestant background.

Thus a student with even the most practical of motives, such as the intention of directing a play, will, if he is wise, try to become not merely expert in technical devices, but also something of a philosopher. If he plans, let us say, to produce a play of Shaw's, he must really read Shaw's prefaces, and he should go on from them to a study of Fabian socialism and biological evolution. But these topics are of course merely a start; the vistas might easily become endless: the Ireland from which Shaw sprang, the England to which he emigrated, the commercial drama against which he rebelled, the Protestant morality which underlies his thought, the contrary impulses of clown and prophet in his nature, his horror at cruelty, his shyness over love. . . . This it not to say that any one man can investigate all such subjects fully, still less an overworked director with an opening date to meet and any number of immediate practical problems to face. This is not to say that without such study an entertaining production of *Candida* or *Pygmalion* may not be made: after all, Shaw's plays, and all good plays, speak for themselves. This is to say, though, that the sureness and depth of an interpreter's understanding will never be great if he is merely a technician.

This book, then, pays attention to the forces of civilization that have molded dramatists, in the belief that knowing them will contribute in practical ways to the improvement of theatrical and dramatic art. At the same time, the plays themselves are our first concern, and we study them because we love great drama. All the arts live through the civilized delight they afford, and an analysis of one of them may increase our enjoyment of it by increasing the range and depth of our appreciation. Unfortunately, some scholars approach a work of art in the spirit of a police surgeon about to perform a post-mortem, and usually the results of their dissections are melancholy indeed. I hope that I have avoided such consequences, and that this book is not a melancholy anatomy.

My intention throughout has been to inquire, not to dogmatize. In view of the long history of dramatic criticism and the impossibility of reaching certainty in matters of taste, the proper attitude of any student is one of tentative inquiry.

If this book should interest professionals of the theater as well as academic students, I would be greatly pleased. Whatever the merits of the ideas advanced, the topics treated certainly deserve any professional's concern. I have mentioned the director. Actors also need critical understanding if they would be more than so many Trilbys waiting to be hypnotized. The proof of an artist is his creative effort; and though that is guided immediately by what we call intuition rather than by reason, the intuition needs to be trained and directed. The sign of a finished artist is not his native genius—though he must of course have that—but his taste, which is the result of broad and humane culture; and this requires a nurture that is not to be got simply from rehearsals and the application of grease paint.

Unfortunately, humane culture and practical experience are seldom brought together, and people who promote them are at times even hostile to one another. The theaterman too often scorns all theory. The school of dramatics too often apes a narrowly professional attitude, preoccupying its students with all manner of techniques such as stage lighting and make-up, and neglecting the psychological, ethical, and social values that make a play significant to an audience. Scholars, on the other hand, too often merely accumulate facts in monographs or forget a drama's theatrical conditions. In time, the development of university theaters along with courses in the drama may do much to bring about effective coöperation between these two groups. But they will not do so if departments of drama concern themselves merely with producing plays for production's sake, so as to gain or keep a place on the theatrical map, and fail to integrate their interpretative efforts with the scholarship and trained taste of teachers whose approach to the drama is literary and theoretical.

It is such fun to work in a theater that a student will often prefer to do it than eat, not to mention study. Of course he might be engaged in worse things. In his knocking together of flats, his applications of spirit gum, his fiddling with floods and borders, his conning of lines, he may even pick up not merely an amount of practical experience which, if he is very lucky, may serve him in a professional career, but also some smatterings of insight into the drama as an art. But in a university, at least, he ought seriously to concern himself first with becoming an educated man and a person of cultivated taste.

I should like to suggest that the chief contribution a university can make to dramatic art is not the training of professionals, though the universities are already doing that, and doing it more than people of the commercial theater realize, but the training of audiences.

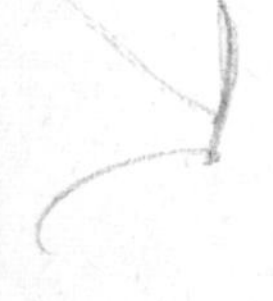

The audience is the jury that passes its verdict upon every new play and every production of an old one. And no play can rise higher than its audience. The universities can do more than any other one agency to send into the theater people who know a good play when they see it and are glad to pay for tickets to a good play. The commercial theater is starving for want of them. The quality of the plays will rise also in proportion as audiences are able to value the play apart from its production; that is, are not dazzled by the glamour of the star and are not merely "actor fans" instead of drama lovers. An ideal audience would not admire fine acting the less for concerning itself first with the play; indeed, it would be more critical of showy histrionics than most audiences are today, and more ready to applaud the genuine artist. It would discriminate between the production and the play, and value the latter according to its deserts.

The theater cannot live without plays; and the proper business of the theater is to produce them in order to bring out their dramatic values, not merely to give parts to actors. The theater is an instrument, not an end. This proposition ought to be taken for granted, as a parallel proposition is in regard to music. Interpretative musicians are finally judged, in spite of ballyhoo, not by their "personalities" but by their interpretations. Toscanini's glory is not that he exhibits himself, but that he exhibits the fullest possible values in the music of Beethoven and Brahms. It is Beethoven and Brahms that the hearer is led to love through his interpretation. But for many a playgoer the star, not the play, is the thing.

Anything, then, that a book of this sort can do to encourage audiences to demand good plays as well as good actors is of service to the theater as well as to the drama. And since actors are the servants of the public, they will respond to such a demand. Indeed, some of them also try to encourage it. Though Bernhardt and Irving were as content to play in mere "vehicles" that showed off their talents as in Racine or Shakespeare, Duse was not; and Stanislavsky became famous because he humbly submitted his own talents and those of his company to the task of sincere and self-effacing interpretation.

He and his partner, as directors of the Moscow Art Theater, saw their artistic task in its proper perspective. Hence the actor Stanislavsky was glad to be guided in critical interpretation by the literary critic and dramatist Nemirovich-Danchenko. In these two persons histrionic and literary abilities coöperated in a common artistic task. Thus they combined forces usually hostile or indifferent; and the result of their combined efforts was a degree of perfection in the art of the theater that has never been equaled, and an immense and ever-spreading influence on serious theater artists throughout the world.

The proper production of great plays is the end of an art theater. The Moscow Art Theater and its directors are justly famous, but it ought not to be overlooked that they are so because they had great plays to interpret. Their revolutionary development of naturalistic acting, in particular, is due finally not to them but to the dramatist Chekhov. When Stanislavsky first considered producing *The Sea Gull* both he and his troupe, as he tells us, found it "monotonous and boresome," and it took all the persuasive powers of his literary partner to make him try it. Then, when he undertook the task, he discovered that to do it properly he had to develop a new way of acting. All the features of his famous "method"—its avoidance of the conventional and its search for the characteristic and individualizing gesture and business, its insistence on teamwork, its never-tiring search for the inner meaning of the role through an imaginative identification of the actor with his part—are exactly what Chekhov's plays required in order to be acted effectively. At that time the conventional repertory was written for conventional acting; Chekhov's plays alone required naturalistic interpretation. Hence it seems that the mild little doctor, with his shy humor and his distaste for theatricality, was the real revolutionary of the theater. Without him the actor would never have been forced to a fundamental alteration of his methods.

Actors are interpreters, and they are a notoriously conservative guild. The dramatist is the creator, and every so often the theater is renewed and rejuvenated by rising to the challenge of a great and original dramatist. This declaration is not a disparagement of the actor; it is simply a statement of his proper function in relation to the author's. The actor has his creative task also, and it is obviously a great and difficult one, but it is creative only within the frame of the author's larger initial creation. Only when playwrights fail them must actors do more than this. Of course, playwrights often do fail them; but we are considering those who know their job.

There is, then, no substitute for good plays. We Americans have a childlike faith in machinery and organization, but if we should erect a model playhouse in every city, assemble the best possible troupe of actors to play in it, and supply the unlimited funds it would need, we still would not have a living drama without plays. Of course, the producer can borrow from Broadway or from the classics; but most Broadway plays are merely articles of commerce or are limited to a metropolitan point of view, and the classics, important as it is that they be produced again and again, can never have the immediate vitality of new plays written by dramatists living in the community and expressing the life of the community.

To encourage the writing of them ought to be the aim of any genuine theater; yet the American theater today seems concerned with almost everything else. It is concerned with the demands of the unions, with the methods of selling tickets, with the competition of Hollywood, and of late it has even made efforts to give the ambitious young actor a tryout less wasteful and discouraging than running the rounds of producers' offices. But for the ambitious young dramatist it offers nothing but difficulties. It makes known that, of thousands of scripts yearly offered to commercial producers, only a handful are worth trying out; and it manages its business so inefficiently that even the tryouts are often such great financial risks that producers cannot afford to take them. It gives the novice no chance to learn his business under professional guidance, and it ignores the efforts of university teachers to train him. Oliver Morosco once offered to produce annually the best play from Professor Baker's "English 47'ers" at Harvard; but this is the rare exception.

If the playwright has one Broadway hit his financial worries are over. He may even be translated to Hollywood to help concoct movies—a possibility which only emphasizes the unhealthy condition of playwriting in this country. The beginner faces nothing but barriers and hurdles;

he who has "arrived" gets such extravagant financial rewards that his temptation to sell his artistic soul for money is often too much for him.

But only the dramatist who overcomes such temptation will write plays of any artistic importance. His plays will entertain, but they will be more than mere entertainment: they will deal vividly and powerfully with the problems of human conduct; they will have form, substance, and beauty. The more we become "drama-minded" rather than merely "theater-minded," the more we are likely to get plays of this sort—plays that will help to keep civilization alive in the world.

ALAN REYNOLDS THOMPSON

Berkeley, April, 1942

ACKNOWLEDGEMENTS

THE CHAPTER on "Melodrama and Tragedy" has its origin in a doctoral dissertation, "Melodrama as a Dramatic Genre," which fortunately is unpublished and buried in the Harvard library; and on an article in the Publications of the Modern Language Association for September, 1928. The chapter, "The Dilemma of Modern Tragedy," is based on an essay with that title in Humanism in America (New York, Farrar & Rinehart, 1930); for permission to use it here I am indebted to the publishers. Parts of the chapter on "Drama and Poetry" are adapted from the essay, "Science, Criticism, and Poetry," which appeared in The American Review for March, 1937.

I am greatly indebted to Dr. James Turney Allen, Professor of Greek in the University of California, for criticism of those parts of the book which deal with Greek drama; and to my wife, Marie K. Thompson, for her expert assistance in revision. Finally, admiring appreciation to my friend Harold A. Small, Editor of the University of California Press, for his skillful and sympathetic work upon my text.

A. R. T.

Contents

THE ANATOMY OF DRAMA

CHAPTER I

The Drama as a Narrative Medium

THE VARIETIES OF NARRATIVE ART

THOUGH STORIES were first told by word of mouth, and their chief future medium may be television, at present the three major narrative mediums are printed page, screen, and stage. Each has its peculiar advantages and limitations, and an understanding of these is useful to the student.

For the moment let us lump together under the label "fiction" not only novels and short stories, but also verse narratives such as ballads and epics, and narratives in dramatic form which are not meant for theatrical performance—the so-called closet dramas. Stage dramas of course are also printed and widely read, and the only way that we can know most of them, in the present state of our theater, is to read them. But there is a vital difference between stage dramas and closet dramas, as indeed between them and all other varieties of fiction: they were written for production and have been, or at least could be, effectively produced.

This difference is made apparent by the fact that it takes special training to read plays. Stage directions are often meager, dry, and technical, and to a novel-reader the dialogue seems bald and incomplete without the auctorial comment and description that accompany it in fiction. The novelist gives us a great deal besides talk, and all this—description, analysis of the character's state of mind, observations on the situation, transitional remarks—enables our minds to slip from one scene to another with hardly a jar or effort of the imagination. A typical novel is thus easy to read. But all these aids to the imagination are absent from the script of a play, and what is left is like a skeleton without flesh and blood. On the stage this skeleton is vivified: the actor, aided by light, properties, and background, fills it out with life. An audience then absorbs the narrative without conscious effort, just as a reader absorbs a popular novel. But, alone in one's easy chair, to read a play so as to fill out its bare skeleton in one's imagination with vivid visualized action and expressive tones, is hard. Even professional playreaders and actors often neglect dramas of marked originality because they cannot fully imagine them as they ought to be produced. For this reason a student of the drama should keep his opinion of a doubtful play tentative until he has seen how it affects audiences when it is competently acted; and he will prefer to see it acted by more than one company, and in different styles. Indeed there are plays, such as the Greek tragedies, which after our best efforts in staging and study remain for us artistically incomplete because we cannot fully visualize their proper production.

In short, just as a score is not the music proper, a printed play is not a complete artistic creation in the sense that a printed novel is, and the reader must learn the art of imaginative production in his mind's eye just as the skilled musician learns to "hear" the music of a score simply by scanning the musical symbols on the page.

Thus the drama has a dual nature which differentiates it from fiction. For playgoers it lives in the theater; for the less fortunate lovers of plays, in books. The theater worker—the actor, the producer, the designer, the director—tends to consider the drama solely in terms of production. To him the playwright's finished product is not a drama, but a "script." The student, on the other hand, tends to think of the drama merely as "literature." Over and over again in the course of dramatic history we find this tendency to consider one of the two aspects of drama to the exclusion of the other; and always it has led to a one-sided development of the art. Thus we find actors and directors ignoring the literary and social values that enrich the taste of cultivated readers, and busying themselves merely with stage tricks and business; and likewise, theatrical reviewers who take a sort of perverse professional pride in approaching a play solely from the theatrical point of view. At the opposite extreme we find scholars who ignore the theatrical function of the plays they study—an error less common today than it was a hundred years ago, especially among Shakespeare critics.

The drama is not literature merely to be read; its proper end is stage production. At the same time it *is* literature. Aeschylus and Shakespeare are poets as much as Homer and Milton, and Ibsen ranks with Flaubert and Dostoievsky among the great writers of the nineteenth century. The classics of drama are literature to all but a few of those who love them, and trained students often feel better satisfied by reading a play than seeing it acted, as did Charles Lamb when he declared that *King Lear* could never be adequately staged. It is not quite wholly true that the drama is properly produced only in the theater; it can be read in terms of a theatrical production. An ideal approach to a play, then, will do justice both to its theatrical and its literary aspects.

DRAMA AND FICTION

The candid playwright must acknowledge the advantages a novelist enjoys. The latter may, for example, expect readers to spend many hours over his book—how many hours such elephantine best sellers as *Gone with the Wind* indicate, not to speak of masterpieces like *War and Peace*. The playwright can expect a playing time of less than three hours including intermissions, exceptions like *Strange Interlude* or the uncut *Hamlet* notwithstanding.

The time at the novelist's disposal allows him a vastly greater scope. He may, like Jules Romains, conduct the simultaneous life stories of some dozens of characters through volume after volume. (Theoretically, he need never stop at all.) He may, like Henry James, trace the course of refined emotions in the supercivilized, with all the details of qualificaiton and explanation painstakingly supplied. Or he may write a "stream of consciousness" novel which attempts to set down everything that comes into a protagonist's head from moment to moment—a task calling for such numbers of words as can properly be reckoned only in astronomical figures. Like James Joyce in *Ulysses,* he may face a reader with a whole series of literary puzzles that take the patience of Job and the ingenuity of Sherlock Holmes to unravel. No matter what he writes, or how much, he will apparently find readers to stick it out with him to the end.

Again, the novelist's medium sets up no formal barriers to the range of his imagination. He can deal with any imaginable time, past, present, or future; with men and women, or with ants or angels; he can set his action in his own backyard or in interplanetary space. In short, he can tell about anything he can clearly imagine. But the dramatist is tightly restricted to only such words and deeds and characters as actors can represent on a stage. And he must leave everything to the actors. He cannot stop the action to whisper into his audience's ear just what his hero happens to be thinking, for the actors alone can speak. The old-fashioned device to avoid this limitation was the aside, which except in farce seems to us too clumsy to be used any more. (O'Neill experimented with it on a wholesale scale in *Strange Interlude,* but the experiment has found no imitators.) Other devices recently developed to express more than the naturally visible and audible, such as we see in expressionistic plays, have been more interesting as experiments than impressive as art.[1]

The drama is also subject to a *greater need for plot.* By plot I do not mean merely a planned sequence of incidents, but a sequence that develops a single course of action from its origin to its conclusion.[2] We know many fine novels that have merely what is called the "unity of the hero." They connect a variety of otherwise unrelated events only by reason of the fact that the hero happens to take part in all

[1] See, in chap. ix, "Strindberg and Expressionism," pp. 341 ff.
[2] See, in chap. iv, "Plot," pp. 115 ff.

of them. Thus the picaresque romances from *Gil Blas* to *Anthony Adverse;* thus *David Copperfield* and *Pendennis.* Other novels have two or more heroes who divide the interest and action among them. Thus *Anna Karenina,* in which the story of Anna and Vronksy runs concurrently with that of Kitty and Levin but does not combine with it. Thus *The Brothers Karamazov,* which indicates by its title that it is about more than one member of a family. Still other novels have, strictly speaking, no hero at all, but instead a social unit like a town, a city, or a sanitarium, as do *Middlemarch, Manhattan Transfer, The Magic Mountain.* But plays that have succeeded with analogous themes are exceptional.[3] As a general rule a play requires a protagonist or hero, and a plot that develops, from origin to conclusion, an action or series of causally related actions centering in this protagonist.

The greater need for plot implies a greater need of eliminating the irrelevant. This is called the "law of dramatic economy." Novels may and often notoriously do wander off the presumed subject, but as long as the digressions are amusing nobody minds except critics who feel that the dramatic rule should apply to fiction. Some readers of Thackeray even prefer his interlarded essays to his narrative, and though most readers probably wish that Tolstoy's lectures on history were cut out of *War and Peace,* shortening it by perhaps a third, nobody has brought himself to do the cutting. The quality of a great novelist's personality is one of the strongest ties that attach a reader to his works, and this quality is often revealed most fully in his digressions. The

[3] See, in chap. v, "Unity of Theme," pp. 163 ff.

dramatist has no such license. He may have the most engaging of personalities, but his job is to create other personalities for actors to impersonate. Audiences are not conscious of any rule, but are always restive when the action of a play is sidetracked. It is curious that this should be so, for the individuals who compose an audience are for the most part also readers of novels.

The chief reason for the greater need of strict unification on the stage is apparently the limitation of time. Since our two and a half or three hours is scarcely enough for presenting the main action adequately, we resent any wasting of it on digressions. We have come to see the whole play in one evening, and want it to go on; we do not have the desultory mood in which we usually read a novel, picking it up and laying it down as suits our whim. In this respect a play is more like a short story: though the novel may meander, the short story may not; at least, the dominant tendency of short-story writers who are most conscious of their genre as an art form, from Poe and Maupassant to Chekhov and Somerset Maugham, is toward a unity and economy similar to those of the drama. The reason seems to be simply that a short story must be short.

Thus we find inherent in the dramatic medium a need of *unity of action*. This ancient term, which comes to us from Aristotle, traditionally meant merely what Aristotle meant by it—a unity of plot, with "beginning, middle, and end, . . . according to the laws of probability and necessity." Physical accidents and chance events, though they may sometimes modify the course of the action, must never dominate it, for traditionally its mainspring must be the effect of some person's will, or a conflict between strong and irreconcilable wills.[4] A hero in traditional drama was a person who willed something hard enough to act in order to achieve it. As we all admire strength of will, a person who exhibits it is admirable, dramatically speaking, even though, as with Richard III, his aims may be reprehensible. Moreover, such a person is the sort from whom a course of interesting action most readily springs. (The relative weakness of *Richard II* as a play is really the weakness of Richard as a character.) Bring two strong-willed persons into conflict and you get a greatly enhanced interest in their struggle. This interest is so keen that modern theorists generally accept the view that the essence of drama is struggle. Unity of action thus springs from the unity of the hero's conflict.

This is the dramatic tradition, and many current plays still conform to it; but in recent times we have come increasingly to concern ourselves with the ordinary mortal who is acted upon more than acting, and less and less with the exceptional hero who wills and fights on the grand scale. The old pieties that fostered heroism have largely passed away, along with the old monarchies and aristocracies. Though war calls forth the greatest physical heroism, this is not easily adaptable to dramatic uses unless it transcends blind obedience to duty, which controls multitudes on both sides of every battle, and unless it arises also out of a religious faith that wins an audience's allegiance. Such a faith, beyond patriotism, was generally lacking in the recent conflict. (The artificial fostering of barbaric creeds in dictator countries is of course the antithesis of humane heroism.) A war,

[4] See, in chap. iv, "Plot," pp. 115 ff.

moreover, is an abnormal condition in modern society, and the emotions that it excites pass quickly with the signing of an armistice. The older opportunities for glory through individual achievement have dwindled everywhere with the increase in economic and social interdependence, with the increase in the power of machinery as compared with muscle, and with the increase in the complexity of social organization. The sciences also have had a large share in destroying the heroic tradition by seeming to demonstrate how petty, bestial, and physically conditioned are all men. A philosophy of flux, a belief that no standards are absolute and that all things change with the shifting forces of a blind and indifferent Nature, has come to dominate the thoughts of modern man. This is the philosophy which we shall refer to as naturalism.

The novel is well adapted as a medium to handle the unheroic protagonists of naturalism, the "little men" who are chosen for their roles not because of any unique and positive character but because of their similarity to the mass of men. The novel not only can tell their story, but can also supply the philosophic commentary that is needed to render such a story generally significant, or take the time needed to set the little man in his significant environment, to demonstrate his representativeness, and to show in detail the complexity of influences that mold and control him. Many novels that deal with essentially unheroic characters of this sort yet manage to impress us with a sense of great or even profound importance. They are usually depressing, as heroic actions are not, but they seem to us true, as many heroic actions no longer do.

The very nature of the drama goes counter to such themes and characters, and hence it is difficult for a dramatist to compensate, as does the novelist, for the absence of a strong-willed hero. We have seen that the dramatist cannot philosophize directly, and he uses a character as mouthpiece only at his peril. Moreover, he has too little time at his disposal to make an adequate presentation of a complex modern environment. The plays that have succeeded in such an attempt[5] are exceptional. Of these *The Weavers* is probably the most notable.

I speak here, of course, of serious plays. Commercial playwrights, like movie writers, usually retain the conventional hero of romance and melodrama, modernized on the surface but still superhumanly competent. So do writers of "popular" fiction. They all appeal to people who are as yet untouched by the more serious effects of modern thought and therefore naïvely responsive to traditional heroics, or to people who are more sophisticated but at the moment willing to escape from whatever is serious.

The naturalist movement in literature, as a matter of fact, was in large part inspired by the feeling that the stagey hero of tradition no longer represented anything real in actual life, and that on the contrary the little man or woman alone could do so. Zola succeeded in putting his theories into practice in his novels, though, to be sure, he was inclined in spite of his theories to romanticize his protagonists; but when he attempted the stage he failed. Nevertheless, his arguments attacking the old drama and urging a naturalistic drama had a wide effect. Naturalistic plays according

[5] See, in chap. v, "Unity of Theme," pp. 163 ff.

with his formula were written in France, but the most successful were the early plays of Hauptmann in Germany. The greatest naturalistic plays were written, with less direct influence from Zola, by Chekhov and Gorky in Russia.[6] Chekhov's plays are populated by characters whose absence of strong will, or inability to exert it, is the very source of the playwright's tragicomic effects. His achievement is extraordinary, for in spite of a minimum of traditional plot and the absence of a hero, and in spite of emphasis on all that negates vigorous, heroic action, his plays have an enduring vitality. Even so, they are not plays for the average spectator, and have seldom been imitated successfully.

We must, then, admit notable exceptions to the principle of heroic action. Yet it remains generally true that the drama requires a plot and a strong-willed hero; the literal meaning of the Greek verb δρᾶν, from which our word drama is derived, is "to do, to accomplish." The novel may deal successfully with themes of frustration and suffering which, as Matthew Arnold said in condemning them for poetry, "find no vent in action."[7] It can describe petty routine and passive endurance. The drama, on the contrary, needs positive and significant struggle. The difficulty for the dramatist is therefore peculiarly great in an age of disillusionment such as ours.

What artistic advantages, then, can we claim for his medium? The first that springs to mind is its much greater concentration of emotional effect. The reader of a book ordinarily takes it up from time to time over a period of days

[6] See, in chap. ix, "Chekhov and Naturalism," pp. 333 ff.

[7] Preface to *Poems* (1853).

or weeks. Emotion cools in the intervals. But a dramatic performance is almost continuous. Again, the novel-reader sits alone and cannot share the emotionalizing influence of a crowd swayed by a common experience. Above all, he does not see with his eyes and hear with his ears the physical enactment of the story.

Even the difficulties of the medium may prove advantageous. At first this statement may sound self-contradictory, for ordinarily we value our instruments in proportion to their ease of operation—as, for example, our automobiles. We do so because they are merely means and we wish to achieve our ends with them as easily as possible. But it is otherwise with human achievements, of which works of art are among the most notable. These we value in proportion to the difficulties successfully overcome. (We often value them also for other qualities, of course.) Thus mountain climbing or playing chess or writing a play. When we contemplate a masterpiece, we admire the skill of its artist, and that admiration is no small part of our delight. Naturally, however, if we are to appreciate the artist's skill, we must understand the difficulties which he has overcome. The tyro may enjoy other qualities in a work of art, but not this. Hence, those who comprehend are better pleased by the mastery of a difficult medium than by mastery of an easy one.

If it be objected that this delight is not an aesthetic one—well, I do not care to quarrel over the meaning of that much-debated adjective. I should say that the objector is using the term more narrowly than I do. In my opinion, any and every legitimate source of delight in a work of art is a part of its total aesthetic effect, and there is no good reason for choosing some sources and ignoring others.

This pleasure in observing achievement is universal. Even a useless stunt like engraving the Lord's Prayer on a pinhead gives it, and the skill of fine athletes and acrobats gives it strongly. Indeed, in this respect, the baseball fan or the chess addict has as thrilling an experience from watching an expert game as the playlover has from seeing a great play. The game lacks the deep human significance of the drama, and it is less rich in complexities and sensuous appeals, but it has similar elements of struggle, climax, and catastrophe. We do not call it a work of art, because we have limited our word "art" to a few varieties of skillful achievement; but the emotional experience is in no small measure the same. Again, though we value an instrument in proportion to its ease of operation, we value the skill of the operator in proportion to the difficulty of his instrument. Mastery of the violin is more impressive than mastery of the mandolin. A poet who writes fluently in a stiff poetic form like the sonnet gives us a special pleasure not afforded by easier forms like free verse. *The more resistant the medium,* other things being equal, *the greater the impressiveness of a successful mastery of it.*

I have emphasized the technical difficulties of the drama in comparison with the novel. Though in sheer bulk of labor the novel requires more effort than a play, it is comparatively flexible and adaptable. It is like clay; the drama is like marble.

There are also the difficulties of subject matter; and these may be made clearer by a comparison with music. Music has no objective subject matter: it is not about anything. (I am thinking, of course, of abstract music, such as a symphony. And even when a composer writes "program music" like Beethoven with his "Pastoral" symphony or Strauss with his tone poems, many listeners prefer not to think about the story or the aspects of outer nature suggested by the program notes, but to listen to the music solely as music.) The materials of music—melody, harmony, rhythm, tone quality—make no reference in themselves to the outer world. The listener never says, "I don't like this melody because it is unlike the melodies I meet on the street." But unless the dramatist is careful the spectator at a drama is always likely to say, "I dislike this characterization because it is unlike that sort of person as I know him in life." The materials of narrative are human beings in what are offered as real situations, and thus both drama and novel constantly and unavoidably lead us to compare their subject matter with the outer world as we know it.

The drama and the novel thus share this difficulty of subject matter, but the novelist can more easily explain, cover up, enlarge, or omit; even, like the narrative poet, he can so charm us by the magic of words that we cease to be critical. But the playwright has only his three hours, his three to five acts, his limited stage; and every moment he must hold his audience enthralled. How make the flowing complexity and interrelatedness of human life fit these rigid conditions without loss of plausibility and with rich significance? How contrive an action that will be unified, growing in intensity, and rounded to a powerful and convincing close? The task is seldom even moderately well performed; there are few technically excellent plays, and perhaps there is none that combines a high degree of technical excellence with loftiness of theme and greatness of characterization. In one or other of these respects obvious faults have been found even in the masterpieces of Sophocles and Shakespeare.

When technique is the primary consideration, Ibsen comes nearest of all great dramatists to being master of his medium, and for this reason alone he affords a peculiar and lasting delight to the student. The more one studies his plays, the more one perceives difficulties of the hardest sort triumphantly overcome. Indeed, the delight in these triumphs endures when the more obvious effects that once excited audiences no longer stir us; Nora's slamming of the door on her husband cannot shock modern audiences as it did those of the 'eighties, but it can still thrill us as a masterly close to a play marvelously constructed.

We may say, then, without straining a paradox, that the limitations of the drama as a medium are an artistic advantage to the dramatist—when he overcomes them. As for the dramatist who fails, he fails so much more definitely than the mediocre novelist that the world is far less cluttered up with bad plays than it is with bad novels.

DRAMA AND FILM

The superficial similarities of the stage play and the screen play are so obvious that the two are considered by many people, including professionals, to be more nearly alike fundamentally than they really are. The consequences of this error are of some practical importance.

It is not surprising that the fundamental differences are overlooked, the superficial likenesses are so striking. Both drama and movie are presented in theaters; both tell stories by presentation; many of these stories have been adapted for the screen from the stage; above all, actors perform in both—often the same actors—and when these actors are stars their brilliance so dazzles everybody that other matters fade into obscurity. Among these other matters, such theoretical distinctions as here concern us become almost invisible.

The main difference is simply that *the stage presents people; the screen, pictures.* Throughout every performance we are all aware of this difference without thinking about it. We consciously notice it only when it is violated—as it would be if Charles Laughton, for instance, should suddenly stick his living head through a hole in the screen, or if a stage producer should run a film as background for living actors. Such a combination would make us immediately aware of each medium as a medium; it would distract the imagination of the spectator from identification with the story, which it is the function of each medium to produce, and instead rouse him to a critical comparison of the effectiveness of stage and screen, or confuse him through the effort to follow the two different kinds of action going on simultaneously.

For this reason one is inclined to lift one's eyebrows at the enthusiasm with which some theater artists have lately been advocating just such a mixing up of stage and screen. Thus Mr. Robert Edmond Jones: "Our dramatists now have it in their power to enlarge the scope of their dramas to an almost infinite extent by the use of these moving and speaking images. Some new playwright will presently set a motion-picture screen on the stage above and behind his actors and will reveal simultaneously the two worlds of the Conscious and the Unconscious. . . . On the stage we shall see the actual characters of the drama; on the screen we shall see their hidden secret selves."[8]

Will the result be what Mr. Jones calls in his chapter heading "a new kind of drama"? A few pages later in his book Mr. Jones himself, in effect, answers this question; he writes: "I want my imagination to be stimulated by what I see on the stage. But the moment I get a sense of ingenuity, a sense of effort, my imagination is not stimulated; it is starved." Mr. Jones evidently finds the drama an inadequate medium for handling psychological themes. Would it not, then, be logical for him to abandon the stage altogether for the screen? To retain the stage action and at the same time to offer a visible (and perhaps audible) representation of the character's thoughts is not so much likely to stimulate the imagination as to starve it. The objections which I raise later[9] to Eugene O'Neill's use of asides for this purpose in *Strange Interlude* would much more hold true of any mixed production such as Mr. Jones describes.

We are always aware of the medium, but we want to forget it, and in successful productions we do almost wholly forget it, in the illusion of the story. Neither medium is clearly superior to the other in its power to create this illusion. The fact that on the screen we see merely photographs does not seem to make the illusion which they are capable

[8] *The Dramatic Imagination* (New York, 1941), p. 18.

[9] P. 394.

of producing any less effective than that which is possible on the stage. I do not hold with the argument, raised by playlovers during the early days of the film, that photographs cannot please us as real actors do. The facts are often to the contrary, for we generally prefer animated photographs of good actors to the personal appearance of bad ones; and if we have to buy cheap seats, we should rather, other things being equal, see a twenty-foot image of an actor than get a second-balcony glimpse of him in person.

According to Professor Allardyce Nicoll, character acting is rarer in the films, and type casting preferable, because "in serious films actor and rôle are indistinguishable."[10] Certainly the fantastic adulation of film stars indicates that the public thinks more of them as persons than as impersonators of roles. We often hear their names used instead of the names of the characters they are supposed to represent: "In this movie Clark Gable falls in love with Claudette Colbert." Unquestionably the star, as a person, serves multitudes of youngsters of the other sex as an object of amorous yearning. But when Professor Nicoll concludes that the drama gives less illusion of reality because it necessarily involves more make-believe and "theatricality," and that stage characters are types whereas film characters are individuals, I find it difficult to agree with him. The film can give a strong illusion, but so can the theater. In both mediums a serious realistic theme calls for strong illusion, whereas a comic theme keeps the spectator in a comparatively detached attitude.[11] A play of Ibsen's or Chekhov's demands that the

[10] *Film and Theatre* (New York, 1936), p. 169.

[11] See chap. iii.

stage actor lose his individuality in the role and build up his part so that the smallest and subtlest details of characterization are convincingly projected. Stanislavsky's art in doing this is famous. In both mediums farce or satire calls for broad comedy types; in both, plays of tragic quality often require simplified and heightened characterizations that represent human beings not as they actually are, but as they might be, nobler or more grandly wicked than in life. Stage settings, it is true, cannot be so fully "realistic" as those on the screen; but that a use of obvious artifice in stage setting precludes strong illusion is not borne out by experience.

In neither movie nor play do normal people ever lose their underlying consciousness that what they are seeing is make-believe. The illusion may be strong, but it is never complete. In both, the degree of illusion varies greatly with the imagination of the individual spectator, the theme and treatment, the skill of the actors, and accidental circumstances. I for one am not prepared to assert that either can create a stronger illusion than the other. Undoubtedly, real people acting are more real as such than photographs of them, but in general the films are more clearly visible, the voices from the sound track are more easily heard, and the photographed background is more convincing than stage scenery. We are always aware that the actors on the stage are not in fact the characters they impersonate, and we are always aware that on the screen we see merely photographs of actors who impersonate characters. Even when all screen photographs are made to appear three-dimensional as well as in natural colors, we shall still know that they are merely photographs: improvements in technique will make the photographs more vivid, but they will not make us think them reality.

A photograph is a picture, and therefore subject to all the necessities of a picture. It must be on a flat surface, or one that seems flat; and it must be bounded by a frame. The flat surface of the screen is one of the elements of film presentation of which we are always aware. That is to say, no matter how stereoscopic the picture may some day be made to appear to us, we shall never expect to see round its corners or step into it. As we read Lewis Carroll's story we may step with Alice through her looking glass; but that is a fairy tale, and in the actual world a film is even less "real" than a mirror, for we know always that the film picture has no depth whereas the image in a mirror reflects the actual depth of the space in front of it. And the film picture is framed, whether it has a special border or not, by the boundaries of the camera image. Everything within this frame is equally definite, and nothing exists, so far as the movie is concerned, beyond it. The picture therefore differs from our vision, which has a center in focus surrounded by a gradually fading fringe of half-seen images, and which shifts so constantly that we see the visible world around us not as pictures but as continuous three-dimensional space.

Again, everything in the film picture, even though seen but for an instant, is as much a part of the picture as everything else, and therefore all parts are equally pictorial. All images on a photographic film are merely silver on a transparent surface. The images of people are silver exactly as much as are the images of chairs; they assume greater importance only through the action of the human intelligence that views them.

As a consequence, we want everything in the picture to have an equal effect of reality. In the earliest films real actors performed against obviously painted backgrounds, as they were accustomed to do in the theater. On the stage this contrast between their reality and the artificiality of their background does not trouble spectators. On the screen it seems ridiculous; to enjoy a screen story we accept the make-believe that a photograph of a man is a real man, but we will not accept the make-believe that a photograph of an obvious painting of a house behind the man is a real house; we demand a photograph of a real house. Of course, the technician fools us with false fronts, superposed photographs, scale models, and other devices; but the point I wish to emphasize is that he must succeed in fooling us all the time. He must never let the eye detect the deceit, for if it does, even for an instant, the effect of the whole is ruined. Indeed, for this reason producers are said to dislike letting the public know too much about their methods. The idea in the familiar expression, "The camera cannot lie," would be more accurately expressed as, "The camera's lies must never be noticeable."

We demand accurate realism in motion pictures. It doesn't matter to us how the producer obtains it, but it must indeed satisfy the eye. Moreover, we see everything very vividly, and we notice details. (The vivider the pictures become in future with improved projection, the more details we shall notice.) If anything appears inaccurate, historically or in the light of our visual knowledge of the world, some of us are sure to notice it and be disturbed. We want to lose ourselves in the story, but incorrect details divert our attention and destroy our illusion. If I should see an American naval officer of 1917 wearing a tunic with lapels, I would be ready to write a letter to tell the movie people off; the screen play might be an artistic triumph, but after seeing that tunic I should hardly be able to appreciate it.

Producers know this danger only too well, and as a consequence have reduced to a science the task of getting accurate surface realism. They know that every film, at least every film of modern setting, will need to sustain the scrutiny of all sorts of specialists, who like nothing better than raising a to-do over minute errors in detail. Hence the visible aspect of motion pictures has become almost as unchallengeable as that of a cyclorama in a museum of natural history. To a somewhat less degree the same is true of sound effects. And to a greater degree than the stage, perhaps, the film seeks accuracy in such aspects of speech as dialect. A further reason for this search after realism may possibly be an unconscious effort on the part of the producers to offset the disadvantages that photographs otherwise have in comparison with living actors.

I call this accuracy "surface realism" to distinguish it from that other realism which is not pictorially visible or immediately audible—realism of characterization, motivation, plotting. Anybody who can see and hear can check the accuracy of surface realism, but to notice poor characterization, flimsy motivation, or melodramatic plotting requires of a spectator some knowledge of life and art, some capacity for reflection and analysis, and some training in good taste. Hence, compared with the number who notice surface inaccuracies, few moviegoers notice these faults beneath the surface, and fewer are troubled by them. Most members of an audience are observant rather than critical. As a consequence, producers who concern themselves merely with the box office neglect fundamental realism and freely use stock characters, stock situations, trite dialogue, sentimentalities, and improbabilities. A movie can get away with unmotivated murder, but not with the wrong kind of "lethal weapon"! The stage situation, however, is much the reverse; it escapes the painful need of surface realism, and it more acutely requires an underlying probability. Let us explore the reasons for this difference.

The fundamental condition of stage performance is that, while the actors are real people, much that is represented in their setting is not real because it cannot be. A stage chair can be a real chair, but a stage mountain cannot be a real mountain. It must usually be a painting of a mountain. No ingenuity of technicians can evade this fact.

Its consequence is that it introduces into play production a clash between make-believe and reality—a clash that has troubled designers almost from the beginning of theatrical history, and that always will trouble them. In the art of mise-en-scène we can see, broadly speaking, tendencies toward two extremes in meeting this difficulty. One is to use a stage bare, or nearly bare, of properties and scenery, and leave to the actors the task of building up an imaginary background by pantomime and descriptive speech. This was the method of the Elizabethan theater, and it is what Thornton Wilder called for in the production of *Our Town*. It is likewise the basis for the art of the Chinese theater, though there a large number of objects and actions have been conventionalized to symbolize reality.[12] The other extreme has been tried out most thoroughly by the naturalistic school, from the 'nineties to the present. It is to make every property on the stage real, if possible; otherwise, to simulate it so carefully as to deceive the eye. David Belasco's settings used to be famous for this surface realism, and the setting of *Dead End*[13] is a recent example.

Dead End called for such details, and so the use of them in that play was artistically justified. But most plays, contrary to the movies, would seem inartistically staged if they were cumbered with such painstaking imitations of reality. The best modern feeling on the subject, I think, prefers as little setting as possible. Certainly, if we had to choose between too little and too much, there is no question that we would ask for too little, at least when plays of imaginative appeal were to be produced. But usually neither one extreme nor the other is wholly satisfactory and each play calls for its own style of mise-en-scène. As a consequence designers compromise: for most plays they show actual objects when such are convenient or are needed in the action, and things that cannot be presented they merely suggest. Modern lighting aids them in this, but more important than lighting, or clever scene painting, is the audience's willingness to let a token or symbol stand for a thing. The outline

[12] See, in chap. iv, "Conventions," pp. 108 ff.

[13] The reader unacquainted with the authorship of any play mentioned in the text of this book will find it in the Index, under the title of the play.

of a groined arch or two, for instance, sufficiently suggested a cathedral in the original New York production of *Murder in the Cathedral.*

To make a stage scene properly and effectively suggestive for the needs of the play requires of a designer much taste and imagination as well as technical skill. Anyone who has considered the matter knows how complex and difficult this art of stage design has become. It is beset with dangers, for an overambitious designer can easily make his settings obtrusive, and lack of dramatic sense on his part may put them out of key with the play. Moreover, he must see that he gives his actors adequate playing space, and he must not make his sets too expensive or hard to shift. When we realize these difficulties we can admire the more our designers' frequent successes.

But the clash between the reality of the actors and the inevitable make-believe of much in their background remains, no matter what is done. Hence the artistic stage designer frankly accepts the situation and ordinarily makes no pretenses of hiding it as does the movie producer. Such pretenses are not natural to the stage as a medium. Thus, with certain minor exceptions, we may conclude that the motion picture requires surface realism; the stage play, a frank make-believe in setting.

Our present theater is fortunately free to employ any kind of setting, from the extreme of what can be shown to the extreme of what can be suggested, without exciting objection—provided the setting fits the play. It has won this freedom only recently. It has won it partly because of the widespread experimentation and theorizing of theater artists of a variety of schools—the romantic Gordon Craig, the "stylizer" Jessner, the constructivist Meierhold, the "epic" propagandist Erwin Piscator.[14] Partly, I think, it is due to the movies. Since the screen can reproduce all visible and audible reality photographically and phonographically, it would be absurd for the theater to compete with it. And the movie houses have drained away from the playhouse the less sophisticated theatergoers, leaving smaller but on the whole more intelligent audiences, which are less impressionable to mere trickery and readier to respond favorably to taste and imagination in design. Only when a play definitely requires extreme realism do we find it employed, for the designer has now won the imaginative emancipation of a genuine artist.

The screen, however, must stick to realism. Indeed, it seems forced by its nature to limit itself to stories that are, on the surface, realistic. It can tackle fantasy, of course, but only at the price of making every sensible element of the fantasy, down to each fairy's bootstraps—if she wears any—accurate and real to the eye. We might be tempted to say that it takes all the surface realism the screen can muster to make some of its scenarists' wilder fancies plausible. (Very young spectators are of course uncritical in such matters. My youngsters apparently found *The Wizard of Oz,* a film of real actors, just as enthralling as *Snow White,* an animated cartoon. I was chiefly conscious of the trickery

[14] Interesting discussions of all these, especially the last, are in Mordecai Gorelik's *New Theatres for Old* (New York, 1941), chap. ix. By Piscator in Germany (before Hitler). the stage was used as a pulpit; he sought a logical demonstration for "agitational" effects, not illusion. Whence, in part, the Living Newspaper productions of the Federal Theater in this country.

resorted to in photographing the former, not to mention the stupidities of the scenario.) But essentially it is not exigencies of plot that make realism necessary on the screen; it is the nature of photography itself. On the stage, however, actors can create fantasy with no visible aids at all save their own bodies and costumes. As the imagination is infinitely more accommodating than the eye, the stage is infinitely superior in this field of narrative. *A Midsummer Night's Dream* was written to be acted on a bare platform, and is still most stimulating to the imagination when performed with a minimum of properties and setting; not all the arts of Max Reinhardt and Hollywood technicians combined could make the screen version of it more than pretentious photographic fakery.

One notable exception to this general assertion must be allowed, and that is animated drawings. *Snow White* and *Pinocchio* proved marvelously effective. (They would have been even more so if the animators had resisted their habituation to farcical gags of the Mickey Mouse tradition!) But this exception is not really an exception, because, artistically speaking, animated drawings are not photographs; they are merely reproduced photographically. A drawing does not represent visible reality as a photograph does; it merely suggests it. Like all good draftsmen, the artists who drew the pictures for these films made no pretense of imitating reality, but on the contrary skillfully exaggerated and distorted visible forms such as human figures to conform to a distinctive graphic style. As a result, Walt Disney's products (and they are truly his, for although animated cartoons require a large staff of draftsmen, one artist dominates the work and sets the style) have the personal, imaginative appeal that we find, for instance, in Tenniel's classic illustrations for Lewis Carroll. The immense popularity of his films indicates perhaps how much the public instinctively prefers the imagination of a genuine artist to mechanical photographic reproduction.

Certainly the range of representation in animated drawings is as wide as the range of the artist's ability to fix his fancies in graphic forms. The possibilities of this medium have obviously not been fully explored. So far as we can see at present, however, they do not involve competition with photographs in the field of realistic narrative: their figures will never displace living actors in such movies. It is difficult to imagine them seriously rivaling either the drama or written fiction, even in the field of adult poetic fantasy such as *A Midsummer Night's Dream,* for they are primarily a pictorial, not a literary, art. If all movies appeal chiefly to the eye, these do so preëminently; and the greater the skill of their artists the greater their visual appeal.

To return to films in general: the screen, as we have noted, employs pictures; the stage, people. Hence, *the screen appeals primarily to sight; the stage, to hearing.* In a movie the sound track is mainly an accompaniment to the photographs. When we attend a play our eyes, on the contrary, mainly confirm our ears.

Proof of this difference is that no movie can be performed on the air without television, whereas plays are constantly being read over the radio and with surprisingly little loss of essential dramatic values. Further evidence is that afforded by foreign films. Actually, a slight knowledge of the language spoken in these films is rather a handicap because it tends to be a distraction. I myself know enough French to follow a good deal of what is said, and no Russian; yet I cannot say that in seeing Russian films I have lost noticeably more of the dramatic values in them than in French films because of my ignorance of Russian speech. Nor do I find that foreign films in general are noticeably less effective for me than those in English. Now and then their subtitles fail to make everything clear, but on the whole little loss results from my inability to follow the details of the dialogue. My experience may not be typical, and I shall readily admit the possibility that if I had understood the dialogue in many films I might have got much more out of them. (I might also have got less. Consider the effect of the words of almost any Italian opera if it should be rendered in English!) I can only say from my general experience that subtitles, though an awkward makeshift, do assist us to get along well enough without understanding a word of the dialogue. I conclude that the dialogue in a movie is not really essential. In other words, the screen remains what it was in the days of the silent film—a medium for visual images. As Professor Nicoll says, "Whereas in general a stage play demands constant talk, a film requires an absolute minimum of words. The essential basis of the cinema lies primarily in the realm of visual images."[15]

We can of course make too much of this difference. Both normally appeal to both senses at once: the drama appeals to the eye, and the film to the ear. Nevertheless, we may expect the highest achievements of the screen to be in pic-

[15] *Film and Theatre,* p. 129.

torial beauty and expressive movement. And even though the strongest effects of a drama are sometimes conveyed in silence, by pantomime or pose, and though business is often more effective than words in conveying details of characterization and action, these visual appeals are, on the whole, subordinate in extent and importance to speech. Moreover, the higher the type of drama the less important they are. Farce and melodrama need them much more than do high comedy and tragedy. Great drama is primarily spoken literature.

Thus far we have considered the formal differences between the mediums. Next, a word about differences in the conditions of their production and presentation. Since the film actor does not perform before an actual audience, and his acting is done piecemeal in short sequences arranged with regard, not to the order of events in the play, but to the conveniences of production, he lacks the stimulation of a living audience's direct response and cannot build up to a climax from one scene to the next, but must, as we say, start each short sequence "cold." To learn how audiences react to him and how to adapt his acting to them he must go on the stage; and now that many film actors begin their careers before the camera, it is being found advisable to send them off for stage experience.

Again, once the film is made, it is, as Professor Nicoll emphasizes, made once for all and unchangeable, whereas a stage production is a new creation at every performance. And finally, the audience cannot respond to a film as it does to a drama. The greater darkness of the movie theater tends to isolate each person psychologically from the crowd, and the uselessness of hissing or applause thwarts his instinctive impulses toward overt expression of his feelings. That these conditions decrease the pleasure of audiences to some degree is probable.

These are handicaps; but I do not think them so important as some writers maintain. The fact remains that film actors can and do learn to act very well before a camera, that audiences respond to film plays very strongly, and that the fixed nature of the film makes it possible for the audience always to see the very best performance the actors are capable of.

It remains for us to consider the differences in the narrative powers of the mediums. Why is it, for example, that stage plays are notoriously less effective on the screen when transferred direct than when freely adapted?

Obviously, the screen is far more fluid and flexible than the stage. Even an Elizabethan platform stage cannot make changes of scene with the ease of the camera; and the realistic settings of most modern plays are expensive and, without elaborate machinery, slow to shift. But it is not merely the practical difficulties of sceneshifting that make dramatists avoid it as much as possible. Each act of a drama is felt to be a subordinate unit of the whole, and a change of scene within the act tends to break up its unity of effect. Its total action is framed in space by the setting as it is in time by the rise and fall of the curtain.

The screen writer, on the contrary, runs great risk of boring the eye with pictorial monotony if he prolongs the fixed view of any single set beyond a few moments. Hence he keeps up an almost continual shifting of scene, either breaking up the natural sequence of an action which on the stage would be played without interruption, or at least moving his camera about from side to side, up and down, close up and at a distance, to give visual variety and varied emphasis on different actors. For the same reason, he makes his actors move about much more than is necessary on the stage.

Besides this, he makes free with temporal order—the normal sequence of events—in a fashion seldom attempted on the stage. The film narrative is far less bound to follow this order. It can be liberal with flashbacks into the past and with alternating glimpses of two actions presented as going on simultaneously. On the stage such effects are usually artificial if not downright awkward; and the more serious the play the less the dramatist can afford to interfere with its illusion by trying them. They were rather effective in *Grand Hotel* because its aim was to get sensational effects of contrast by glimpses into the lives of a number of people all living in the same place. Their employment in expressionistic plays is appropriate because such plays depend for their major effectiveness upon the frank use of artifices. But O'Neill's four-room house in *Desire under the Elms,* any room of which could be opened to view as needed by the action, seemed a clumsy expedient only partly justified by its usefulness in showing two or three simultaneous actions.

Moreover, the "camera eye" can look inward as the drama cannot, and, by a universally accepted convention, show us in pictures what a character is thinking. It can even show the visible word distorted or out of focus, as it appears to a person in an abnormal mental state. It can contrast one scene with another for ironic effect, and it can use symbolic "shots" to express thoughts or emotions. Professor Nicoll illustrates this last device by reference to a film in which a prisoner's state of mind on being pardoned is symbolized by brief shots showing his hands, a bird flying outside a barred window, a rippling stream. Such imaginative use of visual images is probably the film's greatest power for artistic effect.

It is easy and natural for the photographic medium to do these things, for it can show anything that can be photographed. Hence it is unnatural for it not to do so when the story calls for them. It is especially unnatural for it to cease its constant flow of visual images. On the contrary, a law of the screen is that its scenes must be continually moving and changing. Like a sleeper's imagination as it brings dream pictures into the mind to dissolve one into another, the cinema must keep up a constant visual alteration. The pictures are indeed moving pictures; *they must not be still.*

Only written fiction can rival such range and freedom. The novel, indeed, excels the screen in scope, for it can claim many hours' attention. But the screen excels the novel in vividness and rapidity. It makes visible instantaneously and with absolute convincingness people and their physical surroundings, whereas the novelist can only suggest them slowly and dimly with his best descriptive skill, and runs great risk of boring his reader while doing it. This power of the screen is a special advantage when it deals with familiar scenes, conventional types of people, and simple or elemental passions. On the stage or in the novel such material is likely to seem trite or boring; in both these mediums, stock characters, for example, are obviously stock characters. But on the screen the visible variety of physical aspect amuses our eyes and renders us less quick to note underlying commonplaceness. Evidence of this is the popularity of photograph magazines and photogravure sections in the newspapers. In these we stare with bemused intensity at the photographs of people or objects which, seen in life, we would pass by without a glance. We are all children in our liking to look at pictures. And since the physical world offers infinite visible variety, art is not required to put it on the screen. Moreover, the filmed actor is so utterly real to us as a visible and audible person that we unconsciously assume a like reality of his assumed character in the story. Thus it is easier to produce illusion in the film than on the stage, where make-up, distance, lighting, and an artificial background all make us conscious of the theatricality of the actor. Hence the film actor can utter banalities intolerable in drama or novel without annoying us. Because the eye is amused, the intelligence sleeps. If the actor (or actress) is physically attractive, the intelligence sleeps the sounder. This makes the writing of screen scenarios easier than the writing of a good play or novel; indeed, it makes it far too easy.

We thus see that we are misled by superficial resemblances when we consider the cinema and the drama as closely similar arts. In its most important powers as a narrative medium the screen is actually much more like the novel.

The correctness of this view may be tested by adaptations from one of the three mediums to another. To dramatize a novel for the stage usually requires a most lamentable boiling down and cutting out, not to mention unavoidable changes of essential quality. On the contrary, screening a novel is comparatively easy. The brevity of the screen play, which is the principal difficulty, is partly compensated by its visual rapidity, and it can cope with the greatest range in scene and action. Poor screen adaptations are commoner than good ones, but we are considering the capacities of the medium, not the skill of the adapters; and good adaptations are frequent enough to show us something of what it can do. The screening of a drama, on the other hand, usually calls for expansion of physical action and reduction of dialogue, the breaking up of acts into short sequences, and the addition of new scenes to show visibly what is merely told about on the stage.

The superiority of the screen over the stage in range and fluidity is generally considered an artistic superiority. This view is, I believe, a mistaken one. A screen play must be continually on the go from beginning to end. *No intermissions are needed, and therefore none has functional justification.* Even the rare film that takes so long a time as to try the endurance of its audience—*Gone with the Wind,* for example—is usually run without pause. Indeed, an arbitrary interruption would strike us not only as unnecessary, but as inartistic. We come to have our eyes amused, and we want no intermissions. Film exhibitors in this country scarcely dare to turn up the house lights between shows, so compelling is the necessity of keeping the audience's eyes on the screen. Uninterrupted movement from start to finish is the law of the film. This necessarily makes for a fuller absorption of attention, but it is a distinct limitation upon the artistic possibilities of the film as compared with the drama, where intermissions are not merely a relief but a means of building up powerful effects of surprise and suspense.[16]

It limits also the achieving of adequate total effect. I do not refer to the American moviegoer's lackadaisical habit of strolling into a "continuous" show in the middle of a film and seeing it hind end foremost. This habit is not the fault of the medium. I am thinking of the psychological fact that the more concentrated the emotion of a spectator the shorter is the time he can endure it pleasurably. When a film lasts as long as the average stage play, with no intermissions such as the stage play always has, it becomes for many in the audience unpleasantly boring or exciting. Sheer fatigue is also likely, as it is when we have to endure more than three hours of "double feature" programs. In fact, the more exciting a film is, the more unpleasant the strain on the nerves. Being unable to utilize the external relief of intermissions, the producer is forced to seek emotional relief within the film itself. He can, for example, interrupt a serious action with comic relief like that of the old stage melodramas. But this usually results in destroying the unity of effect and the artistic integrity of the film. Or he can relax the emotional tension by softening it down. But this is to weaken the film. Or he can change the subject—with a loss of unity of theme. The screen play of *Gone with the Wind,* for instance, is tolerable in spite of its three and a half hours because, like the novel, it is episodic. The central love story ties the episodes together—after a fashion.

[16] See, in chap. iv, discussions under these headings: "Surprise," pp. 134 ff.; "Suspense," pp. 145 ff.

A final alternative is to make the film short. This is what is usually done.

Most films today are shown in "double feature" programs. If this abominable custom should be stopped, we would undoubtedly return to programs that offer a single feature with a "comedy" and "shorts." It might be argued that the length of a feature is governed by such customs. It seems more reasonable to assume that the custom is the result of the desires of the audience, and that these desires arise in large part from the fatigue caused by prolonged absorption in a single subject.

We should not dogmatize, but the noteworthy fact is that most films are short, and perhaps we may conclude that an hour and a half, or thereabouts, is the optimum length for them. If this is so, mixed programs will continue, and the artistic values of the feature in such programs will continue to be blurred by the effect of the other films. Perhaps, in theory, a beautiful film should remain as beautiful even when just before it begins we are forced to see five minutes of "prevues," and just afterward, twenty minutes of so-called "newsreel" showing mainly bathing beauties and gridiron heroes. But experience surely does not bear this out. A work of real art creates a mood we want to linger over; and when it is destroyed by the ruthless grinding of the projector the effect is as shocking as it would be in the concert hall if right after finishing Beethoven's "Emperor" concerto the orchestra should start in on "Hearts and Flowers." A work of art demands a frame in space or time to set it off from the rest of life and enable us to contemplate it as a whole. At the least there should be, after a powerfully moving cinema play, a few minutes' interval in which the audience might adjust itself to the banalities that are almost sure to follow.[17] This pause is sometimes actually provided.

It is also conceivable that exhibitors may some day make up programs that have something of the same aesthetic harmony that the numbers have in a well-planned symphony program. But, if the optimum length of a well-unified serious film is no more than an hour and a half, this brevity constitutes a more serious handicap; it means that the film writer cannot develop his action as gradually and subtly as the dramatist can. Act I of a play is usually given over, for the most part, to exposition, but the film must start its action much more quickly. Since the camera can set an environment in a few brief flashes, and can make the characters recognizable to the eye in almost as short a time, the scenarist is the less inclined to take us beneath this visible surface. Hence he generally skips complications of motive or subtleties of character such as make up the very essentials of dramatic interest in, for example, Ibsen's plays. Instead, we usually see a few token pictures to introduce the actors, and then immediately plunge into the action. The film is capable of doing more than this, and occasionally it succeeds in doing more; but the need for quick action, in order that the film may be finished in time, is a handicap that will always exist if, as seems likely, "programs" must always be the normal form of movie presentation.

Thus, in spite of its theoretical possibilities, in practice the cinema is a medium which, because it must be continually

[17] While at work on the first draft of this chapter I saw the beautiful French film, *Grand Illusion,* and with it a newsreel, a travelogue, and screened advertisements. At that, the "program" might easily have been worse.

moving, cannot easily pause to allow significances beneath the surface to sink into the spectator's mind; a medium which, because its primary appeal is a succession of visual images, cannot easily center the attention on profundities of human character. Thus the movies can hardly hope to achieve the effects of great drama. *Othello,* for instance, would probably be unendurable were it presented in full, honestly and unflinchingly, on the screen.

If, as some scholars think, Shakespeare's plays were originally produced without intermissions, the fact would not invalidate our principle. Shakespeare's audiences were made up mainly of rough and rowdy males who stood in the pit eating nuts, who were quick to find diversion among themselves if bored or troubled by the play, and who were not much troubled by squeamishness. Modern audiences are fixed in their seats, with inadequate leg room, and by custom are kept generally from emotional outlets except applause or laughter. When Guthrie McClintic produced *Yellow Jack* without intermissions, we are told, "the uninterrupted tension made for an exhausting evening, which probably accounted in part for the play's lack of popular appeal."[18]

But there is another reason why *Othello* is a triumphant work of art on the stage. Though it is an extremely painful story, the language in which it is written is extremely beautiful. Poetry has the power to soften, refine, and transmute into beauty the most terrible actions. Well-spoken poetry has this power in greater degree than that which is merely read. Hence, *the special power of the drama is its unrivaled use of the spoken word.*

[18] Eleanor Flexner, *American Playwrights, 1918–1938* (New York, 1938), p. 47.

The imaginative appeal of language transcends any possible appeal of photographs; for language suggests far more than it says, while photographs show far more than they can suggest. A photograph is a complete thing, definite and finished, but words are full of connotations, or overtones of significance, comprising all the memories and emotions which our constant use of them in the past conjures up in us when we hear them. A single word like "sunset" or "daughter" or "goodbye" may move us in certain circumstances to fancies which, as Browning expressed it, break through language and escape. Sometimes these effects are eccentric, like the emotion of the pious old lady in the anecdote who was so much affected by "that blessèd word Mesopotamia." For the most part, they are such as all of us who have lived full lives can share. When combined by a poet, words have a sometimes transcendent magic.

But I do not need to praise poetry. I do need to remind many people nowadays that great drama is poetry.[19] Much of the world's supreme poetry has been drama—the poetry of Aeschylus and Sophocles, of Shakespeare, of Racine. And there is no reason to believe that drama will not be the medium for much of the greatest poetry of the future. Written fiction, including narrative verse, cannot have the vitality of living speech. And the screen is only in a minor degree an art of words at all.

[19] See chap. x.

CHAPTER II

The Approach to Dramatic Criticism

THE PROCESS OF CRITICISM

THIS CHAPTER is concerned with certain general problems of criticism. It may strike some readers as platitudinous; and for those who are already, so to speak, in a state of grace, it may be. But others will probably find much to disagree with, and still others may not have thought about the matters discussed. To these this chapter may be of use.

The word criticism, as used here, means favorable as well as unfavorable judgment, and includes the honest opinions of the novice as well as those of the specialist. Thus we are not concerned with the special journalistic problems of professional dramatic critics in big cities. As journalists they must report and comment on the acting and all other interesting aspects of the production as well as on the play, and it is often more important for them to write entertainingly than justly. Moreover, they seldom have time to study and mature their judgments. In spite of these difficulties they often write excellent criticism. My point is that these difficulties do not concern the rest of us and so may be disregarded, but that the difficulties of criticism *per se* concern all of us.

In the broad sense everyone who reads such a book as this needs to be a critic. The student of course must write papers and answer examination questions. The director or actor must decide what sort of play he is working on, and how it should be interpreted. The scholar who is anything more than a collector of facts has a critical aim as a matter of course. And the amateur who simply likes to read and see plays wants to deepen his enjoyment of them. He can do so only through enlarging his critical understanding.

At this point some readers may dissent. A good many people dislike analyzing their feelings and picking a work of art to pieces. But real criticism leads to greater pleasure. The fan in the bleachers may howl with rage at times, but at others he is thrown into ecstasy by a feat of skill which an ignorant onlooker misses entirely. A seasoned playgoer cannot lose himself in a play like a child, but no seasoned playgoer wants to return to a childish state of undiscriminating suggestibility. When his experience of life, his ear for beautiful language, his eye for expert pantomime, color, and pictorial beauty, his understanding of technique and structure, his moral sentiments all approve his emotion, the effect he receives from a play is incomparably richer than anything a child can feel.

The full enjoyment and appreciation of great art is not a simple, natural response that one feels without trying; it requires long cultivation. "The judgment of literature is the final aftergrowth of much endeavor," said Longinus; and he was right. To offer a personal illustration, I had my first experience of dramatic emotion in the theater when I was ten years old, on seeing the "sacred cantata" *Esther* as performed by local talent of high school age. The romantic charm of the performance, and particularly of the heroine, laid me under a spell from which I did not recover for weeks. My feeling was probably stronger than any experienced by a professional critic at the performance of a masterpiece. Certainly it was much purer in the sense that it was entirely uncontaminated by judgment, sense of proportion, familiarity with the theater, knowledge of life, or any other adult consideration. But I have no more wish to return to that state of innocence than a music lover who has progressed from Johann to Richard Strauss wants to return to the days when the "Blue Danube" waltz filled him with delight but "Death and Transfiguration" was merely noise.

If we can all agree, then, that it is worth while to cultivate sound critical judgment, our next problem is to decide what the critical task is. I suggest that the purpose of good criticism may be summed up as seeking to answer three questions: What did the author set out to do? Did he succeed in doing it? And, was it worth doing? These questions were first propounded by Goethe in a slightly different form: "What did the author set out to do? Was his plan reasonable and sensible, and how far did he succeed in carrying it out?"[1] The order first given, however, is the order in which the critic should proceed. He should want to know the author's intentions first, and last of all he should try to judge the value of the work. Some critics, to be sure, including Mr. Spingarn, omit the third question entirely: they think that a criticism is complete when it determines the success

[1] Quoted from *Goethe's Literary Essays,* edited by J. E. Spingarn (New York, 1921), p. 140.

of an artist's purpose. I shall have something to say about this view later. At present I shall assume that all three questions should be answered.

How shall we find out what the author was trying to do? If he tells us in a preface or through a character who is clearly and unquestionably his mouthpiece, our task is simplified. But good playwrights seldom express their personal views through their characters, and even Bernard Shaw, for all his prefatory volubility, may not always make his intentions clear. Thus I have found his few remarks about *Candida* far from helpful in explaining his intentions regarding Marchbanks and Morell. The former is usually played "straight" in spite of his absurdities, in order to win sympathy, but it is the preacher, not the poet, who on the whole stands for the things that his author believes in. Or did Shaw aim at showing up impartially the strength and weakness of both for the sake of comic contrast, disregarding social significance? Such is not his customary practice. How we answer such questions makes a world of difference in our interpretation of the play.

If the author has made no specific commitments regarding the play, his general point of view may help us. To know what this is we must read what has been published about him and his environment, and above all we must read other writings of his, especially letters and essays. Such evidence as we can get in this way may be vague, and we should be slow to make positive assertions on the basis of it; but it may give us valuable leads.

The play itself, however, is the best evidence of its author's intentions. If it is well done it speaks for itself, and speaks so clearly that usually our first question can be answered with little or no doubt as soon as we have read or seen it.

Our second question, however, is another matter. Here we are concerned not with what the author meant to do, but with his effect on other people. But each one of us can speak only for himself; we have no accurate ways of knowing whether our impressions are typical, as it is not customary to conduct polls of public opinion on such matters; and often the individual critic can be pretty sure that special conditions make his impressions eccentric. Similarity of the plot to some event in his own life, for instance, may greatly affect his feelings. On a more trivial plane, his feelings may be influenced one way by the companionship of a charming person of the other sex; in the opposite way, by a whisperer in the row behind him. Obviously we must do our best to eliminate such irrelevances from our critical judgment; but we cannot hope to do so entirely, and we may be sure that our point of view is never wholly representative of that of the majority. Indeed, we should hardly wish it to be so; we should want it to be superior. Though, in a sense, a majority vote decides the commercial fate of most plays, it does not decide their intrinsic merit. Nonetheless, we cannot properly take it upon ourselves as individuals to answer the second question without regard to other people.

Personal conditions are not the only irrelevances that a critic must eliminate if he is to judge a play as a play. His response to the acting and the mise-en-scène are also irrelevant, since they are not the work of the dramatist. Of course these things are important and interesting, and if we are people of the theater they are often of more interest to us than the play; but this book assumes that we are, at least for the time being, concerned with the drama *per se,* and that even an actor will find it profitable to eliminate his histrionic interests temporarily when considering the value of a play that he wants to study.

If we have never read the play before seeing it, and must judge it from seeing it once, this task is difficult. It is usually beyond the powers even of trained newspaper critics who must meet a deadline, as can be proved by their many condemnations of good plays or laudations of bad ones according as the one performance they are writing about has affected them. Sheridan's *Rivals* nearly failed at its first production because the critics were enraged at the poor acting of the player who impersonated Sir Lucius O'Trigger.

On the other hand, if we have studied a play and seen it several times in different productions, we easily discriminate between acting and book. We then enjoy the acting in proportion to the effectiveness of its interpretation of the story—a principal reason why playgoers never tire of seeing new Hamlets. We then enjoy the play also for its own sake.

I have tried to show that it is important to make such discriminations; but unfortunately few people ever attempt them. Naturally the majority who go to a "show" for amusement do not, but even the few who have special reasons to be critical are still pretty much habituated to the star system, under which almost all plays short of Shakespeare are mere "vehicles."

Having sifted his feelings about a play and disregarded irrelevant ones, the critic must deal with those for which the dramatist alone is responsible. And here he must at all costs be honest. No matter how strong his reasons for wishing to feel otherwise, let him never pretend to like what he dislikes, or dislike what he likes!

This advice may sound easy, but the pressure of opinion is often too much for us, and we seldom realize that to yield to the opinion of authorities in matters of this kind is to destroy our chances of forming our own taste, which, like salvation, is something we have to work out for ourselves. I do not mean, of course, that we should lightly disregard the opinions of professional critics and scholars. On the contrary, we should generally assume that when they agree they are probably right, and that if they disagree they do so for good reasons which it would be enlightening to understand. I mean that we should distinguish opinion about a work of art from the actual experience of its beauty. We can get the opinion from other people; we can get the experience only by ourselves.

Let us imagine that our critic is a novice, a modest young man who has seen and thoroughly enjoyed *Abie's Irish Rose* and has been bored by *Romeo and Juliet.* He is sure, and correctly so, that there is something wrong with his feelings. Shall he pretend to feelings he did not have? Not at all; to do that would be either hypocrisy or, what is worse, self-deception. He should try instead to find out why he liked the wrong play. That way lies critical insight.

One likely reason for his preference is that, like all normal and healthy young men, he likes love stories, and that the modern play was a love story near enough to his own experience for him to identify himself with the lover and imagine the girl to be actually his own. There is surely nothing to be ashamed of in that; but if he has the inquiring mind which, along with sensitive perceptions, makes a critic, he will begin to wonder whether he did not miss something in Shakespeare's play. Let him pursue that line of inquiry and he may make valuable discoveries about poetry, delicacy of characterization, and even the beauty of a tragic approach to life. As a result, he may come to feel as well as to reason out the values that he missed at first: he may find himself, among other things, responding to genuine sentiment and disliking sentimentality.

The initial data for determining the effect of a play, then, are our own personal impressions, stripped as far as possible of irrelevances; and it is upon them that our critical structure must always be built.

These impressions are strongly emotional, and it is extremely difficult to apprehend our emotions intellectually. We have a few names for them, such as anger, love, hate, and the like; but these names are vague general labels whereas our feelings are always immediate, mixed, confused, and changing. Moreover, they are not a mixture or confusion of concrete objects like a junk pile or a heap of jackstraws, which can be sorted out and definitely classified. They are more like what we might observe if we should look into a transparent chamber through which by different channels a great number of different fluids were flowing in constantly varying volume, some of them interacting with each other chemically so as to change their essential nature, others mixing mechanically, and yet others remaining distinct but with indefinite regions of separation. Should we imagine these fluids to be of different colors, they would exhibit a chromatic flux like the effects of a color organ. They would have no outlines or permanent characteristics to be defined by the intellect.

As we mature, we learn, in spite of the difficulty, to make some order out of our emotional states. Each complex of feeling tends to be dominated by one recognizable emotion. Such complexes tend to repeat themselves in the course of living—not exactly, but approximately so often that we recognize them and often give them names. When we are first seized by a new emotion in our youth—erotic love or jealousy, for example—we are thrown into intellectual confusion by it because we cannot recognize it or foresee its consequences; but with experience we learn to understand it and—sometimes—to deal with it intelligently. We cannot annul it by reason, but we can often act so as to prevent its doing us harm. Thus, a few of us learn to hold our tongues when we are angry.

Aesthetic emotions are seldom powerful enough to do us injury; indeed, for them to be aesthetic at all—according to one theory at least—they must be felt, as it were, at a distance. For this reason we can the more easily objectify and study them. They then become objects of thought in spite of their cloudy indefiniteness, and we can draw critical judgments from them.

Obviously, such judgments differ from scientific or legal judgments since their initial data are matters not of fact but of feeling; and as everyone's feeling is and must be peculiar to himself, inevitably different in some degree from everyone else's and inevitably incommunicable except in crude outline, it follows that no aesthetic judgment can ever be final. It is always limited by the temperamental peculiarities of the individual.

It does not follow, however, that everyone's aesthetic judgment is as good as everyone else's. The old saw that there is no arguing about tastes really means that nobody can prove his preferences correct. But the admission that a geometrical demonstration is impossible in criticism does not involve the corollary that there are no critical standards at all.

Incidentally, the old saw is also wrong if it implies that people should not argue about tastes. The more vital the arts are to us the more we want to argue about them, and the more we argue about them the more we sharpen our perceptions and capacities for discrimination. For the majority of us who are not creators, is there any more civilized occupation? There is surely no more delightful one.

On the question of standards people often go to extremes: they either say that there are no standards at all, as do the impressionist critics, or they try to maintain one definite and rigid set of standards, as do the dogmatists. Anatole France was an extremist of the former type: to him everything was a matter of chance and relativity. The neoclassic critics of the late seventeenth and early eighteenth centuries were extremists of the latter type: they set up Aristotle and Horace as absolute authorities.

If we are candid we must admit, I believe, that we cannot prove the relativists wrong in theory; but we can easily show that they never conform to their theory in practice, and that to do so would stultify all human action. France himself continually made literary judgments on the basis of a set of standards which he had developed in spite of his disbelief in them. If one maintains that aesthetic judgments are merely relative, one must logically maintain that moral ones are merely relative also. But to maintain this is to say that we have no right to prefer one course of action to another. Nobody ever goes so far as this. Our need to preserve our lives, if no other need, forces us to make up our minds about questions of right and wrong. All men have standards of value, whether they believe them relative or absolute.

As for the other extremists, the dogmatists, in this age which is dominated by relativistic theory there is no need to argue that they have gone too far. Nobody nowadays maintains that Aristotle's *Poetics* is infallible. On the contrary, a strong tendency among some critics of an iconoclastic temper is to deny that it has any merit whatever. *The Theatre Handbook*,[2] for example, offers as its entire article on Aristotle three paragraphs: the first, of six lines, giving biographical data; the second, of five lines, quoting S. R. Littlewood to the effect that the *Poetics* is a mere assortment of lecture notes and that it has "gone far to stifle . . . dramatic effort after a score of centuries"; and the third, of seven lines, quoting Brooks Atkinson in a passage heartily agreeing with Mr. Littlewood. Mr. Atkinson speaks of what he calls Aristotle's "system of platitudes and blunders."

It is unnecessary to point out that in a work offered as an authoritative reference on all matters concerning the theater and the drama such an article is inexcusably partisan and inadequate. What is significant for us here is its demonstration of the modern bias against authority. Of course the

[2] New York, Crown Publishers, 1940.

Poetics is no Bible. At the same time, it is full of wisdom; it is extremely valuable and stimulating to the contemporary critic who really studies it, as it was to the critics of the last three centuries. I do not apologize for my own many references to it.

Common sense suggests a middle position between these extremes. Our standards in taste and in morals are the expression of human nature. In matters of superficial choice they vary widely from age to age, and the more superficial the concern the more eccentric and whimsical they are likely to be. In times of peace the United States, for example, is annually swept by some craze—at one time for marathon dances, at another for pole sitting. Should we judge our human standards by such crazes alone, the relativists would seem amply justified. But the more fundamental our concern, the more important it is for human welfare, the less our attitudes toward it are likely to vary. Robbery and murder have always been crimes, and always will be. Cruelty, cowardice, selfishness have always been reprobated; kindliness, bravery, genuine altruism have always been admired. Though evil rulers may for a time try to corrupt whole nations, and though there is some variation even among the free, fundamental moral attitudes are surprisingly stable and definite through the centuries.

In artistic fields there is the same general agreement in respect to masterpieces. The greatness of Homer, of Phidias, of Sophocles stands unquestioned. It is the work of third-rate importance about which there is great variety of opinion. The masterpieces appeal to the most fundamental and therefore the most unchanging of human emotions.

The critic who believes in standards will no longer urge the artist to imitate these masters. Such advice as Pope's:

> Learn hence for ancient rules a just esteem;
> To copy nature is to copy them,

is extreme. Rather, a reasonable critic would follow Arnold in urging the artist to know and emulate the best that has been thought and said. An artist must write out of his own experience and in terms of his own day; he must discover his own methods of expressing what he has to say. Mere imitation would prevent him from doing these things. Emulation, however, will foster whatever capacities he has for largeness of soul, delicacy, power, and depth, such as he finds in the masters. All young artists, as a matter of fact, emulate somebody. The trouble with too many of them is that they do not emulate the highest, but are corrupted by the desire for easy success and money, or are swept off their feet by the popularity of some writer of their immediate time who appeals to strong but temporary interests. In the 'twenties all undergraduates of literary leanings tried to write Menckenese. In the 'thirties those who wrote fiction aped Hemingway; those who tried drama, Odets or Saroyan.

Whether based on masterpieces or not, a set of artistic standards is no rigid set of rules. Indeed, the word "standards" is misleading in such matters because it ordinarily suggests instruments of exact physical measurement like yardsticks. In aesthetic matters standards are, on the contrary, flexible and intuitive; they are matters of tentative rather than definite comparison, because the things compared are matters of feeling.

Feeling needs the training of much experience and the correction of wide knowledge of the subject. Much of the latter it is the proper function of scholarship to supply. Professional critics of Shakespeare, for instance, must either be scholars themselves or know the most important literature of Shakespearean scholarship. (They cannot know it all; life is not long enough.) Otherwise they are sure to misinterpret Shakespeare's Elizabethan language, misunderstand the viewpoint of the audience for which he wrote, overlook the special conditions of his theater, or in a variety of other ways build conclusions on shaky foundations. They are under an obligation to know the relevant facts before they pass judgment, for no delicacy of feeling or brilliance of expression will save them if they do not. Even at best they will make mistakes—or at least other Shakespearean critics will think so.

At the same time, the scholarly accumulation of information is not the end of criticism; it is merely a means. This obvious fact would go without saying, much less emphasizing, were it not that scholarship, especially in universities, is itself a profession, and a fascinating one too. The professor is always in danger of forgetting that what he calls historical or textual criticism is often not criticism at all since it never goes beyond facts to evaluation.

The serious critic needs also something even more important—worldly wisdom. Since he can get this, in any direct sense, only by living in the world, no book can give it to him; but a book may emphasize that without experience of life he can never understand the motives or sympathize justly with the struggles of the characters in a great play.

When he comes to answer our third question, the critic brings to bear upon his impressions of the work whatever scholarly knowledge he has that applies, whatever worldly experience, and, most of all, whatever acquaintance with other works of similar nature. He has stored in his mind a large number of general impressions of other works. If he is properly trained, this storehouse is well stocked and organized, with the best in one group, the second-rate in another, and so on to the downright bad. If his fully studied impressions of the new work patently fit in one place, he can put them there without delay. This is pigeonholing, to be sure; but many a play fits a pigeonhole.

Others, of course, do not, and the critic always runs the risk of wrongly disposing of one on the basis of a superficial examination. A really original creation is much harder to place, and sometimes requires a shelf all to itself. But to some degree it can always be brought into relation to other works. In respect to one of its salient characteristics it is like work A; in respect to another, like work B; in respect to a third, something entirely novel perhaps. Thus, in characteristic 1 it is highly distinguished, in characteristic 2 only fair, in characteristic 3 a relative failure, and so on. There will emerge from such careful comparisons and weighings, ultimately, a fairly clear and coherent "picture" of the work as a whole, which becomes the critic's final judgment of it.

This critical labor, as I have tried to describe it, is highly complex and difficult. Nobody would undertake it voluntarily without a natural inclination in that direction, and in this sense critics, like poets, are born. Again like poets, they become masters only by training. At first the work must be slow, and if the critics are lazy they will shirk the scholarly study it needs, or the final arduous testing of their impressions. If they persevere, however, they reach in time a state of experience and expertness in which they are able to make up their minds quickly and accurately on almost all works they are called upon to judge. Their immediate responses become generally reliable without elaborate intellectual testing and justification. They are then what we call connoisseurs; they have trained themselves to like good things and dislike bad ones, and can jump to conclusions intuitively with reasonable confidence. Such a critic, no matter how well trained, will not offer his intuitive conclusions to a reader without carefully testing them and justifying them, but he will reach them quickly and accurately. He will have, in short, what we call a trained taste.

As I have pointed out earlier, we should wish to train our taste to such a point for the sake of the increased artistic pleasure it affords us. In a larger sense, it is important for mankind that those who are specially gifted in criticism should cultivate their gift. The critic seeks to arrive at such an estimate of a work of art as not only displays its every significant quality, but also shows how far it measures up to the masterpieces of its kind and, finally, judges its importance to civilization. The critic thus becomes, at his best, a defender and promoter of genuine culture and even of morality and religion. He will seldom directly occupy such high ground, but his philosophy, whatever it is, is bound to be implicit in even his most trivial observations.

All of us can therefore undertake such critical work as we are capable of with an assurance of its value.

So much for the critic's general task. I wish next to consider three special difficulties which often beset the student of the drama. They take the form of widespread but mistaken or at least exaggerated opinions. The first is that a play should be a work of "pure" art. That is the aesthete's view. The second is the businessman's view that a play should merely entertain, so as to make money. The third is the view of the partisan or moralist, who demands that the play should be judged solely by the degree to which it teaches a lesson acceptable to him.

There is real need of clearing our minds on these questions because the advocates of each view influence large numbers of theatergoers and students. Practical men of the theater, for example, often adopt a disillusioned if not cynical attitude toward any artistic idealism in the show business. Propagandists, on the other hand, influence ardent idealists among spectators to look with scorn on plays that merely entertain. And aesthetes (I use the word in a narrow sense) have spread abroad among many intellectuals the doctrine of art for art's sake, according to which the pursuit of practical ends of any sort, even the highest morality, constitutes a cardinal artistic sin.

THE IDEAL OF "PURE" ART

One way of considering the doctrine of the "artsakists," as for the sake of brevity I shall call them, is to review the great dramas of the past and see to what degree they have been written from purely aesthetic motives.

It is generally conceded that in the fifth century before Christ the little city of Athens produced more artistic masterpieces than any other community has ever done in the course of a like period in all the history of mankind. Yet the Greeks had no notion of art as an end in itself, but on the contrary judged their drama along with their dance, their music, their painting, their sculpture and architecture, primarily according to its service to the gods and the state. (These ends were not yet distinct, for piety and patriotism were still one.) The artists themselves accepted this view of their function. Aeschylus, of course, was a pious patriot, as his plays make obvious. There is no reason to believe that even the skeptical and disillusioned Euripides regarded himself otherwise than as a promoter of morality and the well-being of his city. His very skepticism is an expression of his earnest dissatisfaction with elements in Greek religion that did not measure up to the highest moral standards. Of course, like all independent moral thinkers, he aroused hostility. Aristophanes in particular savagely satirized him in more than one play. Yet what does Aristophanes put into his mouth, when, in *The Frogs,* he has the character Aeschylus ask him, "What are the principal merits entitling a poet to praise and renown?" He has Euripides answer:

> The improvement of morals, the progress of mind,
> When a poet, by skill and invention,
> Can render his audience virtuous and wise.

Later, after Athens had lost its independence and its ancient pieties, the great age of creativeness had passed, and the city became a seat of learning, the arts were studied academically for their own sake. Similarly Alexandria, in the Hellenistic period, became a center for learning and aestheticism rather than creation.

The Romans, even before they had conquered Greece, were won by its superior culture to an often slavish imitation. Unfortunately, Greek art though admirable was for the Romans an alien and impractical adornment of life, and could not possess the power for social integration which it had had for the Athenians. It became Art with a capital "A": something to be collected by connoisseurs, not something to move the spirit and influence conduct. It ceased to be democratic and vital. The drama in particular leaned so heavily on Greek models that vital native material, such as we find at times in Plautus, could not survive; the theater could not compete for popular favor with the arena; and writers turned to closet drama, literary in the narrow sense. Little of Plautus and Terence, and none of Seneca, has intrinsic dramatic interest for us. These writers are important to the student of the drama chiefly for the light they throw on their Greek sources and the influence they exerted on the playwrights of the Renaissance.

In the Middle Ages drama once more arose from religion, and for a time it had a vitality like that of Greek drama though its form was different. Again the religious influence declined and plays became secular entertainment. But these medieval plays were too rude to be valued as art, and no class of wealthy connoisseurs arose to patronize them. They remained essentially popular entertainment, so that when an interest in art developed in the Renaissance, poets and scholars naturally turned for dramatic models not to their vital native drama, but to the classics.

The growth of aestheticism in the Renaissance was gradual, for the critics were at least nominally Christians and were in some measure influenced by the Church's age-old hostility to the stage, and even those who had least sympathy with the puritan's hatred of secular entertainment unquestioningly accepted Horace's dictum that a poem should instruct as well as please. As for the playwrights, some of them, like Shakespeare, did not concern themselves with theory; but those who did were full of pious professions. There was no drama that was written for art's sake only; at least, none that has survived in the theater. Shakespeare wrote to amuse and gain profit; Racine had pious as well as worldly intentions. The great age of English drama was one in which popular entertainment was the dominating motive in the theater; the great age of French drama, one adapted to the preferences of the Sun King's court and the suspicions of the Church.

In France during the seventeenth and eighteenth centuries, and in England after the Restoration until well into the eighteenth, the tastes of the aristocracy largely controlled the stage, but in the late eighteenth century came the revolutionary age in which the growth of commerce and industry put power into the hands of the middle class. This change affected the drama in two very important ways.

The first was the rapid commercialization of the theater. Since ordinary citizens now paid the piper, they called the tune. And as they could be a source of large profit only if they attended in large numbers, theater managers and playwrights began to develop the methods of modern mass appeal. Though theaters had been businesses before, they had been small businesses, run for the most part by the actors themselves, often supported by aristocratic patronage and monopoly privileges that put them at least partly beyond the need of playing down to the populace. Now they grew into big businesses, run usually by entrepreneurs who hired actors and cared only for profits. This is the condition of most of them in Western nations still.

Naturally, dramatists wrote more and more for mere entertainment. A German, August von Kotzebue (1761–1819), holds the dubious honor of being the first playwright of our commercial era to make wholesale profits. His vulgar, sentimental plays were vastly popular over all Europe, and were translated into French, Spanish, Dutch, Russian, Greek, Swedish, Danish, Rumanian, Italian, and English. The most popular of them, *Menschenhass und Reue* (1790), held the English stage under the name of *The Stranger* down into the 1870's.

A generation later, the Frenchman Eugène Scribe (1791–1861) had an even greater commercial success. He turned out some 374 dramatic works, including *vaudevilles,* melodramas, comedies, *drames,* and operas, and owned a fortune of two million francs when he died. He was an excellent businessman in other respects, too, for through his efforts the modern method of paying authors by royalties was established. His products were slick, machine-made vehicles that carried acting troupes triumphantly throughout the Western world. Their superficial skill and essential emptiness fixed in the critical vocabulary the term *pièce bien faite* (well-made play) as a label for the type.

Scribe's successor to the kingship of commercial playwriting was Victorien Sardou (1831–1908). With equal skill, he had a larger range of subject matter and more pretentious-ness; but time has proved his plays equally hollow. Though no one playwright since his day has gained so overwhelming a success, the majority have had like aims. Nowadays, in this country, as soon as one achieves a "smash hit" he goes to Hollywood, where, in recompense for a loss of creative independence and possible fame, he can get more money.

The commercialism of Kotzebue, Scribe, and Sardou is directly contrary to a devotion to art, and as none of them wrote a single play of any artistic merit they might be considered as proving that the commercial motive destroys artistry. Unfortunately, those who opposed them from pure artistic motives were equally unsuccessful in writing great plays. If Scribe and his like were too "popular" to be artistic, his opponents were too "aesthetic" to be popular; and a good play must combine popularity and artistic merit. During the early nineteenth century most of those who tried to write purely artistic plays were romantics who shone in writing lyrics but not dramas. Not a single first-class play has come to us from the great English romantic poets, though they all, from Wordsworth to Tennyson, tried to write plays. Victor Hugo is the chief name among the French. There is no doubt that his *Hernani* has been popular, but nobody, at least outside of France, would ever think it great.

One of the French romantics, Théophile Gautier, who was a journalist as well as a poet, tried for several years to counteract the popularity of Scribe by violent critiques, but at length wrote in despair (1841): "As for us, four or five years of criticisms have led us to the conviction, confirmed by M. Scribe's successes, that the theater has nothing to do with literature, and that thought has little importance in it. Poetry, philosophy, the study of the heart, analysis of passions and character, caprice, fantasy, style—these excellences, the highest of the [playwright's] art, would surely cause the failure of a play."[3] This view became widespread among the poets, most of whom gave up trying to write for the stage, and when they did write in dramatic form, wrote closet dramas, which strictly speaking are not dramas at all because not capable of life on the stage.[4] The majority of gifted literary men chose rather the purely literary genres—the novel, the lyric, the short story. Only in recent years have they had much encouragement to return to the theater.

Thus we find a strange anomaly in the status of the drama during the last century. Through all previous centuries since Aristotle, writers of plays were universally called poets, and tragedy was deemed the highest possible form of poetic art. This was not merely because dramatists habitually wrote in verse, but because, as Aristotle himself carefully points out, a poet was a maker of plots. Since the commercial and romantic revolutions, this point of view has become foreign to us. When people speak of poets nowadays, they mean writers of lyric verses. When they speak of literary men, they think of lyrists, novelists, essayists. The dramatist is outside the pale.

Some dramatists themselves take pride in their nonliterary and purely theatrical professionalism, and like to remind

---

[3] Quoted by N. C. Arvin, *Eugène Scribe and the French Theatre, 1815–1860* (Cambridge, Mass., 1924), p. 229. The present translation is mine.

[4] Alfred de Musset's little *proverbes* and comedies are an extraordinary exception. One of them was "discovered" accidentally by a French actress playing in Russia where she saw it performed in translation. She introduced it to Paris on her return. They soon became part of the repertory of the Théâtre Français.

themselves that they, like Shakespeare and Molière, live in the theater. But Shakespeare and Molière also lived in the world; that is, however narrow their outer lives may have been, they possessed the humane imagination to look past theatricality into the vital problems of all men, significant for their age and every age. The trouble with Scribe and Sardou (as perhaps also with some contemporaries like Noel Coward) is that they lived only in the theater and, like many highly specialized persons, lost contact with the concerns of nonprofessionals.

Modern commercialism and specialization have tended to drive the fine arts in general into cults which are out of touch with the great public, and to stimulate the development in large cities of connoisseurs who take pride in admiring only that art which is caviar to the general. The cult of art for art's sake is a natural result of this tendency. The artsakist wishes to judge a work solely by its aesthetic value. He is apt to be rather vague about what this value *is,* but definite about what it is *not.* Among other things, it is not anything to do with morality, choice of subject matter, popularity, verisimilitude, or even—for the more radical—meaning. Since the drama is necessarily a popular art, it seldom appeals to these people, who turn in preference to verse, abstract painting, and music. In the last, the least representational of the arts, they sometimes find the aesthetic "purity" they desire.

If their view affected themselves alone, we should hardly need to take account of it, but critics and professors have spread the notion widely. The consequence is that many students of the drama approach a play with the assumption that it ought to be judged solely by its possession of Beauty, and that so far as it is merely entertaining or edifying it is inartistic. We have seen that few, if any, great plays have been written without the intention of entertaining or edifying, and we must conclude that the artsakists make demands which the drama cannot meet. We may also conclude that their demands are unreasonable. A further examination of the commercial motive and the reforming instinct will confirm us in this opinion.

THE COMMERCIAL MOTIVE

All of us will grant that dramatists, like other people, must make a living, and ought to make a good enough one to live comfortably, at least. Starving in a garret is no aid to an artist. At the same time, it is generally felt that writing merely to make money is not only an inartistic motive but one fatal to artistic production. It usually is, as we have seen. Yet some of the greatest dramatists worked primarily for profit.

Lope de Vega wrote the most prodigious number of plays ever composed by a single mortal—the total is calculated variously as between 1,800 and 2,400—and this stupendous productivity was to make money. "I write," he tells us with engaging candor, "in accordance with that art which they devised who aspired to the applause of the crowd; for, since the crowd pays for the comedies, it is fitting to talk foolishly to it to satisfy its taste."[5] Yet in spite of this commercialism, not to mention the haste and carelessness inevitable to such

[5] "The New Art of Writing Plays in This Age" (1609), translated by Wm. T. Brewster, in Barrett H. Clark, *European Theories of the Drama* (rev. ed.; New York, 1929), p. 90.

quantity production, some of Lope's plays, at least, are deserving of critical respect after three centuries.

Molière was the greatest comedist[6] who ever lived, yet he was a professional actor and producer, all too ready to please his audience and his royal patron, and he ridiculed the contemporary pedantry of judging plays strictly according to the "classical" rules. "If the plays that are according to the rules don't please, and those that please aren't according to the rules, it follows of necessity that the rules were badly made. Let us scout the chicanery to which they [the critics] would subject the public, and in a comedy consider only the effect it has upon us."[7]

Shakespeare, it seems, thought little of his plays as art, since he never bothered to print them (though he published his narrative poems), and thought much of the money they earned him, since as soon as he had made a pile, he retired to Stratford to live as a "gentleman" like any bourgeois philistine.

It may be that these geniuses, though they began with mere thoughts of gain, became fired by their theme and ended by writing for art's sake. Many men actually need the spur of some necessity, financial or other, to get to work; but, once under way, some of them are impelled by higher inspiration. If this were all that is to be said for the commercial motive, however, it would not justify it aesthetically. There is more to be said, and it is this: the commercial motive makes a playwright consider his audience.

---

[6] At the risk of irritating some readers I am venturing to use the words "comedist" and "tragedist" in this book instead of the cumbersome "writer of comedy" and "writer of tragedy," or the ambiguous "comedian" and "tragedian."

[7] Dorante in *La Critique de l'école des femmes* (1663); my translation.

Pure art is an admirable ideal, but like holiness it is often best approached by indirection. The ideal of pure art according to the classical tradition was firmly upheld by Addison and Johnson, but when Addison wrote *Cato* (1713) and Johnson *Irene* (1736) their reverence for the ancients did not prevent them from composing very dull plays.[8] And we have seen how unsuccessful were the nineteenth-century poets who wrote plays according to the romantic ideal of pure art.

Perhaps the best example is Goethe. He was intensely interested in the theater and in great drama, as anyone knows who has read *Wilhelm Meister;* and, after he had become the boon companion of the Duke of Saxe-Weimar, he was appointed director of the ducal theater and given a free hand and funds to produce what plays he would in what way he would. He was hampered, it is true, by mediocre actors and an uncultivated audience, but he nevertheless had what might seem an almost ideal opportunity to make effective use of the stage as a medium for poetry. He did produce a large variety of great plays from Greece, Rome, Spain, Italy, England, and France, as well as native works, and he did experiment with staging and acting; but his temperament, encouraged by his associates of the court, was aristocratic and dictatorial, and he despised his audience. "No one can serve two masters," he wrote to Schiller, "and of all the masters the last that I would select is the public which sits in a German theatre."[9] He had only to point to

[8] *Cato* had a temporary vogue because its theme was applied to contemporary political controversy. *Irene* was produced by Garrick in 1749.

[9] Quoted by G. H. Lewes, *The Life of Goethe* (Leipzig, 1882), Vol. II, bk. vi, chap. v, p. 213.

Kotzebue, who happened to be a fellow citizen of his in Weimar, as an awful example of what flattering the public might lead to. In his own works his aim, consequently, was for the most part literary in the narrow sense rather than dramatic, and his plays are all essentially closet dramas. He saddled his countrymen for a hundred years with a theatrical tradition out of touch with the vital social forces that make great acting possible. "Upon the art of acting in Germany," writes Karl Mantzius,[10] "the Weimar School exercised a fateful influence.... Its empty, monotonous, but sonorous declamation, and generalized, plastic style of gesture furnished a convenient shelter for dullness.... To this day the aftereffects of Goethe's schooling are clearly traceable in German acting, and anyone who has attended a performance in the unadulterated classic style at a third-rate Court theatre will feel a lively sympathy for the well-disciplined Weimar public in the trials to which it was exposed." Worse than this, dramatic literature lost the contributions it might have had from the greatest literary genius of his age.

I should not expect a German to agree with this assertion, but it should hardly be difficult to defend before disinterested judges. We need concern ourselves only with those of his plays on which his reputation as a dramatist rests. Of these his first, *Götz von Berlichingen* (1773), is double the length proper for the stage, and is written in a loose chronicle form that imitates all the weaknesses of Shakespeare's dramaturgy and few of its merits. The real literary merits of the play (and they are considerable) lie in its admirable

[10] *A History of Theatrical Art* (trans. by Louise von Cossel; London, 1921), Vol. VI, p. 268.

characterization, particularly of Götz; but these are novelistic rather than dramatic. In short, it was written to be read. Goethe himself admitted, after attempting its adaptation to the stage, that such a play cannot succeed in the theater.[11]

Of *Egmont* (1775–1788) John G. Robertson[12] writes, "Goethe has stretched the limits of dramatic form to the utmost; no other of his dramas, not even *Tasso,* is so deficient in progressive action." *Iphigenia* is a purely literary adaptation of Euripides. As for Goethe's masterpiece, *Faust,* only by cuts and adaptations can a stage play be made out of its first part; its second part is totally undramatic. *Faust* is a great poem, but it lives only in book form. Yet it has all the machinery of a play—all the forms of dramatic dialogue, scene, and act. Coleridge wisely said, "Nothing can permanently please, which does not contain in itself the reason why it is so, and not otherwise." But there is nothing in the purpose or subject matter of the second part of *Faust,* and little in the first, that makes its dramatic machinery necessary. It suffers from the fault inherent in all closet dramas: it utilizes machinery without any real function. Great as it is in power of expression, nobility of feeling, and range of imagination and thought, it remains, so far as dramatic art is concerned, a monument of genius wasted.

"I should like to know," wrote Molière, "whether the rule of all rules is not to please?"[13] In a broad sense this question suggests a truism for all art, since even *Faust,* Part II, in order

[11] "A piece that is not originally, by the intent and skill of the poet, written for the boards, will not succeed." *Conversations with Eckermann,* quoted in J. E. Spingarn's *Goethe's Literary Essays* (New York, 1921), p. 269.

[12] *A History of German Literature* (New York, 1908), p. 321.

[13] *La Critique de l'école des femmes.*

to gain literary distinction, had to please at least the critics who praised it. But in the narrow sense meant by Molière, with reference to plays written for the stage, the rule has a peculiar importance because of the peculiar dependence of the drama on popular suffrage. One who writes for readers alone, like Goethe, can depend on the discerning few. A dramatist cannot.

This necessity of pleasing an audience is galling to many lovers of literature, who would prefer their drama uncontaminated by the impurities of theatricality, and so, when they discuss a dramatist whom they admire, they try as far as possible to ignore his theatricalities. A good deal of Shakespearean criticism during the Romantic period and even later was of this sort, and it took the vehement attacks of a number of scholars like Professor Stoll to bring Shakespeare the practical playwright back into proper perspective. Excellent as was the criticism of Goethe, Coleridge, and De Quincey, it is vitiated by the failure to realize that Shakespeare wrote for a particular stage and to please a popular audience. This is the more to be deplored because, as we have seen, the peculiar glory of great drama is its triumph over the extraordinary difficulties of the medium.

No matter what his inclinations, in his work the dramatist must be democrat enough at least to win audiences. He must win them here and now, for there will be no resurrection of his play later on if he does not.[14] A painting, a lyric, a piece of music may lie unknown for years and then become famous; not so, a drama.

[14] The sole notable exception that proves this rule is the plays of Alfred de Musset, already referred to.

Even Ibsen, who was by nature and philosophy an aristocrat, scornful of the mob and indignant at its follies, forced himself to write for a general audience. It took him years to learn how, but he did, and even grew rich on his box-office receipts. He never, to be sure, wrote merely commercial plays. He even flouted the taboos and prejudices of his contemporaries, as in *Ghosts*. Yet to excite bitter antagonism, as he did, is a good way of filling a theater. One thing he was careful never to do: bore his audience. He throve on denunciation; he would have failed if he had been dull or unactable. He knew his job as a playwright.

Other arts may succeed through the admiration of scattered individuals. A play must win a crowd all at once. If it goes over their heads it will fail financially. If it lowers itself to their bad tastes it will fail artistically. Hence to be both successful and artistic it must win audiences without yielding to their bad tastes. This is a hard thing to do, and only a dramatist who knows his business is likely to succeed in doing it.

In this the drama is like oratory. "There are many audiences in every public assembly," wrote Emerson in his essay on "Eloquence." There are "the boys and rowdies"; there are those of "more chaste and wise attention"; there are those, "capable of virtue," who "are ready to be beatified." And "all these real audiences, each above each, which successively appear to greet the variety of style and topic, are really composed out of the same persons; nay, sometimes the same individuals will take part in them all, in turn." The public in the theater is "capable of virtue" if the dramatist has the art to make the right appeal.

THE REFORMING INSTINCT

Because of the democratic necessities of the drama, few playwrights have been much affected by the doctrine of art for art's sake. There is little in the theater, for example, to correspond to Kandinsky's extremism in painting or to Gertrude Stein's in printed literature. Most plays make plain, unesoteric appeal to the practical and moral concerns of ordinary people. Great plays all do. They may have, also, their subtleties and complexities that delight the connoisseur, but they must always and primarily make the common appeal.

This is exactly contrary to the doctrines of the artsakists. "In a poem," wrote the Abbé Henri Bremond in 1925, "all is impure . . . which is immediately concerned with our surface activities of reason, imagination, and sensibility; all that which the poet seems to us to have wished to express; all that he has in fact expressed; all that we say he suggests to us; all that the analysis of the grammarian or the philosopher deduces from the poem; all that a translation preserves of it."[15] Such "purity" is not for the dramatist; indeed, on such an understanding of poetry, drama is not and cannot be poetry. For drama is always and inevitably concerned with problems of conduct, and every great play must have a moral point of view.[16]

By "a moral point of view" I do not mean one necessarily in agreement with traditional ethics, Christian or other.

[15] *La Poésie pure;* my translation.

[16] An eloquent assertion of this view by Maxwell Anderson is "The Theatre as Religion," an address at Rutgers University, printed in the *New York Times,* October 26, 1941.

I mean simply that the playwright must take sides regarding the debatable courses of action which he presents, and must do so in accordance with ethical standards which his audience is able to infer and respect. The spectators need not wholly accept these standards; sometimes the playwright may even antagonize them, as Ibsen did; but they, or at least the more understanding of them, must feel that the author is sincere and firm in his convictions and that he has serious reasons for holding them.

The evidence of the greatest plays bears out this assertion. Aeschylus sought to justify the ways of the gods to men; Euripides, to challenge archaic moral assumptions. Aristophanes was a pamphleteer and preacher as well as a maker of obscene jokes. And Sophocles, though more detached than they, was a lover of nobility. Of the two great French classical tragedists, the earlier, Corneille, stretched the concept of honor or *gloire* almost to the breaking point, and for this very exaggeration of an ethical standard he has won the admiration of Gallic audiences to this day. Racine was a pious Catholic of a strict and puritanical sect. Of his plays *Phèdre* is considered his masterpiece, and it certainly contains one of the greatest acting roles in all dramatic literature. In his preface to it he writes: "I do not dare yet assert that this play is in fact the best of my tragedies.... What I can assert, however, is that I have never written any in which virtue is more fully displayed than in this. The least faults are severely punished; even the mere thought of crime is regarded with as much horror as crime itself; the passions are presented only to show all the disorder they cause; and vice is painted throughout in such colors as will make its deformity known and hated. This properly is the aim that every man who labors for the public should set himself; and it is this that the leading tragic poets have had in view above all else."[17]

Molière, as comedist, had less exalted aims, and always sought first to amuse his audience, but he was nonetheless ethical, for he was constantly ridiculing excess and folly and praising moderation and good sense. In those days moderation and good sense were popular virtues, in theory at least.

Shakespeare is widely cited as an artist unconcerned with ethics because he is so elusively objective and impersonal: "Others abide our question. Thou art free"; but it is obvious enough from his plays that he shared the common political and social views of his countrymen, and he never leaves us in doubt about his sympathy for goodness or his hatred of evil. He never preaches, but when a dramatist draws one man as a villain and another man as a hero he leaves no doubt which one he favors. Most of Shakespeare's characters, of course, are not merely good or merely bad, they are lifelike mixtures of good and evil; yet our ethical attitude toward them is never confused, we are never beguiled into liking wickedness or scorning nobility. Macbeth, for instance, is both a hero and a villain. That is another way of saying that at one and the same time we admire some of his qualities and reprobate others. But there is none of the moral ambiguity in Shakespeare's treatment of him that there is, for instance, in Euripides' treatment of Medea. We don't exult at his murders, and he does not escape retribution. The way in which the play as a whole illustrates the doctrine of

[17] My translation.

nemesis, indeed, may seem to many moderns who no longer believe in Providence to represent a moral wish rather than the ordinary course of events in life.

In ignoring or disregarding the morality in Shakespeare the disciples of "purity" are forced to ignore the very core of his dramatic power. Benedetto Croce wrote: "An artistic image portrays an act morally praiseworthy or blameworthy; but this image, as image, is neither praiseworthy nor blameworthy. Not only is there no penal code that can condemn an image to prison or to death, but no moral judgement, uttered by a rational person, can make of it its object. We might just as well judge the square moral or the triangle immoral as the Francesca of Dante immoral or the Cordelia of Shakespeare moral, for these have a purely artistic function, they are like musical notes in the souls of Dante and of Shakespeare."[18] Musical notes, indeed! Such a view disregards not only the plain fact that Dante wished to condemn Francesca's adultery in spite of his intense sympathy for her (stern moralist that he was!),[19] and Shakespeare wished to make Cordelia's filial piety shine bright in a naughty world, but also the more significant fact that our attitude as readers or spectators toward these characters is fundamentally dependent upon our own moral attitudes toward them. Croce's position is exceedingly arbitrary, since

[18] *The Essence of Aesthetic* (trans. by Douglas Ainslie; London, 1921), p. 14.

[19] "Alas, how many sweet thoughts, how great desire led these to this dolorous pass!"

"O lasso,
Quanti dolci pensier, quanto disio
Menò costoro al doloroso passo!"

Is it not the tragic emotional clash between the sweetness of this love and the misery of its consequences that causes Dante to fall fainting at the end of his interview with Francesca?

for the sake of a theory of extreme aesthetic "purity" he would eliminate from the great poets, as poets, qualities that are woven into the very texture of their work and that have been a primary source of emotion to lovers of them for centuries.

We need not cite lesser dramatists. The nature of dramatic subject matter makes a moral attitude on the part of the playwright necessary. No one will deny that Arnold was right when he said that conduct was three-fourths of life. Our very self-preservation, not to mention our happiness, depends on our conduct, and the problems of choice between courses of action that constantly confront us are therefore of primary importance to us. They are consequently of primary interest to us in drama. Indeed, a dramatic plot cannot be constructed except on the basis of some such choice.[20] Even if the dramatist should deliberately avoid all ethical implications arising from it and all partiality for or against it, his audience would not. They would certainly judge his play primarily by their moral feeling toward the conduct of its characters. Every playgoer can verify this assertion from his own experience. We do not demand that the playwright agree in all particulars with our attitudes; we may even violently disagree with his on one issue or another; but we do demand—instinctively if not consciously—that he stand for something morally respectable, even if it be mere animal energy. And we prefer that he stand for something that we can also admire. If he does not actively sympathize with the characters we like and disapprove the characters we dislike, he must at least be impartial or we

[20] See, in chap. iv, "Plot," pp. 115 ff.

will have none of his play. Just as we are all partisans in life, forever taking sides for and against the conduct of our fellows, so we are all partisans in the theater, which mimics life in action. The very essence of dramatic emotion is our participation in the struggles of human beings.

Perhaps I may seem to have labored this point, but I deemed it necessary to do so in view of the confusion which the artsakists have caused. Their criticisms have generally been justified so far as they have been leveled at crude preaching and moralizing when these are injected into narrative art where they do not belong. We rightly resent obvious propaganda. The business of the playwright is not to preach but to present, and we want to draw our own conclusions. But wanting to draw our own conclusions is quite a different thing from not wanting to draw any conclusions. The true dramatic way of dealing with ethics is not to talk about the consequences of a choice, but to show them. (Abstractions may be beautiful in particular speeches: "The quality of mercy is not strained." But a play as a whole is and must be a concrete presentation.) It is not inartistic to be moral; it is, in the drama, inartistic to be abstract.

As a consequence of the moral implications in all dramatic action, dramatists face a practical difficulty. The stronger their moral feeling toward their material, the more likely they are to write powerfully, but also the greater their temptation to preach. Too indifferent an attitude will leave us cold; too fervent a one will probably offend us. The difficulty is especially acute when, as is usually the case, a dramatist wants to build his play on a morally significant theme. To bring out the moral significance strongly he must make the plot a demonstration or apologue, but to give his audience a strong illusion of reality he must make his characters convincingly human. He can seldom meet both requirements fully, because they conflict. Real people are complex creatures, driven by a great variety of motives, whereas the clearest form of apologue is one in which the characters are abstract virtues or vices personified. Concrete individuals seldom fit abstract theses. Thus the dramatist with a thesis faces a dilemma: *forcing his characters to fit the thesis renders them unreal, but subordinating his thesis to lifelike characterization renders it confused or insignificant.*

The dramatist is rare indeed who can combine a powerful ethical theme with living characters in a unified action, dramatically moving and psychologically convincing: there has been only one Ibsen. Ordinary dramatic propagandists let character go, merely selecting "types" such as the selfish middle-aged capitalist, the idealistic young radical, the self-sacrificing mother, the spoiled daughter of the rich, and so on. They try to make these types individual enough to seem real on the stage, and often depend greatly on the actors to help them. Even as careful and sensitive an artist as Galsworthy too often failed, in the script, to make his characters much more than ethical types. When, on the other hand, a playwright becomes enamored of the variety and mystery of human character, he is likely to develop his characters at the expense of his theme. Ibsen usually kept his theme strictly before him, but his nature combined the poet of character with the moralist, and once—in *Peer Gynt*—the poet got the upper hand in spite of the playwright's initial intentions: he started out to make Peer a symbol of Norwegian vacillation and selfishness, but he ended by making him a universal character. The acting versions of the play rightly omit as much as possible of the satire of the original and set Peer's human drama in the foreground. As a poem of character alone the play has become a classic, but so far as Ibsen's purpose is concerned it is a failure.

This interest in character for its own sake has grown in modern times. The novel, which depends less on plot than the drama does, has helped to cultivate a taste for striking personalities. Thus we remember characters in Dickens like Mr. Micawber or the Fat Boy long after we have forgotten what happened to them. A great many readers have learned to like such characters so much that they care, or profess to care, very little for the story proper. Such people sometimes even feel that in most plays the plot is too obtrusive. It is not surprising, therefore, that some modern plays should have been written to satisfy this taste, and that occasionally they have succeeded. They are the more likely to succeed on the stage, indeed, because they naturally give the actor who plays the interesting character a fat role. Chekhov's plays had other interests for Russians of his day, but now their chief appeal is that of character. William Saroyan's work, so far, depends mostly on the exploitation of human oddities.

This interest in character is certainly legitimate, but it alone will rarely suffice to hold an audience for a whole evening. We shall see, when we come to discuss plot, that what we call character in a play is known to us only by what the *dramatis persona* says and does, and that the sum total of what the *dramatis personae* say and do constitutes the action. Oddities and surface characteristics of personality can interest us for a short time, but when we attend a long and serious play we want to get beneath the surface. When we do that, motivation and therefore plot become vitally important.

Characterizations are an aspect of plot when it is fully developed; and plot is the consequence, in large measure, of character. In other words, they are not separate qualities in a play, but different aspects of a single creation. We separate them in our minds for purposes of criticism or because one interests us particularly. The playwright's chief interest usually determines ours. The plot of *A Doll's House* roused tremendous interest when the play was first produced because it illustrated Ibsen's challenging moral views on the relation of a wife to her husband, but now that this battle has been pretty well fought out (among Americans, at least), the play holds us more by its subtle and vivid characterization. (It might indeed be more successful today if played as a high comedy than as a sort of tragedy.) To make a lasting moral appeal a play must deal with some universal ethical problem. When its interest is only in some temporary question its life will scarcely be longer than that of an editorial or any other exercise of propagandistic journalism. The aesthetic issue is not one of propaganda versus "pure" art, so called, but propaganda for local or temporary causes versus propaganda for universal ones.

During the 'thirties our Marxian critics made frequent attacks on the ideal of purity in art. (The title of one excellent article was "Farewell to Purity.")[21] From my point of

[21] By Haakon M. Chevalier, in *The Modern Monthly,* March, 1934.

view, the trouble with them, so far as they were orthodox, was that they esteemed art only in proportion to its service to the proletarian revolution, and I cannot believe that the proletarian revolution is of universal human value. And if we feel also, as many of us do, that Marxian critics have too often been actuated more by hatred of their opponents than by love of what is good in humanity, we may conclude that by just so much they are attacking art itself. Great art, great drama in particular, can only be created by men of good will.

Obviously, good will alone does not make a dramatist; but neither does technical skill alone. Succeeding chapters will be concerned with the latter; I do not wish to disparage it. Nevertheless, the value to us as human beings of what a dramatist has to present remains the ultimate test of his work.

CHAPTER III

The Illusion of Reality

IDENTIFICATION AND DETACHMENT

An interesting account of the illusion created by a play is, unexpectedly enough, given by a psychiatrist: "There is one . . . psychological process . . . intimately related to . . . phantasy construction. . . . This process, technically known as 'identification,' is of considerable importance, and in its minor degrees is frequently manifested in normal mental life. It consists in identifying ourselves with another individual, either real or fictitious, so that we experience his joys, sorrows, and desires, as if they were our own. So long as the identification holds we feel that he is part of our personality, and that we are living part of our lives in him. . . . One of the best instances is afforded by the reader of a second-rate romantic novel. The explanation of the interest which this type of fiction arouses lies in the fact that the reader identifies himself with the hero, lives with him through a series of astonishing adventures, falls in love with the heroine, and lives happily ever afterwards. The novel, in fact, permits the reader to experience the fascinations of day-dreaming without the trouble of constructing the imagery himself. An even better example is presented by the audience of a melodrama. Everybody who has observed the gallery during an entertainment of this kind is aware that its inmates are living on the stage, and always, of course, in the part of the hero or heroine. The illusion of reality which attaches to the play allows the day-dreaming to be conducted much more efficiently than in the case of the novel—hence the greater popularity of the drama. It is because the audience insists that the day-dreaming should be catered for, that the playwright is compelled to provide a liberal supply of peers, and to cast his scenes not too far from Mayfair."[1]

As this passage suggests, the degree of illusion varies with the naïveté or suggestibility of the spectator. The gallery gods are more spellbound than the people in the stalls. The illusion also varies, as we know, with the skill of playwright and actors. Lastly, it varies with the kind of play. Our psychiatrist singled out melodrama for his illustration of strong identification; not tragedy, still less comedy. All good plays, when properly produced, will create some degree of illusion, but normally certain kinds create much more than others. In general, noncomic ones create most, comic ones least.

The reason for this lies in the nature of laughter. If at this time I may deal briefly with a much-debated topic, I propose that the sense of the ridiculous is mainly a sudden perception of incongruities that are not painful to us who laugh though they are often painful to the objects of our mirth, and that its essence is an awareness of difference or contrast, especially a difference from the customary or habitual.[2] Children see outward and visible incongruities such as the

[1] Dr. Bernard Hart, *The Psychology of Insanity* (Cambridge, Eng., 1920), pp. 158 f.

[2] See, in chap. vi, "The Nature of Comic Laughter," pp. 206 ff.

contrast between a father's usual expression and the one he wears when he makes a face. Adults see inner incongruities such as the difference between a person's pretensions and his performances. Whichever the approach, laughter, or the impulse toward it, comes only when the observer is insulated for the moment from sympathy for the object of his laughter. Children think it funny when an old gentleman falls on an icy pavement; adults put themselves in the old gentleman's place and feel alarm or sympathy. Detachment is essential to laughter, and hence comic plays must keep the spectator in a comparatively unidentifying state of mind.

DRAMES AND COMEDIES

Comedies, then, tend toward detachment, while noncomic plays, such as tragedies, melodramas, problem plays, and the great mass of modern realistic dramas, tend toward identification. We have no convenient general name for this latter class. To call them "serious plays" implies that comedies are not serious in any sense. Since the word "serious" may mean either "solemn" or "important," and its implied opposite either "nonsolemn" or "trivial," to speak of noncomic plays as serious might suggest that a melodrama like *Dracula* is important and a comedy like *The Circle* is trivial. We might refer to the class as "plays of identification," but it must be remembered that our distinction is one of degree and that comedies rouse some identification. The French often use their general term *drame* as a loose label for "serious" plays that are neither regular tragedies nor melodramas; it is a usage that started in the eighteenth century when the appearance of middle-class sentimental plays forced critics to find a place for the new species along with the old ones. For us the term has the merit of being colorless and neutral and yet distinct from the inclusive English word "drama." I shall therefore use it for all noncomic plays the effectiveness of which depends on rousing strong identification.

A melodrama creates a stronger illusion in the mind of the susceptible spectator than does a tragedy, but any drame that does not cast a spell will fail. It will fail, that is, as a drame, but it may occasionally succeed as a farce. For several decades after the French Revolution, popular audiences in Paris swallowed spellbound the silliest melodramas; but at length they began to grow conscious of the silliness. Then it occurred to Frédérick-Lemaître, a leading actor, to burlesque his role in an especially silly piece called *L'Auberge des Adrets* (*The Inn at Les Adrets*). To everybody's surprise the result was a smash hit. The hero-villain, Robert Macaire, became famous, and Lemaître was encouraged to write a sequel by that character's name which throughout should be a deliberate burlesque. Similarly, in the 'twenties, George Cohan turned *The Tavern* into a roaring farce. His success started a series of revivals of old melodramas that has continued ever since. *The Drunkard* and *After Dark* and *The Streets of New York* have been popular in our time because audiences have come to laugh at them.

I should hesitate to lay much stress on the difference between drames and comedies with respect to identification were it not for this striking transformation that takes place when the sublime, or the melodramatically "serious," becomes the ridiculous. At the one kind of play, we are absorbed imaginatively into the action; at the other, we are pushed away from it and observe, insulated from sympathy, pity, or fear, but with our eye alert for anything to laugh at. At the one, we are participants; at the other, lookers-on. I suppose laughter is an emotion, or the expression of one; at any rate it has the peculiarity of being a refuge and a relief from emotions of other kinds. It is markedly so in the theater, as the old-time melodramatists knew when they provided for every tear a smile.

This difference, then, must lie deep in our nature, and may well account for the endurance of the Greek division of the drama into tragedy and comedy. Indeed it applies to plays of all times and countries. They differ extremely in outer form, subject matter, style, and methods of production, and any classification on the basis of such characteristics would entail hopeless difficulties; but to speak of a play as a tragedy or a comedy, or, more broadly, as a drame or a comedy, refers us to the dominant emotional effect, which in respect to degree of illusion is strikingly uniform throughout the history of the theater.

This broad assertion is of course subject to qualifications; we have already seen how the melodrama of our grandfathers becomes the burlesque of our day. Again, the difficulties of adaptation often make successful production of old or foreign plays a touchy business. A Chinese play, for instance, may move Orientals to tears and yet strike Americans as merely odd or funny. But adequate presentation implies that what is permanently human in a play should be carried across to the audience despite peculiarities of form or expression. If a play has won its initial success merely by appeal to local prejudices or sentimentalities, it can hardly gain its intended effect in an alien environment; but those which possess some degree of what is called universality will move audiences in the same fundamental way, though usually with less intensity, almost everywhere. Certainly little can be more remote from us today than the social customs and religious beliefs that gave rise to Greek drama; yet, when adequately produced, *Oedipus* or *Antigone* moves us with pity and fear, and *The Frogs* or *Lysistrata* convulses us with mirth. The more we think about it the more amazing it is that this should be so.

The necessity for identification in viewing tragedy is not apparent to all theorists. Professor G. G. Sedgewick finds in tragedy's ideal spectator an attitude of irony combined of "superior knowledge" and "detached sympathy."[3] His discussion suggests that in all tragedies, not merely those like *Oedipus the King* in which irony is intended and emphasized, the spectator is to see an ironical contrast between the hero's condition and his fate. Thus *Othello,* to Mr. Sedgewick, is ironical.

I cannot follow him here. Ironic effect is a discord between painful and comic emotions, as I shall try to show later.[4] But there is no amusement for a normal person in Desdemona, or Othello either. An audience Olympian enough to be ironical while watching *Othello* could turn anything to comedy. Many themes of tragedy and high comedy are, to be sure, alike in the abstract, as has often been observed; and, as I argue later,[5] the highest emotional effects of tragedy

[3] *Of Irony, Especially in Drama* (Toronto, 1935).

[4] Pp. 142 ff.

[5] Pp. 270 ff.

grow out of thoughtfulness. At times, even in a tragedy, the discords of ironic amusement may sound out momentarily and horribly, like the yells of the fiends when Orpheus sings in hell. But a consistent attitude of detachment would simply make tragedy impossible.

A CLASSIFICATION OF PLAYS ACCORDING TO ILLUSION

Classifying *Oedipus the King* as a drame or *The Frogs* as a comedy makes no difficulty, for their emotional impact upon us is definite and powerful. Most plays, however, are much less intense in effect, and often less definite: they may appeal alternately or even simultaneously to mirth and to the emotions of identification. The classification of such plays is not easy.

I can imagine a reader with a certain turn of mind asking mentally, at this point, "Why try?" He may even quote to himself from Polonius' pedantic listing of dramatic types: "tragedy, comedy, history, pastoral, pastoral-comical, historical-pastoral, tragical-historical, tragical-comical-historical-pastoral." The answer, of course, is that if we would examine the nature and laws of any sort of subject matter, classifications are primary necessities. To understand the drama, we must segregate its varieties. We must be sure, however, that they are real varieties and not the arbitrary groupings of pedants.

Classifications can be made on the basis of any sort of characteristic, and the historic labels that have come down to us for various types of plays show this variety. "Tragedy" and "comedy" were at first merely the names of certain religious rites, and it was accidental that they became attached later to types of drama. "Farce" means "a stuffing"; that this name rather than another was the one that became attached to early French slapstick was also accidental. "Melodrama" is a late Renaissance name for opera, being compounded from the Greek words for song and drama; mere chance gave it its present meaning.[6] Other terms, such as Polonius' "history" and "pastoral," refer to subject matter; they ceased to be useful when the Elizabethan vogue for dramatizing English history and for bucolic plays ended. These, and others of the sort, being descriptive labels, are usually self-evident, and are freely used or invented as the need arises: "problem play," "proletarian drama," "war play," "fate tragedy."

Terms that refer to dramatic effect are more generally useful in a book of this kind. An old one is "tragicomedy," which, as its form indicates, designates a play that begins in tragic vein but ends happily. A tragicomedy is usually a melodrama unless distinguished by qualities, like those of *The Winter's Tale,* that raise it above the level of mere popular entertainment. The best label for most of Shakespeare's comedies is "romantic comedy." Another term constantly used in this work is "high comedy." I suppose the adjective "high" was originally used to distinguish such plays from mere farces, but it now means something more specific—a play that is not only well written, well characterized, and theatrically effective, but also built on a comic idea or theme which, considered abstractly, is seriously significant to civilized and mature people. Thus Maugham's

[6] See p. 257.

The Circle shows how young people in love do not profit by the example of their elders. Such a theme might be the basis of a tragedy. The term "comedy of manners" is a common designation for the English tradition that includes *The Way of the World, The School for Scandal,* and Maugham's comedy, but for the purposes of this book it is too vague and ambiguous to be very useful: many comedies that are not high comedies deal with manners.

Two fairly recent terms that we shall have frequent occasion to apply to plays are "naturalistic" and "expressionistic." I discuss both later on:[7] here a word of explanation may be convenient. A naturalistic play is one that attempts to show life with scientific objectivity and painstaking realism: "a corner of nature" or "a slice of life," to use the descriptions of its advocates. Expressionistic plays, written principally in Germany in the 'twenties, are formally the direct opposite of naturalistic ones since they avoid any literal representation of life, and instead distort it (as outward expressions of mental attitudes and states) and indulge in fantasy and extravagant symbolism, usually to suggest to an audience some abstract theme or subjective struggle in the mind of a character or of the author. Often this subjective experience has a nightmarish or even insane quality.

The degree of illusion which plays of a certain type normally produce may be represented graphically. We may put those of high identification at the left, and those of relative detachment at the right, and indicate the probable variation of their effect on different spectators by arrows (⟶ and ⟵), as on the page opposite.

[7] See, in chap. ix, "Chekhov and Naturalism," pp. 333 ff., and "Strindberg and Expressionism," pp. 341 ff.

NORMAL DEGREE OF ILLUSION IN TYPICAL DRAMAS

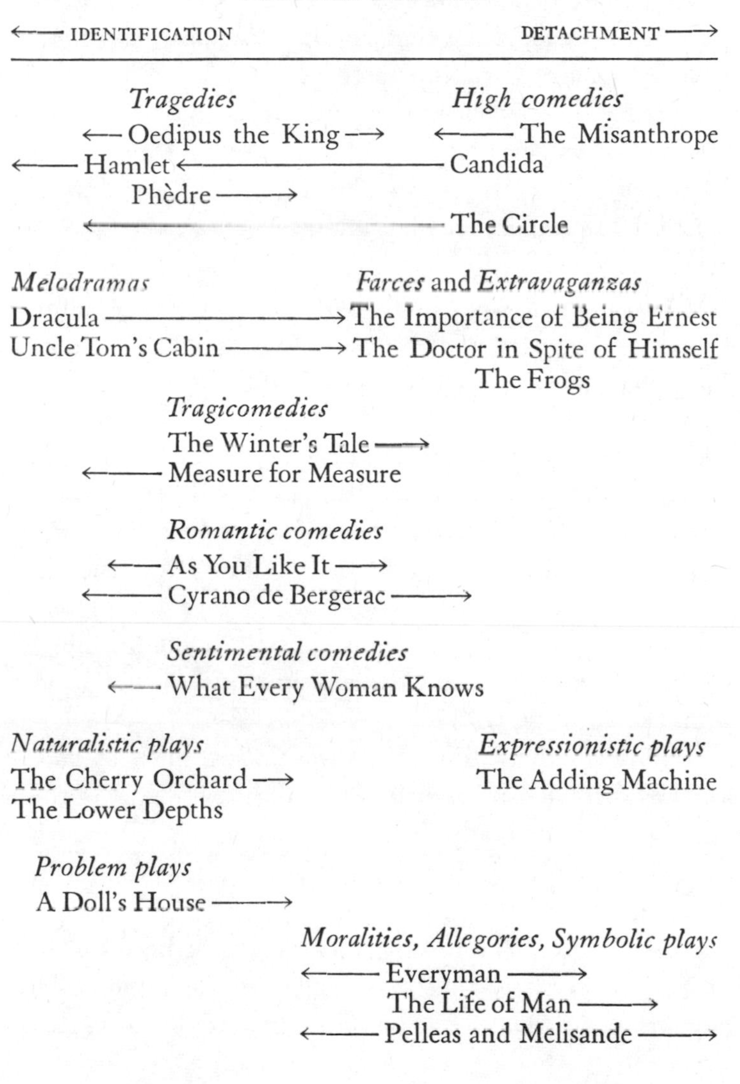

No doubt, readers would like to move some of these plays to right or left, but the general grouping is, I believe, fairly representative of an audience's response. The variation is greatest for melodramas that can be farced, as I have indicated by the arrows running across to farce.

Granted that any such a grouping is subjective, it has, I think, a real value. It helps a student to look for the essential quality of a play, and it raises questions that are of great practical importance in play producing. I should like to mention a few of these.

I once saw Sothern and Marlowe play *The Taming of the Shrew*. After the wedding journey in which Petruchio puts Kate through so many rough-and-tumble hardships, they arrive wearied at his house and she sits down by the fire to take off her wet footgear. At this moment Petruchio, as Sothern played the role, stood behind her and pantomimed that he was really touched by her bedraggled condition and would like to caress her. He stretched out his hand tenderly and then drew it back as if controlled by a sense of duty. "No," he seemed to be saying to himself, "though it hurts me more than it does her, this punishment is for her good. I must go through with it."

Why did Sothern thus sound the solemn notes of duty and love? Obviously, in order to keep the sympathy of the audience. But sympathy is out of place in a farce, which should be played for all it is worth as a farce, as the Lunts played it.

Historically, such a misinterpretation as Sothern's is explained by the fact that sentimentality was abnormally popular in the theater during the nineteenth century. Psychologically, it is explained by the fact that actors desire "sympathetic" roles and are tempted to use any means to gain sympathy, even to the extreme of doing violence to the spirit of the play. Shakespeare thought it "a most pitiful ambition" in the clown to try for laughs at the wrong time. Would he have been more lenient toward the "lead" who drags sentiment into a farce?

For certain other attempts by Shakespearean actors to work for sympathetic identification the poet himself may be blamed. According to the Elizabethan stage tradition which Shakespeare inherited, the Jew was a stock comic villain—so grotesquely avaricious as to be funny. But great as Shakespeare's comic gifts were, still greater was his power of imaginative sympathy. Hence, once his mind set to work on Shylock, the caricature that was first intended became a human being, the puppet of farce turned into a man, even a man of tragic qualities. The poet himself destroyed the detachment of comedy, and actors naturally have followed him.

We may forgive or even disregard Shakespeare's destruction of comic detachment in *The Merchant of Venice* because of the tragic power of his characterization and the marvelous role it gives an actor. Nonetheless, a play that violates the dominant mood goes counter to our universal desire for unity of effect. If it succeeds, it does so in spite of the violation.

The classical tradition was dominated by this desire for unity, but Shakespeare was a dramatist of the medieval tradition, which freely mixed the sublime with the ridiculous, the terrible with the farcical, and he was always less concerned with the emotional unity of his plays than with the poetic reality of his characters.[8] Hence none of his comedies can be classified as a high comedy, and only two or three of them as straight farces. Most are of a mixed type—tragicomedies or romantic comedies. They excite identification for the romantic leading characters, who in this respect are contrasted with the often farcical clowns, and they are full of scenes that touch on melodrama or sentiment.

Molière, on the other hand, wrote in the classical tradition, carefully avoiding identification and maintaining the comic tone. He had had instruction in the classics at a good school, and though he poked fun at the "Rules" (as did Shakespeare) he violated them little. He lived in an era when Frenchmen sought order and good sense after a period of disorder and fanaticism; and the great classical works which his period produced have marked the spirit of French literature in contrast to English. The French prefer clarity, logic, and unity; the English like a muddle. In particular, the French like their comedy straight; the English, mixed. This is not to imply that English artists are not the equal of the French, but it does mean that they generally shine for other qualities than the classical.

Though Molière was a master of the technique of maintaining detachment,[9] actors and audiences so lust after identification that his masterpiece of high comedy has been misinterpreted from the time of his death to the present. Contemporary comment indicates that the part of Alceste, the hero of *The Misanthrope,* as played by the dramatist, was a comic one; and Molière's intention seems clear from

[8] See, in chap. v, "The Greek and Medieval Traditions," pp. 168 ff.
[9] See, in chap. vi, "The High Comedy of Molière," pp. 214 ff.

the full title of the play (usually shortened today): *Le Misanthrope ou l'amoureux atrabiliaire* (*The Misanthrope; or, The Atrabilious Lover*). And if we look for absurdity in Alceste's character we find an abundance of it. He is so vain of his plain-speaking, for example, that he is willing to risk a duel rather than say that a sonnet is pretty. In a jealous rage over his sweetheart's flirtations he tells her that "fortune, demons, and wrathful heaven never produced anybody so wicked," yet when she refuses to be contrite, or even to defend her conduct, he makes an about-face and begs for a kind word, finally saying that he wishes she might be reduced to misery so that he could have the pleasure of supporting her alone by his love. He is a thoroughly extravagant young man.

Yet after the dramatist's death his protégé, Baron, played Alceste sympathetically. Then Jean-Jacques Rousseau, the sentimental philosopher, wrote a famous letter attacking stage plays, in which he interpreted Alceste as a noble victim of a corrupt society.[10] The tradition of the Comédie Française, which has maintained the play in its repertory to this day, has, I understand, been consistently that of Baron. Criticism has only recently emerged sufficiently from the sentimentalism that enveloped France after Rousseau's time to speak out forcefully for Molière's real intention.[11] If the dramatist had suspected how his play might be misinterpreted, he no doubt would have made the comedy in Alceste's character unmistakable. Since he did not, the play which in many respects is the world's greatest high comedy

[10] *Lettre à d'Alembert sur les spectacles* (1758).

[11] See G.-M.-A. Michaut, *Les Luttes de Molière* (Paris, 1925), pp. 207 ff., esp. p. 222.

requires special interpretation before most readers, unaccustomed to the detached, high-comic approach, are able to appreciate it.

It will be noticed that in the diagram I put *Oedipus* and *Phèdre* somewhat to the right of *Hamlet*. Like *Hamlet* they both are acknowledged masterpieces of tragedy, but unlike it they are in the classical tradition: they not only have a stricter unity, but they are also composed according to strict formal conventions. The action of the former, for example, is interrupted by the lyric interludes of the Greek chorus, and in both the dialogue reaches its height not in passionate realistic argument or intimate personal confessions like Hamlet's soliloquies but in long, eloquent speeches, or *tirades* as the French call them, which analyze and describe the passion of the speaker rather than expressing it in a lifelike manner. The successful delivery of a *tirade* demands the highest elocution and, like a well-rendered operatic aria, thrills an audience by its virtuosity.

Such artifices diminish identification. When they are part of a living convention, to be sure, audiences are rarely conscious of them as artifices.[12] The Greeks, for instance, probably did not think of the choruses as interruptions of the drama proper. Nevertheless, the more artificial a convention is, the quicker the playgoers will be to note any departures from it, or any inexpertness in its use; and when they do, dramatic illusion is endangered. When an audience applauds a *tirade* it is not losing itself in the action, but admiring the actor's technique.

Thus in the performance of any elaborate poetic tragedy,

[12] See, in chap. iv, "Conventions," pp. 108 ff.

whether formally classical or not, there is always the possibility that the conventions may cause detachment. From one point of view this may be actually an artistic merit. According to the theory of "aesthetic distance," an observer must be somewhat detached from a work of art if he is to appreciate it as such.[13] But this theory is better suited to painting than to drama. The contemporary connoisseur of painting consciously observes the form and is careful to disregard the subject. He would consider it philistine to take notice of its story value. Fortunately, such one-sidedness does not prevail over dramatic critics, who cannot scorn the desire of the unsophisticated and normal spectator to forget form in the story. The dramatic critic is always unavoidably at a certain aesthetic distance because he is always aware that the play is a play, and it adds to his pleasure in seeing a fine play to recognize its formal excellences as it proceeds. But if he should cultivate an attitude like that of the art critic, he would increase aesthetic distance so far as to destroy the primary pleasure which the play is designed to afford. He will differ from his colleague, then, by participating fully in the illusion while he is seeing the play; he will apply his powers of conscious analysis and discrimination afterward.

We are most conscious of the formal beauties of a poetic tragedy when we are least under its dramatic spell. They thus compensate us somewhat for the decrease in the illusion which occurs when we see the play several times or study it. Nevertheless, such beauties are secondary, and the more obtrusive they are to the spectator the less his illusion

[13] See, for example, H. S. Langfeld, *The Aesthetic Attitude* (New York, 1920), chaps. iii and iv.

is likely to be. Thus for English-speaking audiences *Hamlet* is much more "real" than *Phèdre*.

In expressionistic plays formal features are so very obtrusive that an audience can scarcely feel any illusion at all. Hence I put *The Adding Machine* far to the right. Mr. Zero and the other "characters" are sarcastic caricatures, not living people. But though the play creates as much detachment as a farce, it is not meant to be funny, for its theme is a bitter indictment of machine-ridden commercial civilization. Thus the technique and the theme clash violently. Now, a detached audience must be kept laughing or it will quickly grow bored. When people first see a thoroughgoing expressionistic play the novelty of it amuses them for a time, and its obscurities may excite their curiosity; but such interests do not last. *The Adding Machine* has lived in the anthologies, where it can be read, but not on the boards. And the directors of little theaters and other troupes that try artistic experiments should bear this fact in mind whenever they are tempted to indulge heavily in "stylization" or any other disillusioning effect in a play that is not full of laughs.

Allegories and highly symbolical plays like *Pelleas and Melisande* are often almost as abstract as an expressionistic one, and hence fall to the right of center in the diagram. When we see an allegory we are conscious of its double significance, and in proportion as we are preoccupied with interpreting the represented action in terms of its allegorical meaning we are kept from losing ourselves in it. The theme, moreover, is abstract, and food for thought rather than feeling. Similarly with symbolical plays, or indeed with thesis plays: when seeing them we are likely to grow so much concerned with puzzling out the meaning of the symbols or considering the validity of the thesis as to lose interest in the story or belief in the reality of the characters. Spectators of course differ, and some will enjoy a play like *Pelleas and Melisande* simply as romance, but anyone familiar with Maeterlinck's philosophical essays of the period can hardly avoid seeing Melisande's doves that flutter about her head while she gallivants with Pelleas as a symbol of the author's comforting but dubious notion that the soul is incorruptible no matter what the body does; and the blind men, the driven sheep, and so on, as symbols of his deterministic view of human fate.

So far as the majority of an audience are concerned, *laughter alone is an adequate compensation for a loss of identification.* Hence abstractions and obtrusive technical devices can be used with least danger in comedy, and often are helpful. They may help to emphasize the idea on which high comedy is built and the satirical points in farcical extravaganzas like *The Frogs,* all of which interest the intelligence rather than the imagination. In unintellectual comedy they help to keep us detached. The grotesque mask of Greek comedy and the painted face of the circus clown insure that we shall not identify ourselves with their wearers.

It might be objected that the Greeks used masks also in their tragedies, and a highly conventionalized style of presentation, and yet created a degree of illusion. The reason for this seems to be that every aspect of the tragedy, including the masks, was designed to idealize the characters and their deeds so as to make them more heroic than life, whereas every aspect of the comedy was idealized in the opposite direction so as to make the characters meaner and uglier than life. (I use the word "idealization" to refer to all modifications of nature to express an "idea." Hence a comic caricature is an idealization.) We willingly imagine ourselves nobler than we are, but refuse to do the opposite; hence their tragic idealization increased or at least did not interfere with illusion, while their comic lessened it.

To an Occidental seeing a Chinese play for the first time its extraordinary conventions are highly disillusioning; but they are not so to a Chinese: to him an actor in full regalia, decked like a Christmas tree, his countenance hidden behind lurid paint, prancing solemnly about and switching an imaginary steed, for all the world like a child playing horse, is a real warrior going a journey. Use and wont make such frank symbols real. Indeed the most obviously unlifelike methods may at times create strong illusion: children are enthralled by puppet shows. Hence the point at which artifice and symbol endanger illusion varies greatly. But the broad distinction that we have drawn between plays of identification and plays of detachment remains valid and should help a director by sharpening his perception of the nature of dramatic illusion and suggesting the degree of it that he should seek to arouse.

CHAPTER IV

The Sources of Dramatic Effect

THE ESSENTIALS OF PRODUCTION

IN THE LIGHT of our conclusion in chapter i that the drama is primarily an art for the ear rather than the eye, the anxious elaboration of backstage paraphernalia which we see in many modern productions seems unessential. If we ask how much we might eliminate and still gain a dramatic effect on an audience, I think we may answer, Everything except *a good play and actors.* The actors, of course, must be in a place where they can be seen and heard, but they need not stand behind a proscenium arch, beneath a fly loft, facing an auditorium of plush-covered seats. They do not even need an elevated stage: Greek drama was acted on the flat, circular "dancing floor" at the bottom of the semicircular auditorium. They can get along without special costumes, and even without special properties except those that are essential to the action. Such properties, moreover, need not be imitations of reality. In a pinch a stool can serve for a throne, a stick for a scepter. If we provide such essential properties, the actors can get along on a bare stage, or even on the ground.

"I have seen the suburban amateurs of the Shakespeare Reading Society, seated like Christy Minstrels on the platform of the lecture hall . . . produce, at a modest computation, about sixty times as much effect by reading through 'Much Ado about Nothing' as Mr. Irving with his expensively mounted and superlatively drilled Lyceum version." So wrote Shaw. He was at this time (the late 'nineties) out for Irving's hide, to be sure. Elsewhere, however, he sums up the matter succinctly without special pleading: "The more scenery you have, the less illusion you produce."[1]

It is well to remember this in our day of elaborateness and expense. Settings and paraphernalia may add to the dramatic enjoyment, and nothing said here is to be understood as advocating the elimination of a complete staging from normal productions. I wish to emphasize what is essential; and the mounting is not. Too often, indeed, it obscures what is, or covers up the weakness of a poor play. To know a good play from a bad one, therefore, we might put them to the test of an unadorned performance. *How dramatic is a play when performed in daylight on a bare stage?*

This test must naturally be applied with reasonableness. Some plays call for special effects and cannot be fully produced without them; but such plays are more often melodramas or farces than works of serious artistic purpose, and I believe that the test would be a good one even for them.

We should remember that the careful stage realism which we are accustomed to is a comparatively new thing in the theater, and that for centuries our ancestors saw what plays they did see, and enjoyed them, under conditions often approaching those of our test. The fact that we are used to

[1] *Dramatic Opinions and Essays* (New York, 1906), Vol. I, p. 274; Preface to *Overruled*.

a thing makes us expect it or even demand it, but does not prove its necessity.

Striking evidence that accessories are unnecessary is the success of Thornton Wilder's *Our Town* (1938). With no scenery at all and no properties beyond a few chairs, a table or two, a couple of ladders, and a plank, it portrayed vividly the life of a New England village. The actors suggested minor accessories by pantomime. The boy and the girl, for example, sipped imaginary ice-cream sodas in an imaginary drugstore, sitting behind the plank set up for a counter. Such things were disconcerting at first to a good many playgoers, and tended to make for a detached state of mind. A further influence toward detachment was the stage manager, who acted as chorus and commentator, occasionally played supernumerary roles, shifted chairs about at need, and told the actors when to come in or go out. Yet for success the play required a strong illusion of reality, and on the whole I think that the illusion was as strong as it would have been if aided by all the elaborate realism of conventional productions. At least, the author lost nothing essential by doing without realistic settings, and he gained extraordinarily in freedom to present his action swiftly, flexibly, and imaginatively. The stage manager's comments added philosophic significance to the simple story, and the actors were free to work their spell on the audience by their own art alone.

Our Town was written to be produced in this fashion, and so is better adapted to our test than plays that were not. Moreover, if it had been written less sincerely and poetically its very avoidance of accessories might easily have seemed a self-conscious and "arty" convention. A drama intended for a realistic production would no doubt seem thin and sketchy if produced on a bare stage, but if it were a good play it would nonetheless retain much of its power. This is shown by the effectiveness of a good "reading rehearsal" (a performance by actors who read their lines while acting). Since they must hold the book or manuscript in one hand and keep their eyes on it, their freedom of movement is much hampered and they cannot develop elaborate pantomime or subtlety of interpretation. It is a rough sketch rather than a finished performance. Yet anyone who has seen a good play thus performed by competent actors will agree that it can be surprisingly enthralling. A good play is still moving when acted with open books. Sometimes a play is read by actors who sit in a semicircle and rise to read their lines. Even this method will transmit much of the dramatic power, as Shaw indicates.

Furthermore, we can get along without a full cast. Consider the success of monologuists like Ruth Draper or Cornelia Otis Skinner, who can play only one role at a time, and often give us merely one side of a conversation, like a person telephoning. And the popularity of play readings, in which one actor reads all the parts from the book, shows how much of the essential dramatic value is kept with an absolute minimum of presentation. Finally, the effectiveness of radio presentations shows that we do not even need to see the actors.

Elaborate settings and business not required by the action are likely to obscure essential dramatic values. Directors especially are tempted to err in this fashion, and when they do we may call them "virtuoso directors." Until recently the director was merely a stage manager whose function was subordinated to that of the actors, or he was a leading actor who combined both functions; but the present century has developed a class of specialists who control the entire production, often autocratically, in accordance with their interpretation of the play. When such a director is a man of taste, he can insure the artistic unity of the play to a degree previously impossible; and indeed most of our directors have a proper view of their function as self-effacing interpreters. But sometimes they succumb to the desire to shine at the expense of play and players.

All who take part in a production may help to misinterpret a play. The scene designer's inappropriate settings will do harm to it; but they are likely to be of minor influence and obvious. The actor's misinterpretations, of course, are common and often fatal to new plays; but experienced playgoers can usually recognize them for what they are. Recognition of a director's errors is less easy, because he does his work through the other artists. At times, however, we can detect them, particularly when he is using a play to show off his virtuosity.

In such a production the leading roles will probably not be given to actors of renown, as their performance may obscure the director's. In any event, the ensemble will be stressed. This may be an artistic gain, as it saves the play from the interpretative distortions which are an evil of the star system; but unhappily it gives the director a chance to shine instead. Thus he makes much of crowd movements and spectacular tableaus at the expense of the legitimate dramatic interest, or plays tricks with lighting and sound effects that distract from the action proper. Sometimes he uses an unconventional method of staging, such as mixing the actors up with the audience. Like Meierhold in Russia during the 'twenties, he may make them perform on a "constructivist" set that is all ramps and platforms. He loves "theaters of the five thousand" with immense crowds. Or, if he goes in for intimate productions, he loves to "stylize" them out of all reality and reason. The virtuoso director, or "régisseur," as he likes to be called, is fond of plays that are hard to "put over," especially those that require special ingenuity in staging. Thus he enjoys staging works of Strindberg or Pirandello or Maeterlinck that call for much symbolism or distortion; farces in the tradition of the *commedia dell'arte* that call for skillful clowning and acrobatics; medieval moralities that call for elaborate make-up, costume, and pageantry. I am not suggesting that these plays are not good plays, worth producing; I am saying simply that the virtuoso director likes to produce them because his work can show up well in them. And a good many directors of amateurs in little theaters follow his example in this.

When Max Reinhardt produced *Six Characters in Search of an Author* he largely rewrote the play, adding several roles and innumerable gags, presumably comic. Perhaps Pirandello's drama needed this handling for a foreign audience; I suspect that, played straight, it would seem to most American playgoers not merely queer, but, before the evening was over, boring. When I saw Reinhardt's production, however, I was as much conscious of Reinhardt in it as I was of Pirandello, and I did not feel that the director had improved on the dramatist.

His productions of *The Miracle* and Maeterlinck's *Sister Beatrice* were all cathedral windows, church music, dim religious lights, and the choreographic evolutions of girls in nuns' dresses. When he produced *A Midsummer Night's Dream* in an oak grove at the University of California he provided a mist with real smoke that proved overpoweringly atmospheric. For Puck he procured a Hollywood juvenile who did all manner of gay skippings-about among the trees. After the first three or four acts, he made the audience walk a quarter-mile up the hill to the Greek Theatre, where, with a long flight of steps from orchestra to high stage, he put on a wedding pageant that reminded me of an ensemble scene in a musical review.

Max Reinhardt's productions have been many, varied, and influential; they undoubtedly entitle him to an important place in theatrical history. My experiences with them must have been unfortunate; for I have never been able, in seeing any of them, to forget the director and give myself up to enjoyment of the play.

Though a novice at writing plays may be thankful for the collaboration of experienced director and actors, a dramatist who knows his business has a right to expect self-effacing interpretation. The better a director's work with a good play, the less we should be aware of it. This makes it difficult for him to become famous; but this is his job. "While interesting directing and acting can make a live and at times thrilling theatre," writes Lee Strasberg, "no great theatre can exist except through the medium of great plays and playwrights; and the director is born to serve the play."[2] "Stagecraft at best is nothing more than the tail to the poet's kite," says Lee Simonson.[3]

CONVENTIONS

I have been speaking frequently of conventions, and their importance warrants a special examination. In the broad sense a convention, according to Webster, is a rule or usage based on general agreement. Since the stage cannot represent everything in a lifelike manner, many substitutes for direct mimicry of life have from time to time come into use. When well established, they are called "stage conventions." In the widest sense, all aspects of a dramatic performance might be called conventions since audiences agree to make believe that they are real; but I use the term to refer rather to those devices and methods which are peculiar to particular stage traditions. Thus, acting as such is not called a convention, but a particular style of acting, such as the strut and orotund delivery of the old-time tragedian, is. Again, experimental devices in modern productions are not, strictly speaking, conventions, because not generally accepted in theatrical usage, but it will be convenient here to treat them as such.

It is important for the student of the drama as well as the student of the theater to know the major theatrical traditions and their conventions. Otherwise he is in danger of misinterpreting plays that are written for them.

We cannot help noticing the conventions of the Chinese stage, but we may well overlook our own, especially those

[2] In *The Theatre Handbook,* article "The Director."
[3] *The Stage Is Set* (New York, 1932), p. 40.

used in modern naturalistic productions that are made as lifelike as possible. Yet it is conventional in them for the actors to face the audience most of the time, to "balance the stage" by not crowding all to one side, to speak exit lines on a pause at the door, and to do many other things that are not "natural" but that make, or are thought to make, the acting more effective. And the naturalistic style shares with other styles of production such conventions as the act divisions, the curtain, the use of a spotlight to make an actor visible in a dark scene, and so on.

Our familiarity with the realism of the movies and naturalistic stage plays should not blind us to their artificiality or prevent us from enjoying other systems of convention. Our easy, amused patronage of the Chinese conventions, for instance, as though they evidenced a childish naïveté which we in our superior Occidental wisdom have outgrown, is wrong both historically and artistically. Historically our realism is the exception, not the rule, for almost always the theater has sought not to imitate life but to make its presentation more expressive, splendid, and beautiful than life. The Chinese conventions are highly sophisticated rather than naïve; they are the result of centuries of experience. And once their language is learned they are highly expressive, and to the Oriental they are doubtless beautiful.

Many conventions are the result of convenience or necessity; others, of the search for greater expressiveness and beauty. The latter in particular will not be imitative of life in any literal sense, and they all depart from life in one of two ways: either by being tokens of it, or substitutes for it. The groined arch that I mentioned earlier, which stood for a cathedral, is a token. If such tokens become highly conventionalized through long use, they may lose their original resemblance to reality and become what we call symbols. The colors in the facial make-up of Chinese actors no longer suggest life, but are symbolically interpreted: white means wickedness; red, honesty; and so on. Typical substitute conventions are the soliloquy, the reading of a letter aloud, the aside. Such substitutes are valuable not in proportion to their realism, for by their very nature they are unlike life, but in proportion to their effectiveness in dramatizing the story.

We may review a few of the many conventions used at different times by way of further illustration. To take token conventions first, in Greek drama the scene building at the rear of the circular acting space was accepted according to need as a palace or a temple or a cave, and the chorus of fifteen men did duty for a throng of citizens. In like fashion an Elizabethan "army" might be half-a-dozen supernumeraries, and a Chinese one can be indicated by a single "super" carrying a banner.[4] In the nineteenth century a wing or two, cut out and painted to represent trees, did satisfactory service in suggesting a forest. Chinese actors need much less: to indicate a door one merely raises his foot as though stepping over a threshold, and two actors manage to suggest a sanguinary battle between armies by engaging in a whirling sword dance. In the production of ancient Sanskrit dramas in India, we read,[5] the use of symbolic gestures was so highly developed as to become a veritable sign language in which the movements of the hands were almost as definite a means

[4] A. E. Zucker, *The Chinese Theatre* (Boston, 1925), chap. vii.

[5] R. K. Yajnik, *The Indian Theatre* (New York, 1934), Pt. I, chap. ii; A. B. Keith, *The Sanskrit Drama* (Oxford, 1924), p. 367.

of communication as our deaf-and-dumb alphabet, and no doubt were far more beautiful.

Substitute conventions have been equally universal, and sometimes, when they materially aided in dramatizing the story or heightening its emotional effect, they have been more important. The Greeks sought to give a visual dignity to their tragic actors by garbing them in an unlifelike Oriental costume, masking them, and putting high boots on their feet to raise their stature. The singing of the choral odes served like our curtain to indicate a time interval of indefinite extent. On Shakespeare's stage a change of physical scene was made merely by the actors' leaving it empty for a moment. The Spanish theater of Lope de Vega followed a like convention, and Lope himself was so little enamored of scene painting that he was opposed to writing plays for theaters that used it.[6] The French audiences of the seventeenth century expected their tragic actors to wear ostrich plumes in their headdresses, and costumes never seen on sea or land, and to declaim their *tirades* at the top of their voices. Shakespeare's use of the soliloquy enabled him to tell the audience just what his hero was thinking and feeling. In the eighteenth and nineteenth centuries everybody agreed to assume that an aside was inaudible to the other actors though heard in the gallery. They agreed on this convention because it was so useful in getting the story told clearly and quickly, and because in comedy it had such rich possibilities of contrast between thought and action. The textbooks all record that Ibsen got rid of the aside, but in an age less ridden by realism than ours it may well return.

[6] H. A. Rennert, *The Spanish Stage in the Time of Lope de Vega* (New York, 1909), p. 98.

Conventions are justified by their expressiveness, not by their realism. Above all is this true in the conventional use of language, which is the primary medium of the drama. Every poet who writes drama wants to use unrealistic language because of its greater expressiveness. Hence, prior to the nineteenth century, verse and "poetic diction" were universally employed in all plays that had any literary pretensions, and indeed for many centuries in every sort of play. The linguistic conventions of Greek tragedy were the most elaborate of all. They included for dialogue anapests or, more usually, iambics; for choruses half-a-dozen complicated meters, with many subtle variations, in complex stanzaic form; Doric dialectical forms in highly lyrical passages, unfamiliar fine-sounding words, and sometimes startling figures of speech. The poets of Rome and the Renaissance imitated them as well as they could according to their personal abilities and the capacities of their languages. Shakespeare's blank verse and diction fastened themselves on the tragic drama of both England and Germany until very recently, and today poets in England and America are experimenting with variations upon it that may be more suited to our modern speech rhythms and tastes.[7] The entire history of the drama indicates that ordinary language is less expressive than heightened language.

We must remember that a device is not strictly a convention until it is generally accepted by audiences. The conventions of the Chinese theater are rooted in immemorial custom; those which German expressionists experimented with in the 'twenties were generally puzzling or amusing

[7] See, in chap. x, "Verse in Modern Tragedy," pp. 383 ff.

rather than dramatically expressive. Some of the latter, however, have become widely enough understood for dramatists to employ them today if they find them useful.[8] Indeed, it is remarkable how quickly we adapt ourselves to the most unrealistic devices when the dramatist who uses them has anything vital to say with them. I have cited *Our Town*. Of the Chinese theater, Professor Zucker writes, "As a Westerner learns to recognize its conventions, he quickly becomes used to them, and soon he is as little disturbed by the make-believe of the oriental theatre as he had been before by that of the occidental." When I heard that Eugene O'Neill was reviving the aside in a tragic play I doubted that it could be accepted by a modern audience, yet a few minutes after the curtain rose on *Strange Interlude* I found that I had adjusted myself to the device. It has not been imitated; but not, I think, because it is too unrealistic. I think the trouble with it is that it is too literal in a psychological sense. One of our keenest delights in following excellent dialogue is to guess the motives and *arrière-pensées* behind the spoken words. This pleasure O'Neill's device denies us, for after each "spoken" speech in his play the character himself tells us in an aside exactly what he is thinking. Sometimes these thoughts are ironically amusing because of their contrast with what the character "says," but this amusement, legitimate as it is in farce or high comedy, is wholly incidental if not out of place in a play of so somber a tone as *Strange Interlude*. A device, to be poetically expressive, must stimulate rather than confine the imagination.

Thanks to the wide experimentation of the last few dec-

[8] See, in chap. ix, "Strindberg and Expressionism," pp. 341 ff.

ades, many of us are now trained to accept almost any convention. There is only one requirement that an intelligent modern audience should make: *whatever convention is used must not distract from the central concern of the drama, but must if possible express it more fully and beautifully than it could be expressed otherwise.* Realism is right for Chekhov but wrong for Toller's *Man and the Masses.*

Audiences are far more adaptable and imaginative than many producers are aware; they will accept almost any convention, however strange, and even feel deep illusion, but only on condition that the convention serve directly as the right means of telling a story about human beings. The "actors" may even be wooden puppets, but what they perform must stand in our imaginations for what real people like ourselves would do and feel. "Imitations," wrote Dr. Johnson, using the traditional term for what we would now call artistic interpretations, "imitations produce pain or pleasure, not because they are mistaken for realities, but because they bring realities to mind."

A dramatist may be free with his conventions within these conditions, but to move us at all he must have a moving story to tell. *Our Town* was a partial failure outside of New York City, not because its conventions were strange, I believe, but because it did not have a strong enough plot. It was delicate and profound in its insights, delightful in its characterization, deeply moving in individual episodes; it concentrated, as a play should, on the spoken word, and its language, though plain and colloquial, was poetically conceived and uttered. All these did not sufficiently sustain it on the road, because it lacked "action."

PLOT

Mere talk for its own sake is never justified in a play, even when it is first-rate talk, beautiful, eloquent, or witty. If good enough in such ways, it may, to be sure, get into anthologies and be enjoyed as "literature," like Shakespeare's incidental songs. (In the plays these songs have a partial dramatic function, at least, in enhancing the mood.) We may sometimes tolerate inconsequential talk in a play that is otherwise dramatic, provided there is not too much of it, but it is always better omitted. The principle of dramatic economy decrees that dialogue must advance the story. The end of the drama—its primary end, at least—is to rouse an emotion, and in this it is similar to a lyric poem. But, unlike the lyric, the drama rouses emotion primarily by what the characters do, not by what they say about themselves or each other, or about life in general. Hence *dramatic talk is that which causes changes in the situation,* not that which philosophizes or analyzes feelings or indulges in reminiscences. But when a novice writes a play, he is nearly always tempted to make his characters talk about their feelings when he wants the audience to share them. Thus the young man to his sweetheart: "Do you remember, darling, that evening in Havana when the tropic moon sank behind the palm trees and the native spirituals drifted cloyingly across the still water of the lagoon along with the fragrance of jasmine?" She answers in a husky "Yes," and they both "pause," looking meditatively at the landscape on the backdrop.

In moments of weakness even professionals do this sort of thing, though presumably in better style. There is a great deal of it—some of us would say a great deal too much of it—in the more aspiring efforts of our leading American tragedists, Maxwell Anderson and Eugene O'Neill. I suppose that most English-writing dramatists have been led to the indulgence mainly by the example of Hamlet's soliloquies. It also gives them a chance to indulge a weakness for "fine writing." But such talk is always bad when it is not dramatically justified, and the finer the writing the more pretentiously bad it is. But, on the other hand... if it is really justified by the dramatic situation and cannot be omitted without weakening the action, it may be supremely good! The test is whether it can be omitted without loss. Here is the point where the artist proves himself by ruthless cutting.

In judging a play, however, we must bear in mind that the dramatic relevance of dialogue is not always obvious. We must apply our test broadly and flexibly; we must always consider the ultimate aim of the dramatist as well as his immediate business. Much of the talk in Chekhov's plays seems irrelevant, yet it is exactly by means of this desultory and inconsequential chatter that Chekhov achieved his dramatic purpose. In comedy particularly we must remember that dependence on illusion is less than in drame, and that therefore amusing inconsequentialities are not necessarily harmful. If we omitted Oscar Wilde's epigrams from his comedies, what would be left? Again, dramatic action may be inner as well as outer, and speeches that seem not to advance the action at all may really develop the spiritual struggles of the speaker. The *tirades* of Corneille and Racine do this; likewise Hamlet's soliloquies. And when a long speech does this and is written with eloquence it may create the most powerful effect in the play. A good many playwrights who have learned to shun the long speech merely because it is long miss opportunities for fine dramatic effects. Meagerness and poverty of language are one of the chief weaknesses of modern drama.

Fortunately, we also have a few dramatic poets. Consider the extraordinary power of the Christmas sermon in *Murder in the Cathedral*. When I first heard this piece of pure pulpit eloquence the majority of the audience seemed to be of Jewish descent and therefore presumably unresponsive to the Catholic theology underlying it, yet it held them rapt. It was dramatically moving because it deepened the spiritual meaning of Becket's martyrdom as an act of heroism.

Past generations knew better than we the dramatic power of eloquent debate and oratory. Greek tragedy is full of them, Shakespeare makes superlative use of them—for example, in Brutus' and Antony's funeral speeches. When we occasionally hear effective oratory on the stage today we are the more responsive to it because of its rarity. An instance is the Lincoln-Douglas debate in *Abe Lincoln in Illinois,* where the playwright lets Lincoln speak his own inimitable words.

The law of dramatic economy, then, must be applied imaginatively. All parts of a play should contribute to the total effect sought, but they may do so in unobvious ways. Especially is their contribution likely to be indirect in plays of spiritual and symbolic value. Becket's spiritual progress to a state of readiness for Christian martyrdom is the essence of *Murder in the Cathedral,* and his sermon shows this even though it holds back the physical action. But the long apologies of the murderers later on in the play are an artistic outrage. They are written satirically in the style of an Oxford debate, and are scarcely more in keeping with the rest of the play in this respect than an excerpt from Pope's satires would be in the Sermon on the Mount. They divert us entirely from the protagonist without contributing anything to the action. Considering Mr. Eliot's professions of classicism, it is strange that he should have shown such insensitiveness to propriety and unity.

To observe dramatic economy a play must have continuous "action." But this word "action" is ambiguous. In ordinary usage it means bodily action—all muscular movements except those of speech. In this sense, moving our hands and legs is "action" but wagging our tongues is not. This distinction is often justified in life, as when we wish that a person would "talk less and do more"; but when applied to the drama it leads to a grave misapprehension, for it causes people to overlook the fact that *the principal form of dramatic action is speech.* The novel tells its tale by written words; the movie mainly by pictures; the play mainly by spoken words. Pantomime and business are also action—usually,—but the chief form of action is dialogue that unfolds the plot. Thus Prometheus, because engaged in a superhuman struggle of will and fortitude against Zeus, is acting, in a dramatic sense, throughout Aeschylus' play, though he is nailed to a rock and motionless. It is this literally Titanic struggle that thrilled Aeschylus' audience, and it is not less evident to an audience because it is made manifest through words alone, and because the antagonist never appears in person. Yet an excellent critic will say of *Prometheus Bound,* "There is no action in it"![9] Thus the common meaning of the word brings confusion into our judgments.

The unity of effect at which the dramatist aims is usually gained by a unity of action, and the two terms "unity of effect" and "unity of action" are thus often used synonymously. But the action is a means to the effect, and sometimes, as we shall see later,[10] other means are used successfully without it. Nonetheless, the vast majority of plays stand or fall by their unity of action, and justify Aristotle's emphasis upon it.

They also justify his view that the plot is the foundation of drama. As we saw earlier, the complete plot constitutes the drama itself; the synopsis that we usually refer to as the "plot" is only its skeleton. We also noted that since the dramatist cannot, like the novelist, talk about his characters, we know them only by what they do (which is mainly what they say); and what they do constitutes the action. Thus, characterization is known to us only through action, and action is the principal concern. Those who have objected to Aristotle's emphasis on plot seem really to have understood the word in a very narrow and undramatic sense, with the consequence that one critic has even been led to the ridiculous conclusion that the philosopher's "taste inclined to good detective stories and melodrama."[11] This critic, and many other people, have been misled by their narrow definition of plot to suppose that actually a melodrama has more of

[9] Edith Hamilton, *Three Greek Plays* (New York, 1937), p. 91.

[10] Chap. v.

[11] Mary M. Colum, "Literature, Ethics, and the Knights of Good Sense," *Scribner's Magazine,* June, 1930, p. 601.

it than, let us say, a tragedy by Racine. Except in a purely quantitative sense this is not so. The action of a melodrama is merely more physical and outward. In Racine outer events are few and simple, but the inner events are highly complex and beautifully plotted.

A plot in Aristotle's sense, which is the one we are using, is not any series of events connected with a hero or a theme, but *a course of action that shows a purpose from its rise in an individual's will, through a struggle against obstacles, to a decisive conclusion.*

Purposeless action has, as we say, no "meaning," generally and dramatically. We always want to know why a thing is done, in order to understand it, and we are dissatisfied until we do. Since most purposes are obvious enough, dramatists rarely fail to make them clear. They are more prone to confuse our attention by dividing it among several purposes. We can hardly say dogmatically that one single purpose must always be the inciting force of a plot, but the dramatist who introduces more than one runs the danger of confusion. We should therefore assume that the purpose must be single. Note, however, that it is the purpose, not the motives. A single purpose usually results from several motives; it is the consequence of a variety of desires and impulsions. Too great simplification of motive would render a character unlifelike.

The purpose must be the free choice of a responsible person, and it must lead to action that he wills to perform. The agent must, in short, exercise free will. Some accident may force him to act, but his course of action must be of his own choosing.

I do not propose to argue about free will. The question that concerns us is not its objective existence but its necessity for dramatic effect. A fatalist feels that choice is illusion and struggle futile, for what will be will be, regardless of what we do. To such a view life itself is vain, and the mimicry of life in the theater doubly so—the very shadow of a dream.

The modern doctrine of determinism, based on late nineteenth-century scientific thought, teaches that all our acts are strictly the result of physical causation and that if we knew all the factors influencing them—hereditary and environmental—we could determine what they would be exactly as the astronomer calculates the future movements of the planets. Though recent physics seems to have undermined this doctrine by introducing the principle of indeterminacy, it is still a widespread view and often colors our thinking about ourselves. It is similar to older fatalisms in that it denies free will and hence the moral significance of conduct. If one genuinely believes it, he tends to see men as mere squirming parts of a blind nature and hence essentially insignificant. That plays continue to move even such determinists is a sign that few men are able to accept such a view emotionally, with all its implications, and suggests that the traditional view that men are free and morally responsible is not only something we *want* to believe, but something we *must* believe, if we are to find any significance or hope in our lives.

If these conclusions are sound, it follows that the deeper a play goes in its study of human conduct the more firmly it must be based on the assumption of free will. A farce may be able to evade such matters by confining itself to the superficialities of life, but a tragedy cannot. Most of the tragic plays of recent times have failed to be fully tragic, I believe, because their power has been undermined by deterministic assumptions.[12] The tragedies of the past which we acknowledge to be great have all been based on the assumption that man possesses moral freedom.

A contrary opinion is rather widely held regarding Greek tragedy, and therefore requires consideration here. On this view, the Greeks were fatalists. Most of their extant tragedies support the opinion no more than those, let us say, of Racine; on the whole, I should say, they support it rather less, since Racine believed that all men are predestined either to salvation or damnation. But Racine is not charged with fatalism, because we know that the theology of his religion maintained the existence of free will as well as predestination. What the Greek dramatists thought about the matter must be mainly inferred from what their characters say in their plays. And in two plays there seems to be evidence of a belief in fatalism. These are *Prometheus Bound* and *Oedipus the King*.

In the former play, according to the argument, Zeus himself is described as being bound by fate, and in the latter Oedipus is shown to be a mere victim of fate. The idea of fate was of course present in Greek thought, as it has been in that of other peoples, and it is emphasized in these two plays. But to make fate dramatically significant the poet would have to represent his protagonist as absolutely subject to it. This is not the case. Prometheus chooses freely when

[12] See chap. viii.

he befriends men and when he defies Zeus; his defiance is a powerful exaltation of moral freedom. Zeus also is shown as choosing freely when he ignores the warning of prophecy and overwhelms the Titan by an earthquake. Oedipus acts with extreme energy to do what he thinks right. It happens that, ironically, everything he does brings him step by step to his downfall, but that fact does not lessen his "inward liberty." His choice is free, even though his fate is predetermined. "Inward liberty and external necessity are the two poles of the tragic world," as Schlegel puts it.[13] He chooses according to his character. "Oedipus' destiny was his character,"[14] and character is what we make it. Sophocles was obliged to accept the fatalistic frame of the story as it came to him from legend, but he pushed the barbaric extravagances of the legend into the background, humanized his hero, and in every way possible within the frame showed him as a strong-willed shaper of events. At each stage "it was obviously possible for the victim to do something else—if only he had been someone else."[15] He has a "tragic flaw" that makes an audience feel him to be partly to blame; if he had been less impulsive, quickly suspicious, and imperious, his fate would not have overtaken him. Sophocles made him thus from a sound dramatic intuition. A mere passive victim might be pathetic, but he would not be tragic.

In general the Athenians of the fifth century B.C., far from being fatalists, were active, hopeful, and inquiring, with a

[13] A. W. Schlegel, *Lectures on Dramatic Art and Literature* (Bohn ed.; London, 1886), p. 67.

[14] H. D. F. Kitto, *Greek Tragedy* (London, 1939), p. 139.

[15] *Ibid.*, p. 140. See also Abby Leach, "Fate and Free Will in Greek Literature," in Lane Cooper, ed., *The Greek Genius and Its Influence* (New Haven, 1917).

strong faith in man's moral dignity and responsibility. But skeptical speculation and political corruption and defeat soon destroyed the spirit that had made their great tragedies possible. The later Stoics were fatalists, cultivating a contempt for life and death that makes a tragic spirit impossible by rendering tragic events trivial or merely physical. The plays of Seneca, the Roman Stoic, illustrate this. Even in Euripides the skeptical attitude had begun to weaken tragic power. His minor plays tend toward wry comedy or melodrama, and even in his greatest there is unmitigated horror, as in *Medea* and *The Bacchae,* or hopeless suffering, as in *The Trojan Women*. The latter, indeed, might more accurately be called a "pathodrama" than a tragedy.

Belief in freedom is necessary, but so also is a recognition of the force of circumstance. Our modern concern with biological and social forces makes us more keenly aware of circumstance than our ancestors were, and we demand that the characters in our serious drama be clearly products of their time and place. We hardly tolerate one who acts, as it were, in an environmental vacuum or without hereditary influences, like the old-fashioned hero whose characteristics are simply "given." We want more recognition of "destiny," even when we believe in freedom. Some critics with strong social views, influenced by this attitude, even maintain that no play is worthy of respect that has not what they call "social significance." Hence they tend to disparage plays of the older tradition that deal primarily with the individual and his ethical problems.

This attitude easily becomes unreasonable. In the first place, no drama can exist except as embodied in individuals.

Furthermore, in times when society is well settled, fixed assumptions about manners and ethics become so widely accepted that they are taken for granted; and during such periods playwrights are justified in showing a character as acting in the frame of those assumptions according to the rules they imply, and in not questioning the assumptions themselves. Such plays may now seem to lack "social consciousness" merely because they play a game according to unchallenged rules. Now that the rules are challenged, a contemporary playwright must of course recognize the fact. But he must still deal with the individual and his will, no matter how much he may emphasize his environment. And the individual must be real as a distinct personality, in order to give the play that quality of life which it needs to move an audience.

We shall assume, then, that an act of free choice begins our dramatic action, or begins the chain of events that the drama presents. Somebody wanted something and tried to get it. This initial act may have happened long before the play opens. If so, it will be recounted or suggested to the audience. If it is something universally understood, like falling in love, we seldom need any explanation; a hint of the facts will suffice, as in *Antony and Cleopatra*. Philo's opening lines,

> Nay, but this dotage of our general's
> O'erflows the measure,

give us the situation and suggest the dramatic conflict. The element of will here is less in the falling in love itself—which is likely to be a sort of fatality, as the legend of Cupid and his arrows suggests—than in the course of action that the lover chooses as a result of falling in love. And incidentally, since love involves two parties, love dramas sometimes have two protagonists whose wills are joined. Thus Romeo and Juliet share our interest, and Antony and Cleopatra might also, except that Shakespeare gives special development to Cleopatra's character.

Even with obvious motives it is usually necessary to explain to the audience the special circumstances that are involved. Macbeth has a latent will to power, but we must know how this is set in motion by the prophecies of the witches, the accident of Duncan's visit, and the urgings of his wife. Here the explanation is actually dramatized before us in the first act, but in many plays it is simply recounted.

Which method of exposition, dramatization or narrative, shall a dramatist use? The Shakespearean method was to start at or near the very beginning; sometimes before. Thus we see Romeo before he falls in love, and because the tragic conflict arises out of the feud between the two houses the play opens with a street brawl that dramatizes it. The Greek method, on the other hand, begins close to the catastrophe and requires that we learn about the preceding events—or the "back story," if we may coin a term—through retrospective narration in the dialogue. Euripides simply sends a character out at the opening of the play to tell the audience directly, in so many words, what has happened—the well-known "Euripidean prologue."

Thus the "point of attack," or commencement of the dramatic action on the stage, may be far back or far forward in the line of events. Each method has its merits and defects.[16]

[16] See chap. v, "The Greek and Medieval Traditions," pp. 168 ff.

Both methods have been extensively employed and both have produced masterpieces. Whichever method is used, we want to know quickly what the protagonist is after, and why. The sooner we know this, and also know the opposition to his will that causes the dramatic conflict, the sooner we are plunged into the dramatic action. If the conflict is too long delayed, we grow restless and bored. We must have enough exposition to make the situation clear, but after that we expect "things to happen."

The opposition that the protagonist meets causes him to shift and alter his plans, but all these shifts must be causally connected so as to show always their relation to the initial purpose. What is often referred to as "logic" or "inevitability" in a plot is primarily this clear coherence in purpose. A few chance events—events that cannot be predicted from the initial circumstances or that do not arise reasonably from them—do not destroy this sense of logic, because accident is to be expected in life. A certain amount of accident, indeed, is practically necessary for mere plausibility, as well as to provide an element of the unexpected so that the ending will not be a foregone conclusion. Too much, on the other hand, would not only be implausible, it would break the chain of causality. Similarly it would be broken by a shift of interest from the original protagonist to another. Hence the need for a hero.

EMOTION AND CONFLICT

Dramatic conflict may arise from accident or the intentional opposition of others or contrary motives within the mind of the protagonist himself, or it may be a combination of these.

In any case, interference with the will of the hero sets up a struggle that we call the *complication,* which in the typical plot grows more intense. This rise in intensity, not its pinnacle, is correctly called the *climax.* (The Greek word means literally a ladder, and in rhetoric, if not in popular usage, it still means an emotional ascent.) The pinnacle is the *crisis.* The crisis is known by the fact that its issue decides the outcome of the protagonist's struggle; it is the turning point of the play. What follows it, whether for good or bad fortune, is the *catastrophe* (literally "a sudden turn, an end, close"; *not necessarily a turn for the worse*). Other terms are falling action, denouement, resolution.

According to Gustav Freitag, who followed Aristotle, a play is thus divided into two parts, the rising and the falling movement, with the crisis in the middle.[17] His diagram of this is a pyramid. A serious objection to his division lies in his placing the crisis so far from the end. According to him, the turning point comes when the inciting force of the protagonist's will *first* meets with opposition, since thereafter, in a tragedy, the opposing force or "counterplay" gains more and more to the end. This division is logical enough, though in the nature of things it does not seem compelled to fall square in the middle; but it is made solely on the basis of action and reaction, whereas the effect on an audience is a much more important consideration. In terms of effect a good plot has an increasing tension or climax almost until the end. Though the tension is often relaxed in Greek

[17] *Technique of the Drama,* 1863 (translation, 1896). *Poetics,* XVIII: "By the Complication I mean all that extends from the beginning of the action to the part which marks the turning-point to good or bad fortune." (Butcher's translation, which uses the terms "Complication" and "Dénouement" for rising and falling action.)

tragedy earlier than our taste allows, in order to permit a quiet close with "calm of mind, all passion spent," it comes well beyond the middle even there. Modern practice is to put it as late as possible, lest the audience start walking out before the curtain. The beginning of the ebb in the hero's fortunes may be a turning point to the eye of analysis, but the event that finishes them for good or ill is what impresses an audience. In terms of tension, then, the rising action follows a long ascent; the falling, an abrupt descent. According to Freitag's scheme, the crisis in *Hamlet* is when the hero spares the king at his prayers; but not until he runs him through and falls fainting from the poison does the spectator feel the relaxation that marks the emotional close.

According to either scheme, the conflict grows and is resolved, and with the resolution the plot ends. A resolution in which the hero succeeds in his purpose is called a "happy ending," and in superficial usage it distinguishes a comedy or a melodrama from a tragedy. The differences among these types are not so simple as that; but so far as the main movement of the plot determines what sort of play we are going to have, it does so in this fashion. Thus a plot has, as Aristotle said, a beginning, a middle, and an end. This is one of the observations in the *Poetics* that certain modern critics call obvious platitudes, but apart from the fact that somebody has to utter a platitude first and is a genius if he manages to utter a great many of them first, as Aristotle did, this particular one is less obvious than it sounds. It really points out the three essentials of a plot: the purpose that leads to action, the conflict, and the resolution.

Why should a conflict be necessary? Aristotle did not

speak directly about it, and it was not insisted upon specifically by later theorists before Freitag and Brunetière.[18] The last-named critic gave the opinion such currency that it is now a dogma with many people. I should like to suggest that though conflict is ordinarily the chief source of dramatic interest, it is no absolute necessity. There are plays that succeed with little or none of it. As William Archer points out,[19] there is little or none in *Agamemnon:* our emotion there arises mainly from our terrified observation of a ruthless murderess preparing and executing doom on a proud victim ignorant of his fate. In *Riders to the Sea,* which is widely acclaimed as a great modern tragedy, the chief effect arises from the succession of deaths cumulatively impressing upon us the ruthless destructiveness of the sea and the despair of the mother. The greatest tragedy that depends on pathos alone is *The Trojan Women,* though even here Euripides introduces a debate or agon—a verbal struggle—as though it were practically a requirement of Greek drama. This agon is between Helen, who would exculpate herself with her husband, and Hecuba, who wants Menelaus to put his wife to death. This agon has ironic relevance in demonstrating the futility of the entire war, as the cause of it will go unpunished. Otherwise it is irrelevant, and that Euripides introduces it suggests the need for some sort of conflict in sustaining dramatic interest in a long play. *Riders to the Sea* is too short to need it.[20]

[18] Freitag: "The essential nature of the drama is conflict and suspense" (*Technique of the Drama,* 1896 ed., p. 109). Ferdinand Brunetière, *Etudes critiques,* Vol. 7, pp. 153–207 (Archer's ref.). See also selections from Brunetière and Archer in Clark, *European Theories of the Drama.*

[19] William Archer, *Play-Making* (Boston, 1912), chap. iii.

[20] See the "law of proportional intensity," p. 133 below.

The rarity of the exceptions proves the rule: for the most part both tragic and comic interest is mainly sustained by conflict. *Without conflict we would not be moved enough to enjoy the play throughout.*

In life our intensity of emotion varies, as a rule, in proportion to the difficulty we meet in satisfying our desires. The pangs of love, for example, like the pangs of hunger, arise from deprivation, and the well-mated have no "story," as is properly indicated by the valedictory formula of the fairy tale: "They lived happily ever after." Desires grow passionate as steam generates pressure, according as they are prevented from their natural outlets.

Again, there is a progression in feeling in proportion to its intensity, from indifference to pleasure and from pleasure to pain. The spectator at a play wants to feel neither too little, for then he is bored, nor too much, for then he is distressed.

Our capacity for sympathy, however, is limited at best, for even when we see our dearest ones suffering in real life we seldom feel a fraction of what they endure. It is far less than that in the theater, where we know that the sufferings we see are imaginary. Thus the intensity of our vicarious emotion in the theater lags far behind the intensity of emotion simulated by the players. Mild feeling on the stage leaves us cold, and a convincing representation of agony may rouse us merely to the pleasurable degree of response. It is in this sense that we may be said to "enjoy" suffering.

Some critics, reasoning from this pleasure that people seem to get from observing the ills of others, have concluded that dramatic emotion is a barbarous heritage from bellicose and cruel ancestors. "At comedy as at tragedy we come to see suffering," writes Emile Faguet.[21] If we were moved only by suffering, there would be more plausibility in this theory, but we obviously rejoice in the good fortunes of the hero and admire noble deeds. *What we want above all in the theater is to be moved,* and any kind of emotion will please us there so long as it does not exceed the optimum of intensity. The point on the scale of feeling at which this optimum registers its presence varies with individuals. Unimaginative and cruel people relish sadistic thrills and may even demand fact instead of fiction—like the Romans, for instance, who abandoned the theater for the arena; or the hearty English of Elizabeth's time who preferred bearbaitings to plays and executions to either. But other sorts of emotion can also be cultivated, for the rousing of which the theater may be even more satisfactory than ordinary life. Thus people go to the theater to enjoy, as they usually cannot outside, romantic love, heroism, magnificence, and formal beauty.

"Accurately conveyed emotion is the great fundamental in all good drama," writes Professor Baker.[22] As far as it goes this statement is true, but since our emphasis on emotion in this discussion is likely to cause some readers to reach one-sided conclusions, it will be well to make one or two qualifications. Emotion is what we want, but it is excited in us by a variety of things. The most direct and obvious source is the simulated emotion of the actors; but we can also be moved by the beauty of style and structure of the play, by the moral issues implied in the action, and even by philosophical generalizations. Emotion aroused by comedy, in

[21] Avant-propos to *Drame ancien, drame moderne* (Paris, 1903).

[22] G. P. Baker, *Dramatic Technique* (Boston, 1919), p. 46.

particular, does not depend on sympathetic identification, but is actually stimulated by intellectual detachment. All these sources of emotion, however, are likely to be insufficient for a whole evening unless they are sustained by conflict. A love-making can sustain one scene, like the opening one in *Liliom,* and the agony that results from conflict may sustain several, as in *The Trojan Women*. But generally a love scene merely starts or concludes a play, and hopeless suffering alone, long continued, is almost sure to prove intolerable. I have already quoted Arnold's observation that situations afford little poetical enjoyment "in which suffering finds no vent in action."

Incidentally, special circumstances may affect our susceptibility to painful emotion. Serious war plays, for example, except as they encourage the hope of victory or preach against the enemy, can hardly be enjoyed in times of war. During a war audiences prefer to forget their dread and sorrow, and flock to such escape media as romance, farce, and sex shows.

Sound instinct prevents dramatists from often attempting plays of hopeless suffering, but they constantly write plays that have too little struggle. To these plays we may apply a principle under the name of the "law of proportional intensity": *the longer the performance, the greater the emotional intensity needed to hold an audience.* One-acters need conflict less than full-length plays. They need not explore the profounder passions, indeed can seldom deal with them adequately; and hence they need less plot and may be mere dramatized anecdotes or character sketches. In this they resemble the short story. Interest can be sustained for twenty or thirty minutes by oddities of personality or local color, or by the initial impact of a striking situation without a complete development of its consequences. A one-act mystery or horror play may even end in mystery or inconclusiveness. Most of Dunsany's plays—*The Glittering Gate,* for example—end thus. We often enjoy a weird or puzzling ending when it comes quickly.

The mood that such plays induce can hardly last a whole evening, however; and the majority of short plays as well as long ones rely on conflict. The difficulties of plotting a long play begin in earnest with the second act, or as soon as the definite conflict is introduced. Here the dramatist confronts problems that the novelist and screen scenarist can evade. When the action of a novel runs thin the author can often fall back successfully on description or philosophic commentary, or he can divert us by an easy change of scene and character. The scenarist can always divert our eyes with interesting pictures. But on the stage no secondary interests will serve after the first act.

Freitag said that "the essential nature of drama is conflict and suspense." The conflict is in the characters; the suspense, in us as we watch them. Unexpectedness in their acts also causes us surprise. These two effects on the audience, surprise and suspense, are so often referred to and so important that they warrant separate discussion.

SURPRISE

Since a surprise is unexpected it cannot be repeated. Once a joke is told or a mystery solved, we want no more of it. This is the great limitation of the effect.

In the broadest sense everything that happens in an unfamiliar play is surprising since it is unexpected, but ordinarily we apply the name only to the big, startling surprises. This usage will be unfortunate if it leads a student to overlook the little surprises, for the big ones are better suited to melodramas than to serious plays, and it is the cumulative effect of many scarcely noticed but ingenious and delightful surprises that wins the most lasting appreciation. The big ones, however, are obvious and hence easily studied. Some of them are so obvious that the adjective "theatrical" gets its special meaning of "sensational" from them.

There are several main sources for them. One is the mise-en-scène. Our first sight of a spectacular setting, just after the rise of the curtain, surprises us. Likewise, an occasional effect of sound or lighting. But the surprise value of such things is generally inverse to the sophistication of the audience. The people who went to see Boucicault's melodramas in the late nineteenth century were naïve enough to be amazed by his carefully devised "sensation scenes," but present-day spectators, familiar with the movies, are less impressionable. The normal effect of mise-en-scène, as we have seen, is that of a fitting background for the action.

Surprises arising from plot are more important. When such a one is especially well devised and startling, it is called a *coup de théâtre.* (For this phrase, literally a "stroke of the theater," which conveys the idea of a sudden dramatic turn of events, there is unfortunately no good English equivalent.) The most obvious of the coups is reversal of situation. In Alexandre Dumas's *Tower of Nesle* the villainess, who happens to be also queen of France, is blackmailed by the villain into making him prime minister. But she steals the compromising paper and suddenly hurls him into a dungeon. First reversal. When she goes down there to gloat over him, he suddenly announces that he has another compromising document conveniently deposited with a third party, who will reveal it at a definite time unless he is reinstated. Second reversal. And so on. These startling revolutions of melodrama are often called peripeties, after Aristotle's term (περιπέτεια) for a reversal of fortune, but they aim at surprise merely whereas a true peripety does more, as we shall see in the discussion of suspense.

A skillful coup is effective partly because novelty itself is pleasing; partly because we enjoy the ingenuity of the dramatist in devising it; and chiefly because when properly prepared for and "sprung" it gives us a release of pent-up emotion. We can applaud or laugh and so let off steam.

Good mystery plays end with a major coup when the murderer is identified, for we are surprised and pleased. (Poor ones have identifications also, but these we either suspect in advance or consider farfetched and improbable: it is a cliché that the least-suspected person in the cast will turn out to be the villain.) In general, all good melodramas depend on a succession of coups, the biggest of which are put at the ends of the acts to give them "strong curtains" that will carry interest over the intermissions.[23] Since the action is built carefully to achieve the sudden release of strong feeling, these effects are literal "claptraps." And there should really be nothing disparaging about the term applied

[23] The best "curtains" combine surprise with suspense; see "Suspense," pp. 145 ff., below.

to an honest thriller when it actually traps applause, for great ingenuity of a special kind is required to do it: the plot must be planned intricately and to the last detail, and the production must be just right in pace, timing, incidental business, and stage effects, as well as in the more obvious requirements of acting. In actual usage, however, the term "claptrap" has come to refer not to coups that hit, but to those that miss.

Effective farce depends even more on surprise than does melodrama since the peculiar nature of laughter requires a *sudden* release of tension, and hence surprise.[24] The point of a good joke is something prepared for but unexpected. And to put a joke across the footlights successfully is even harder than to put across a melodramatic effect, for a slight mistiming or an accidental diversion may spoil a laugh. The consequence is that good farces are all too rare and deserve a warm welcome when they appear. The explosions of mirth they excite are accurately referred to as belly laughs: the Homeric gods enjoyed them on Olympus. The sharing of common emotion increases it several-fold, for laughter, as we say, is contagious. This mass emotion is impossible for a solitary reader, and less strong in the darker movie house with its photographs of actors.

Such strenuous surprises as those of melodrama and farce are out of place in plays of greater subtlety and significance. Coups call attention to themselves and make so crude and violent an effect that they would ruin the tone and illusion of such plays, especially for modern audiences that have been trained in the sober realism of the naturalistic tradi-

[24] See, in chap. vi, "The Nature of Comic Laughter," pp. 206 ff.

tion. Our grandfathers were less sensitive to the improbability of melodramatic reversals and trickery, and accepted as "realistic" their so-called "well-made plays" that were little more than complicated series of theatrical artifices. Even Ibsen, who did more than any other man to change all that, employed theatrical surprise. William Archer long ago called the tarantella scene in *A Doll's House* Ibsen's "last concession to Scribe." Yet surely Scribe never devised a better coup, in a merely theatrical sense, than that which ends Act I of *Ghosts*: "Oswald! Are you mad? Let me go!"

We object to a coup only when it does not come off; when it does come off, we are delighted by it without recognizing it as a kind of artifice. Hence in a way it is a pity that naturalism has made us so sensitive to what we call the "artificiality" of Scribe's and Sardou's and even Pinero's coups, for we miss thereby a great deal of innocent pleasure that our ancestors enjoyed. Of course we find a compensation in the greater pleasure we can gain from plays that meet our exacting standards. At the same time we must be on our guard against a tendency to condemn all artifices of the theater along with the cruder ones. In a broad sense all plays are nothing but artifices. Good art differs from bad, with respect to artifice, merely in concealing it from its intended audience; and we may say that when a coup wins its effect without calling attention to itself it is both good "theater" and good drama.

A crude coup, however, is sure to distract cultivated spectators from the central theme of a serious play. In revues, farces, and thrillers they will accept and enjoy such things, but as they want the effect of probability and logic in realistic drames, they are especially prone to object to surprises of staging in them. Sudden turns of plot may be so managed as not to disillusion them, but a stage effect without functional justification is sure to be artistically shocking. It is here that the director turns showman. Of course he sometimes has the excuse that his script cannot hold our interest on its own merits; but the right way of remedying a weak text is not to call in scene designers or musicians or electricians, but to create a more dramatic action. If this cannot be done, the director should look for a better play. At least he need not pretend that a poor play is artistically important.

Surprises of plot and staging are proper in serious drama when they direct attention to the drama, not to themselves. The stronger they are under this condition, the more powerfully effective they are. Hence they are always tempting. But exactly in proportion to their power to startle they are dangerous to use, for the playwright can never be sure that a big coup will not startle an audience out of its illusion. When he seeks a powerful emotional effect, therefore, especially with a critical modern audience, he must depend mainly on suspense.

For those minor effects which keep an action lively, however, surprise is indispensable. It has been observed that good literary style is largely a matter of minute surprises that not only startle the reader imperceptibly but also delight him because of their happy appropriateness. Hobbes's description of the wretchedness of the savage, for example, has become famous because of the effectiveness, in this sense, of the word that ends the passage: "There is no place for industry, no culture . . . , no account of time, no arts, no letters, no society, and, which is worst of all, continual fear and danger of violent death, and the life of man solitary, poor, nasty, brutish, and short." When Emerson described the person who "boils over" into oratory at the least provocation as having "a two-inch enthusiasm, a patty-pan ebullition," we are startled by the figure and delighted by its homely vividness and suitability. In like manner, though in higher degree, fine poetry is filled with surprises, for every just word combines unexpectedness with superlative appropriateness. Examples are countless; Shakespeare's sonnets are supreme:

> Th' expense of spirit in a waste of shame
> Is lust in action....
> Past reason hunted; and no sooner had,
> Past reason hated, as a swallowed bait,
> On purpose laid to make the taker mad:
> Mad in pursuit, and in possession so;
> Had, having, and in quest to have, extreme.

Thus also dramatic dialogue. An instance from a current hit is the curtain line that ends *Life with Father,* where comic surprise is prepared for by sound as well as delightful characterization:

> CLARENCE. Going to the office, Father?
> FATHER. No! I'm going to be baptized, damn it!

Ibsen affords classic examples in more serious vein. For instance, Dr. Stockmann (in *An Enemy of the People*) has been mobbed trying to reform the town, and Mrs. Stockmann laments, incidentally, the damage to his trousers.

"Oh, dear!" she says, "and they are the best pair you have!" To this he rejoins, "You should never wear your best trousers when you go out to fight for freedom and truth." Or consider Nora's symbolic rejoinder to Torvald when he has shown himself a mere male egotist, incapable of the "miracle" that she had dreamed of. Krogstad's letter comes with its news that the danger of blackmail is past, and Torvald fatuously imagines that everything can be again as it was. When Nora goes quietly into the next room, he calls after her, "What are you doing in there?" and she answers, "Taking off my masquerade dress."

The plays of Jean Giraudoux, the late French dramatist, depend for their success to an extraordinary degree upon a constant succession of small surprises arising from unexpected turns of wit or fancy. These effects often have philosophical overtones that make them memorable. Consider two or three in varied mood. In *Paris Impromptu* a good play is said to be one which makes the audience feel happy the next day: "Perhaps they didn't understand it but they understand everything else today—the fine weather, life, the leaves of plane trees, the silky ears of cocker spaniels. Obviously a well-written play!"[25] Jupiter asks Mercury (in *Amphitryon 38*) what happens after he has won a mortal woman. Mercury: "Truly nothing in particular; it's just as it is with Venus." In *La Guerre de Troie n'aura pas lieu* (*The Trojan War Will Not Take Place*) Hector, in the course of his address to his soldiers who have died in a recent campaign, says, "War seems to me the most sordid and hypocritical recipe for equalizing humanity."

[25] Quoted from the translated text in *Theatre Arts* magazine, March, 1938.

In these and in the innumerable smaller effects of good dialogue there is much more than surprise to move us; but surprise is one of the effective elements, and its value may be very great.

IRONY

The examples of stylistic surprise just given are many of them amusing because of the unexpected incongruities they involve. Incongruity—or, more fundamentally, contrast—is so important a factor in dramatic effect (as, indeed, in all art) that we should be justified in devoting at least a section of a chapter to it alone. But we shall deal with comic incongruities in connection with comedy; the broad effects of contrast are touched on elsewhere. While contrasts are not necessarily connected with surprise, but may persist (as in contrasting characters) throughout a play, those which usually impress us most come upon us suddenly and are more likely to be contrasts of event than of character. Hence I should like to add a few words here on the most striking of all such effects not purely comic—the effect which we call irony.

I suggested earlier[26] that though most tragedies involve a contrast between the hero's expectations and his fate, this contrast is not ironical unless comic as well as painful. The most familiar dramatic device for gaining this emotional discord is to have the hero unconsciously use ambiguities of language which have a harmless meaning to him but another and ominous meaning to us. The famous use of this verbal irony is in *Oedipus the King,* and it is so poignant there that we are apt to think it the essential "Sophoclean

[26] P. 87.

irony." But it is in a sense merely a sort of wink to the audience to make them notice the real dramatic irony, or irony of event, which underlies it. If it were eliminated the latter would remain, though it would be less impressive.

More common in Sophocles than this verbal irony is his way of presenting his protagonist as joyful on the very brink of disaster. He makes notable use of irony of both sorts in *Electra,* less striking use in *Ajax, The Trachiniae,* and *Antigone;* but the first *Oedipus* remains preëminent among his plays for them.

These meanings of irony were not general before the nineteenth century, though the Greek poets obviously used the effects consciously. In 1833 Bishop Connop Thirlwall first discussed "Sophoclean irony" in an essay[27] which gave the term the currency it has enjoyed ever since. There is no sound reason, however, for limiting the term to Sophocles, as Euripides used dramatic irony with perhaps equal frequency and force. (Thus we find it with wryly comic or sentimental emphasis in *Alcestis, Ion, Iphigenia among the Taurians, Helen;* with cruel bitterness in *Medea, Andromache, Heracles, The Trojan Women, Iphigenia at Aulis;* with savage horror in *Heracles, Hecuba, Electra, Orestes,* and—above all—*The Bacchae.*) No doubt "Sophoclean irony" will remain in common usage, but "dramatic irony" is in every way preferable as a general term.

Contrast in general, a tragic reversal in particular, are not necessarily ironical. They become so when comic and painful effects clash. There is something, for example, grimly

[27] "On the Irony of Sophocles," *Philological Museum* (Cambridge, Eng.), Vol. II, pp. 483–537.

humorous about the tricks which fate plays on poor Oedipus if we can see them with the icy detachment of an Apollo; they are the cruel practical jokes which the god plays.

> As flies to wanton boys, are we to the gods;
> They kill us for their sport.

We who sympathize with the victim cannot be amused; instead, we are shocked. Thus tragic irony affects us much more deeply than mere calamity. In comedy, on the other hand, incongruities are not felt as ironic unless they involve pain as well as laughter. *Arsenic and Old Lace,* for example, utilizes the ambiguous language of "Sophoclean irony"—harmless meaning to the victim, ominous meaning to us—without the slightest ironic shock.

> WITHERSPOON. You don't see much elderberry wine nowadays. I thought I'd had my last glass of it.
> ABBY. Oh, no . . .
> MARTHA (*handing it to him*). Here it is!

The most fundamental kind of irony is the expression of a conflict in the soul of the poet. When he is a person of deep idealism whose ideals are frustrated by experience yet persist in claiming their moral superiority, and when he has at the same time a keen sense of incongruity, his very view of the world may become grimly or bitterly ironical. The clash between the comic and the tragic is then not merely an effect of the work of art, as in serene-souled Sophocles, but an expression of the poet's own clash of spirit, as in Euripides. Many puzzling problems of the latter's tragedies can best be solved, I believe, in terms of his inner discord. Among other great dramatists the most ironical in this sense, and the most like Euripides, is Ibsen. No play ever written is more compact of philosophical irony than *The Wild Duck*.[28]

SUSPENSE

Unlike surprise, suspense does not arise from a particular incident or stage effect; it is a state of feeling induced by the entire action already witnessed. In its broadest sense it is simply our interest in the story as a story. We feel it as a vague, agreeable anticipation even before the curtain rises, and it becomes specific when events are shown which lead us to wonder what their consequences will be. We do not call this interest suspense when it is at a low intensity, as it is at the beginning of the first act, but there is no psychological difference except in degree between the suspense of Act I and that of Act III. In both we are eager to see what comes next. Anticipation is the life of narrative and the essence of suspense. When there is no more to anticipate the story ends—or should!

A surprise cannot be repeated effectively. Moreover, it is like a piano note, strongest when struck and ebbing quickly away. But suspense, as its literal meaning indicates, is like a taut cord, and during a well-constructed drama it is like a cord gradually being pulled tighter. This is the psychological "rising action" or climax. At the crisis it must, like the cord, be relieved or snap. Relief is artistic when the dramatic resolution is reached before our emotional tension

[28] For further discussion of Ibsen see pp. 179–181 and, in chap. ix, "Ibsen," pp. 316–333. I develop these views on irony at length in a study of dramatic irony now (1946) in preparation. I have not used "irony of fate" here because it is merely a rather pretentious term for dramatic irony of a tragic kind and is badly spoiled by popular misuse.

reaches the danger point, for, if things go too far, spectators find relief by breaking the spell of illusion, like a sleeper who wakes to be rid of a nightmare. Nervous folk in the theater are apt to giggle, for instance, when painfully agitated. I have heard giggles at a horror play like *Dracula;* they indicated that the adolescents were having a fine time shivering. I have also heard them at the tragic crisis of *John Ferguson,* when they were distressing to the more controlled among us. For the weakmindedness of a few spectators we did not blame the playwright. Sometimes, however, he goes too far for the nerves of reasonable people, and then he certainly is at fault. A fair illustration is the ending of Hauptmann's *Before Sunrise:* the heroine commits suicide with a hunting knife, offstage are heard the yells of her drunken, lecherous father, and the curtain falls upon the continuous screaming of the maid. Such a heaping up of horrors justifies incredulous laughter.

Suspense does not, like surprise, depend on the spectator's ignorance of what is to follow. It is strongest when the spectator knows or at least suspects the outcome, as when we see a swimmer helplessly drawn to the brink of a waterfall. The Greeks were familiar with the legends used by their tragic poets, and from the mere title of a new play could guess what its main action was likely to be; yet they enjoyed suspense. Much repetition of a play may weaken suspense for us, but will not altogether destroy it, as those who have seen *Hamlet* many times can testify. To know the ending does not relieve our feelings; it may, on the contrary, increase them. Tragic emotion itself seems to be largely this painful anticipation, rendered endurable and even delightful by beauty of style, form, thought, and character. And the sense of doom which makes so powerful an attack on our feelings in *Oedipus the King* or in *Ghosts* is a consequence of our anticipation of a tragic outcome, and depends on our knowing something of what that outcome is.

Tension can be laxer in comedy than in drame, for comedy depends generally on a series of laughs and its construction proceeds from joke to joke. Though each joke builds up a climax of anticipation, it is touched off by a surprise; and even when the general action follows a line of rising interest, our minds are not centered so much on the outcome as on what occurs by the way. We might say that through the showing of a drame of normal construction we go a journey to reach our destination, but we travel through a comedy mainly to enjoy the trip. Exceptions admitted, the drame depends more on suspense and consequently must build up to a more adequate ending, both emotionally and logically, whereas the denouement of even a great comedy, such as *Tartuffe,* may be a mere makeshift without doing any essential injury to the play.

Though even farce needs some suspense, a drame stands or falls by it. (This is merely stating in another fashion that a drame must have "action.") But to rouse it is merely the beginning of the problem. Bad plays often have fine first acts; it is what happens afterward that causes the trouble. To plot a complication is easier than to find a satisfactory resolution, and to raise expectations and then disappoint them is fatal. Many plays, like the hero of the old-style tragedy, may be said to die of the fifth act.

Major errors in plotting can generally be avoided if the

playwright finds satisfactory answers to two questions: Is the central conflict one that is adequate to sustain interest? Is the outcome of the conflict a genuine settlement of it?

Too little conflict makes a thin play. Too much—such as a combat to the death between blood-maddened maniacs—will probably be unbelievable. Between the extremes are the proper conflicts, which will seem to us real and important. Plays usually become old-fashioned, indeed, merely because their conflicts cease to seem important. One theme sustained innumerable dramas from the days of the Elizabethans down (excepting, of course, Restoration comedy) to the First World War: feminine chastity. A powerful conflict could be developed between a man's love for a woman and his horror at any deviation on her part, even in the distant past, from what was called the path of virtue. But that theme no longer seems important to most people. Real jealousy of a present rival, indeed, still moves us: *Othello* maintains its vitality. But not a play in which we are expected to be agitated by seeing the hero's soul torn between love and social disapproval of his wife's past, or a merely retrospective jealousy: *The Second Mrs. Tanqueray* is dated.

To find a real conflict is only half the battle. Faked resolutions have been common enough ever since Euripides ended his plays with gods from the machine. Few of his theophanies serve merely to cut the knot by divine intervention (as do those in *Electra* and *Orestes*), but he certainly set a bad example to lesser dramatists. Beginning with Aristotle the critics have very properly frowned on resolution by *deus ex machina*. Another form of fake ending is the violent death of a chief character when there is no adequate justification for it in the main action of the play. When a playwright can find no strong resolution otherwise, he is often tempted to kill off his hero or heroine. Death is so final! But the more violent and decisive an action is, the more fully must the playwright motivate it; and such an act as suicide needs to be prepared for throughout an entire play, or an audience will be unready to accept and be moved by it. Three instances of well-prepared suicides, in widely different plays, are those of Othello, of Hedda Gabler, and of Treplev in *The Sea Gull*. Hedda, in fact, has nine motives for ending her life![29]

The ending of the last act must be a resolution; the endings of the other acts, or of the scenes in them (if there is a break in time or place between scenes), should be bridges to maintain suspense across the gaps of intermissions. I have already mentioned the usefulness of an intermission as a breathing spell when suspense is too strong. When it is too weak the intermission may, on the contrary, be time enough for the spectators to realize that they are bored. In reaction from the melodramatic coups that used to end the acts, some modern playwrights have gone to the opposite extreme of letting their curtains fall on nothing of any importance. Sometimes understatement may be a kind of emphasis, to be sure; and Chekhov could sustain interest with almost no plot.[30] Few dramatists, however, have Chekhov's genius, and

[29] As listed by H. J. Weigand in *The Modern Ibsen* (New York, 1925): 1, terror of poverty; 2, dread of motherhood; 3, defeat by her stupid rival Thea; 4, the befouling of her aesthetic ideal by Lövborg's messy suicide; 5, physical and mental exhaustion; 6, Judge Brack's hold over her; 7, the fascination of the thought of death in accordance with her ideal of "doing it beautifully"; 8, desire to prove that she is not a coward; and 9, a diabolical delight in shocking the survivors.

[30] See pp. 336 ff.

an understatement which is really no statement is worse than the theatrical coup: better obvious artifice than nothing. A really fine "curtain" will be well prepared for, surprising yet convincing, and a powerful stimulant of anticipation for coming events. When it is all these it is something to thank Heaven for! A good example from a recent melodrama is the ending of Act II, scene i, of *Ladies in Retirement,* by Edward Percy and Reginald Denham. The murderess' nephew has unexpectedly arrived at the victim's country home where his aunts are living, and at the end of the scene is left alone. He does not know that Miss Fiske is dead, but he does know where she used to keep her cash box: inside the old brick oven. He finds a padlock on the iron door; he picks the lock and swings the door open. We have already guessed that the body has been stowed away inside, and we have an anticipatory thrill of horror while he works on the lock. We half expect him to find the body, or evidences of it. Instead, he is confronted with a blank brick wall. This gives us a shock of surprise. In a moment we reflect that the murderess had too little time to cremate her victim, and to wall up the remains is a reasonable thing to do; yet we are nonetheless thrilled by the visual proof that our anticipation was justified. And we are sure that the evidence of the oven will bring retribution on the slayer. With that momentary glimpse of the blank wall, and the nephew's surprised and suspicious exclamation, the curtain falls.

Such effects the drama alone can give. We have seen that the screen cannot, for it has no justification for act divisions and must be in continuous movement. The novelist may try to end a chapter on a similar effect, but chapter endings are instantly skipped over by the hasty eye of the reader, and even if he should pause to let the emotion sink in, it can never have the powerful sensuous effect that eye and ear receive from a "strong curtain" in the theater. We should never scorn such things on the ground that they are "theatrical." No less theatrical are such masterly coups as the one we mentioned earlier, at the end of Act I of *Ghosts*. It grows from character, it symbolizes the theme, it combines in the most powerful degree surprise and suspense.

At times there is so much suspense in a play that it strains the spectator's nerves. To avoid this strain, melodramatists formerly provided subplots with "comic relief," but, though Shakespeare also used it, the device seems too crude for our modern realistic plays. The central conflict itself, however, may in some degree be handled so as to afford relief without loss of unity. Almost all major dramatic conflicts involve an antagonist—the villain of melodrama, the "unsympathetic" side in realistic and tragic plays. In unfolding the struggle the playwright will show first one side acting, and then the other, in a series of thrusts and parries. This alternation is well illustrated by A. E. Krows in what he calls the "plot" and "counterplot" of *Hamlet*. He analyzes these in two columns,[31] noting in the first what Hamlet does, and in the second the king's actions. As thus outlined the thrust and parry of the play become strikingly evident. (Those who still think of Hamlet as passive and weak-willed should study it.) Thus in a well-constructed play action and counteraction may advance the plot and build up the climax. Normally, we identify ourselves with the hero, and the

[31] *Playwriting for Profit* (New York, 1928), pp. 86 ff.

dramatist naturally provides us with longer scenes in which he is active. But if relief is needed, a shift to the point of view of his opponent may afford variety without weakening the action.

A subplot is a surer form of relief; but it is a hazardous one because it shifts the attention from the central action. If, however, it can be made to bear logically on this action by way of contrast or wider illustration, it may enrich it with broader significance. Laertes thus introduces a secondary interest in *Hamlet* and at the same time deepens the significance of the hero's tragedy by contrast. Like Hamlet, Laertes must avenge his father's murder, but unlike Hamlet he chooses violent, reckless, and treacherous means. He "acts" where Hamlet "hesitates." It is as though Shakespeare were trying to forestall the very criticisms which impulsive people have leveled at Hamlet for delaying his revenge. Laertes proves an easy gull for the king, who turns the youth's lust for vengeance to his own ends; and when he dies, he confesses his own fault and praises Hamlet.

We want to be kept in suspense for a reasonable time, and a delay caused by some diversion from the central action enables us to enjoy anticipation without loss of interest or irritation—provided the delay is caused by something relevant to the main action and is not too much prolonged. The beginning of the fifth act of *Hamlet* is a remarkable instance of such a delay—remarkable because it is so very much prolonged and runs so close to irrelevance. No doubt Shakespeare introduced the gravediggers for the practical reason that the clown in his company needed a part, and the comedy of their scene is so low that Voltaire, as we may recall, found it totally indecorous in a tragedy. "A grave is dug on the stage," he wrote, "and the gravediggers talk quodlibets worthy of themselves, while holding skulls in their hands. Hamlet responds to their nasty vulgarities in sillinesses no less disgusting."[32] Yet even this crude comic relief is made to heighten the universal quality of the tragedy by becoming a sort of earthy meditation on mortality. French tragedy sometimes makes its characters so decorous in manner as to seem unlifelike. Hamlet's meditation over Yorick's skull reminds us, with a qualm of uneasiness, that in mortality he and we are one and must at length "come to this." I do not believe that Shakespeare reasoned all this out; but the fact remains that he made of the comic relief something close to sublimity, and thus a virtue of necessity. Any other dramatist would ruin his play with a delay like that.

When suspense is very greatly excited, the dramatist faces a dilemma. On the one hand, his desire for unity leads him to maintain the singleness of his action even at the expense of his audience's nerves; on the other, the introduction of diversions may ruin the artistic unity of his play. The solution of the problem does not lie in any absolute rule, but, as so often happens in human affairs, in a compromise arrived at by tact and long experience.

Most plays, however, suffer rather from too little suspense.

[32] Quoted in the Variorum edition.

CHAPTER V

Unity

UNITY OF ACTION

In chapter iv it was suggested that unity of effect, the end of drama, may be gained by other means than unity of action. I wish in this chapter to explore the various sources of single effect that are to be found in important plays. And first it will be well to supplement with a historical review what has already been said about unity of action.

Aristotle thus formulated it: "Unity of plot does not, as some persons think, consist in the unity of the hero. . . . The plot, being an imitation of an action, must imitate one action and that a whole, the structural union of the parts being such that, if any one of them is displaced or removed, the whole will be disjointed and disturbed. For a thing whose presence or absence makes no difference is not an organic part of the whole."[1]

The influence of this doctrine has been enormous. Though the *Poetics* did not become known to Western nations until the sixteenth century, it soon thereafter became a Bible for literary theory. From the *Poetics,* from Horace's "Art of Poetry," and from a study of ancient drama, particularly Roman drama, critics fashioned the Rules, and strange as

[1] *Poetics,* Butcher's translation, chap. viii.

it seems to us in this day when artists generally pride themselves on breaking traditions, the dramatists endeavored to obey them. Corneille forced his romantic materials into neoclassical molds, and Racine's plays are models of formal correctness. Even Molière, in spite of his laughter at the Rules, generally found the classical method the best. These three great dramatists in their turn were models for their successors in France and most of Europe down through the eighteenth century, and their influence has not yet ceased. Though Victor Hugo, in his famous manifesto for romantic drama, the preface to *Cromwell* (1827), inveighed against the unities of time and place, and though he violated the unity of action also in practice, nevertheless he upheld the latter in theory. His contemporary Scribe cared nothing for theory, but his "well-made plays" were painstakingly unified in spite of farfetched coincidences and psychological improbabilities. His influence dominated commercial dramaturgy in both Europe and America for many years, and can still be seen in the light comedy and society drama of today.

This French tradition, then, has been powerful in spreading the doctrine of unity of action both among serious artists and commercial playwrights. But tradition accounts less for the dominance of the unity than does its appeal to our sense of logic and form. In all our constructions, from watches to bridges, from sonnets to tragedies, we seek after these qualities. Our desire for efficiency is gratified when our handiwork performs its functions cleanly without waste effort. And especially do we desire efficiency in the theater, where our time is limited.

A like case cannot be made for the other two of the so-called "three unities"—the unities of time and place.

First, they were not doctrines of Aristotle's, but were imposed upon the *Poetics* by his Renaissance commentators. As for time, he merely noted the prevailing custom of tragedy as he knew it: tragedy "endeavours, as far as possible, to confine itself to a single revolution of the sun, or but slightly to exceed this limit."[2] He makes no reference to place.

People who have really read the *Poetics,* from Dryden to the present, have known these facts and proclaimed them, yet the phrase "Aristotle's three unities" has been so widely parroted during three centuries that the task of overcoming the error seems hopeless. Even textbooks preserve it. One of the most recent says, "Aristotle . . . laid down in his *Poetics* principles for the making of the best drama. Among these was the recommendation . . . that the action should be represented as occurring in one place, within one day, and with nothing irrelevant to the plot."[3] And the *Theatre Handbook,* which goes out of its way to disparage Aristotle, shows its ignorance of him elsewhere by stating: "In the *Poetics* are declared: the importance of the 'unities' (of time, place and action). . . ."[4] Faced by such endurance of untruth in spite of the dictum that truth will prevail, one needs to shout the latter. The best one can do typographically, within the decorum permitted by editors, is to use italics: *Aristotle makes no mention whatever of unity of place. He mentions "one revolution of the sun" as a time limit generally ob-*

[2] *Poetics,* chap. v.

[3] *A Handbook of Drama,* by F. H. O'Hara and Margueritte H. Bro (Chicago, 1938).

[4] In the article "Drama, theories of."

served by Greek tragedists. The only unity that he positively recommended for practice was the unity of action.

The Renaissance commentators did not blindly misread Aristotle; they were misled chiefly by the practice of most ancient tragedies. Not knowing the historic reasons for this practice, they naturally ascribed it to intention, and sought theoretical justification for it; hence their error.

Tragedy arose from a religious ritual that required the services of a chorus throughout the entire performance. It was only gradually that dramatic interest was introduced into the songs sung by this chorus; and after the dramatic interest became dominant the songs not only ceased to be the principal concern, but came more and more to be merely a means of indicating intermissions between acts, like our dropping of a curtain. But in the fifth century B.C., when all the tragedies we still possess were written, the chorus was considered a necessary part of the performance; no one dreamed of doing away with it. At some period later than Euripides the odes became so obviously irrelevant that they were omitted or, as in Seneca, made purely ornamental interludes. It was then that the tradition of five acts, no more and no less, proclaimed as a law by Horace, arose.

During the great age of Greek tragedy, then, the chorus still kept something of its original function as a participant in the action, and it was a dangerous strain on plausibility to ask an audience to imagine the passing of days or weeks while a group of men actually stood before it singing three or four strophes. But the convention was so well established that shorter periods such as an hour or so, or even sometimes a day or more (as in *Agamemnon*), might be indicated as passing, and the spectators would accept it without protest. For the same reason it was not plausible to shift the scene of action while the chorus stood stationary. Sometimes a shift was made by having the chorus go off and come back again, as by Aeschylus in *The Eumenides,* when he changes the place from Delphi to Athens. (This shift also involves, of course, a long time interval—long enough for Orestes to travel from the one place to the other.)

The Renaissance commentators, however, rationalized their Rules on the theory that the three unities gave a play greater verisimilitude. Probably also the implausibility of medieval "simultaneous settings," in which any place from heaven to hell had a station on a big stage at one time, stimulated their efforts after something more logical and unified. And in seventeenth-century France people were weary of the violence and confusion of the long religious wars and anxious for order and good taste.

For a time, no doubt, the strictness of the Rules served a useful purpose, but when they became a straitjacket to "poetic madness" or imagination, a change was needed. The romantics effected the change, turning to Shakespeare for a model and rashly imitating his looseness of construction in their zeal for his freedom of presentation. Today we never think of obeying the two minor unities except when they serve our particular purpose, but we still generally believe in unity of action.

Even this unity, however, is no longer held to be universally necessary, for situations occasionally arise in which its abandonment seems justified. Such situations are exceptional, but they deserve consideration.

UNITY OF THE HERO

One of the other interests besides plot which may give to a narrative an effect of unity is what Aristotle called the "unity of the hero." In the *Odyssey,* for instance, many things happen which are unrelated to each other by probability or necessity and which could be omitted without injury to the rest, but since they all happen to Odysseus we feel that the epic is a unity.

So many novels are episodic in the same fashion that no one thinks of criticizing them on this ground. When Defoe published *Robinson Crusoe* and *Moll Flanders,* he pretended that they were actual autobiographies; and so compelling an effect of unity is gained by this device that writers of fiction have used it ever since. Biographical novels, like biographies, naturally begin with birth or near it and go on for any convenient length of time until ended arbitrarily by some event that gives an effect of finality. Marriage used to give such an effect, but has lately—for good reason—seemed less conclusive. Death is final in a physical sense, at any rate; and if such novels have no better reason for stopping they can always stop with that. Aristotle's objection, however, that there is no logical necessity for the events in such stories, remains valid. In the strict sense they are without plot.

But there is no arguing against a tradition which includes the masterpieces of Fielding, Thackeray, Dickens, and Meredith—to mention only four great names of English fiction; or against our obvious experience of unity in reading such novels. When the hero is a vivid, living character we identify ourselves with him and assimilate all that happens to him exactly as we assimilate to ourselves all our own heterogeneous experiences. There is no psychological force with a stronger drive toward the feeling of unity than this assimilation of experience into our lives. It is not logical; it is biological. It is based on our very instinct for self-preservation, since we cannot preserve our individuality unless we make our experiences of the world our own.

Novels, then, need no more than an effective hero for unity. But what of plays? If they could run as long on Occidental stages as they did in the Middle Ages or do in China, undoubtedly many of them would be as episodic as medieval and Chinese plays, and only a central character would bind the episodes together. Our desire for unity is weakened when we face so great a mass of incidents, and even if the plot were classically constructed we would find it difficult to see its structure as a whole. But we can keep our attention on the hero without such effort; he is our guide through the labyrinth. On the other hand, in the normal evening's performance we can easily observe the plot as a whole, and there is no time to waste; limitation of time and our desire for logical unity combine to discourage loosely episodic biographical plays.

Nonetheless, plays of this sort are occasionally successful; for example, *Victoria Regina,* which in printed form contains twice as many episodes as can be played in one evening, but which even in its acting version conveys an aesthetically convincing impression of a woman's life. Furthermore, a play like this offers an actress a rich role, and stars would continue to demand biographical plays for vehicles even if critics should agree with Aristotle in condemning them.

It would seem, however, that a play which depends on biographical unity alone must have for its central figure a hero in the full sense of the word—a person so dynamic and significant in himself that our interest in him persists and grows, no matter what he does or suffers. Give us such a character to absorb our attention and we will hardly be conscious of any lack in plot. Though we cannot enjoy the special satisfaction that well-rounded dramatic construction affords us, a full and rich identification may be nearly as satisfying.

Furthermore, our modern attitude toward plot is less demanding than was that of the past, for science has taught us that there is no evidence of a controlling design in our lives and that therefore a formless narrative gives a truer picture of reality than a formed one. Our ancestors, on the contrary, believed in an intervening God, Providence, or Fate, and were often unwilling to accept a fiction which did not at least suggest divine intervention. Today, when we read a play like Zacharias Werner's *Twenty-fourth of February,* in which fate brings retribution exactly on the anniversary of the crime, and by an exact reversal in which both father and son are punished in fulfillment of curses, we can see nothing in it but improbable, melodramatic plot manipulation; the Germans of 1810 thrilled with superstitious terror at the way it demonstrated the working of Providence.

The change in attitude has been gradual, but the new point of view was clearly stated as long ago as 1880 by Zola in his series of manifestoes in favor of naturalism. He maintained that plot is an artificial thing which by its very nature deforms and falsifies the flowing casualness of life. Although the naturalistic school which he fostered is no longer a "cause," its products have influenced the tastes of playgoers who have never heard of it, making them more critical of manipulated plots. Evidence of this change is the fact that the masterpieces of the 'nineties in the school of contrived action such as *La Patrie!* are now as outmoded as buttoned boots. No matter how much we may admire Sardou's skill in contrivance, Shaw's epithet is the final word: "Sardoodledom."

Of course no play can be successfully put together without some manipulation of events, and in an absolute sense Zola's theory, applied to fiction, is an impossible one. But where our ancestors found some philosophical or religious or superstitious sanction for chance, coincidence, and other handy ways of botching a plot together, we do not. We want at least the semblance of designlessness in our plays. Hence our desire for unity is the more easily satisfied by the biographical method.

When the play is built around a dominant character we may be satisfied with the unity of the hero alone, but if he is a weakling some other force is needed. In either case, unity is enhanced by other forces. One such reinforcement is the interest we take in a general theme or idea for which the hero stands. The hold that *Peer Gynt* has on Norwegians is only in part due to the great vitality of the hero; it is also due to their recognition of Ibsen's satirical intention in making Peer representative of certain national characteristics. The play is not merely a dramatized life; it has elements of allegory. The theme thus reinforces the unity of the hero—though both together, in this play, scarcely suffice to compensate for the looseness of the construction. Even when a dramatist has no specific theme in mind, if he creates a thoroughly vital character thoughtful people are sure to see in it universal significances, and so attach some thematic unity to the play that contains it.

Unity of theme, then, may fortify unity of the hero, as of course it fortifies unity of plot. But can unity of theme alone hold a play together?

UNITY OF THEME

Though art and entertainment are secondary matters to the playwright with a message, he must hold his audience if he is to gain a hearing at all. Therefore, unless his theme is of vital importance to them, he must rely also on other sources of interest. But this involves him in difficulties.

A thesis play is an argument from example, and to be effective it must convince us that its mimic action represents realities and is both fair and typical. This is difficult, particularly in a play with a hero who must be both a vital human being and an abstract idea. Since real people are compounded of complexities and even contradictions, they seldom fit these conditions. As we have noted earlier,[5] unskillful propagandists are continually getting caught in this dilemma. Usually their "characters" are mere abstractions like the Virtues and Vices of the old morality plays. On the rare occasions when they come to life, our interest in them as persons distracts us from the thesis. Even skillful

[5] P. 78.

dramatists seldom manage much better. The only play by Dumas the Younger that still holds the boards is *Camille,* which is also the only play he wrote *con amore*. Ibsen is the one notable exception. It is amazing with what extraordinary force he dramatized his problems and at the same time embodied them in living characters of enduring vividness and truth. *Rosmersholm* and *Ghosts* combine, in unmatched power, unity of plot with unity of character and unity of theme.

We have just remarked that a thesis play is an argument from example. In scientific fields such arguments follow a definite method. The social or medical investigator, for example, collects a great number of case histories of all types which fall under his survey, and in his report, along with his statistical results, cites carefully selected ones to illustrate each type. He may use the method of random sampling, widely successful in polls of public opinion, so as to get a cross section of his material. A few novelists have attempted something of the sort, as, for instance, John Dos Passos in *Manhattan Transfer* and *U.S.A.* The method is difficult in the restricted compass of a play; but it has been tried.

The first notable attempt was Hauptmann's *The Weavers* (1892). Leftists have celebrated this play as revolutionary in subject matter because it shows extreme social injustice under a capitalistic entrepreneur. It is not a typical propaganda play, however, because it does not obviously take sides. It appears, at least, to present simply a series of historical incidents as they probably happened. Such lessons as we draw from it are implicit in the conditions it depicts, and are not preached by the dramatist. To the student of dramatic form it is revolutionary chiefly in method. It has no hero. In the first scene we see a few of the weavers, timid, starving, ill, pleading hopelessly with the manufacturer's overseer. Next we have a "close-up" of a typical weaver in his home: we enter his hut and see the dreadful life his family leads. The third scene illustrates how the landlords, tradesmen, farmers, and even the clergy, combine for self-interest with the manufacturer against the weavers. Then the desperate uprising begins. We observe the manufacturer himself, surrounded by his family and retainers, at first arrogant and self-justifying, then fleeing in terror when the mob attacks his house. As a closing picture we see the one piously submissive weaver who has stuck to his loom shot down by a stray bullet—a touch of perhaps overobvious pathetic irony. Clearly, if Hauptmann had disregarded theatrical limitations he might have multiplied such scenes indefinitely and increased the logical force of his presentation with each, so long as each added to our understanding of the revolt. Clearly, also, being under the necessity of limiting the number of scenes, he chose carefully just those that would make his picture as accurate and full a cross section as was possible in the playing time.

The Weavers has had a profound influence on subsequent dramatists concerned with social problems. We see it directly in Toller's *Machine-Wreckers* and we suspect it in many Soviet and American dramas of the 'twenties and 'thirties. But these plays have followed Hauptmann's in subject matter rather than technique. Toller's play, for example, is unrealistic and full of special pleading. The distinction of Hauptmann's play in its kind is its convincing humanity and relative absence of overt bias. It preaches best because it simply presents.

This method, then, has the special advantage that it puts the playwright under no compulsion to distort character for plot or partisanship but permits him to show each character as he is in life because he is one of many who illustrate the theme and because his very peculiarities help convey its many-sidedness. In spite of the variety that results, the theme, in *The Weavers* at least, integrates the whole.

The difficulties of the method, however, are obvious and great. A writer of Hauptmann's objectivity but with less genius for character creation would be sure to produce a mere series of sociological case histories. A writer with less objectivity could not refrain from overemphasis and distortion. Hence it is unlikely that many playwrights will be as successful in making theme alone the unifying element in their dramas.

The Weavers is in one sense a "history" because the events which it depicts actually took place in 1844 and the dramatist's grandfather had a part in them; but that is not why it interests us today. Its thematic vitality lies in the continuance of the problem it presents. There have been periods, however, when audiences less literate and less educated historically went to the theater, at least in part, to learn about past events. Such were the Elizabethans who enjoyed Shakespeare's "histories." For them the plays had value as information as well as entertainment, and they were the more willing to accept a loose series of episodes so long as these showed the important events in the reign of some English king.

Shakespeare's best "histories," however, except *Henry IV,* are unified also by having the king as protagonist. Furthermore, *Richard III* and *Macbeth* recount the rise and fall of men with dominating characters and thus conform broadly to the plot pattern of tragedy. It is after their model that historical plays have usually been written since then. Such plays have the conventional unities of plot and hero, and hence depend little, if at all, on historical interest. *Henry IV,* Parts One and Two, is exceptional because a minor character, Falstaff, got out of his creator's control and stole the show. (Shakespeare had to kill him off to make the king central in *Henry V.*) *Henry IV* thus survives on the boards with cuts and adaptations as a sort of broad comedy interspersed with melodrama and unified only in part by the presence of the fat knight in the comic scenes. In general, then, we may conclude that historical interest is insufficient alone to unify a drama, but that it may be an aid under special circumstances.

Similarly with setting. Elmer Rice's *Street Scene* joins together incidents from the lives of several people only because they happen to live in the same tenement or to be passing by on the street. A good deal of our interest in this play at first comes from the chance it gives us to go slumming. Our curiosity about others' lives, of course, is a basis for all interest in fiction; but such a play as this claims serious attention as a picture of actualities in a particular social environment. Nevertheless, under the most favorable circumstances, curiosity could hardly by itself sustain a long play; and it does not sustain *Street Scene,* which quickly holds attention by plot interest.

Unity of theme, we conclude, succeeds only when the theme is of vital importance to the audience, and even then it almost always needs reinforcing by the time-honored dramatic interests in plot and character.

We have now surveyed the objective sources for unity. But from a subjective point of view what we call unity in a work of art is a matter of feeling, and since feeling varies indefinitely with the individual we cannot deal with it by the definite and easy method of classification used thus far. Indeed, it involves us in so many difficulties that to avoid it altogether, as do most studies of dramatic form, would be convenient. But such a procedure would leave out of consideration some of the most interesting and important of modern dramas, and for that matter some of the most striking qualities in Shakespeare. In other words, in some plays we feel a unity not accounted for by interest in plot, hero, or theme.

Our approach to this subjective unity will be surer if we begin with a consideration of the two great traditions of Western drama, the Greek and the medieval.

THE GREEK AND MEDIEVAL TRADITIONS

Though a unified plot appeals to our sense of form when we study it, its effect in the theater is in proportion to its immediate impact. Its primary appeal is to emotion rather than to reason, and its method of centering our concerns in the protagonist's struggle and building them up climactically, is justified by its efficiency in rousing emotion. And it is highly efficient. It is like an airplane, the form of which is determined by its function. Though no one Greek play is perfect from this point of view, the Greeks discovered and stated the principles on which an ideal play of this type must be built, and all who follow them are working in the Greek tradition.

The medieval tradition is very different. A medieval play is like a Gothic cathedral—complex, aspiring and earthy at the same time, and full of incongruous figures such as gargoyles and angels that symbolize the antithesis in medieval religions between heaven and hell. To the Greeks there was no such underlying religious antithesis, for their gods, though conceived on a superhuman scale, remained essentially human in a psychological sense, being neither superhumanly good nor bestially wicked like the saints and devils that haunted the imagination of the Middle Ages. Greek art reflects the Greek belief in a humane universe, and medieval art reflects the conflict that is inherent in medieval faith.

The authors of the mystery plays could put into them anything they liked from the vast store of Biblical narrative. Later this store was increased when they drew upon the saints' legends. Here was the farce of Noah and his shrewish wife, mixed up with sermons from Almighty God. Here were the realistic horrors of a martyrdom and the melodramatic pitchings of sinners into hell-mouth; here were the pathos of Isaac's sacrifice and the high tragedy of the Passion. There was no unity of action, for there were many actions; no unity of effect, for each action produced its special effect. Yet the audiences found such incongruities natural, because the whole performance represented, not the rational universe of the Greeks, but the terrible and mystical universe of the medieval Christian.

Formally, the two modes present striking differences. The Greek puts its point of attack close to the catastrophe, usually on the last day of a long series of events, and informs the audience of previous events by narrative prologue or explanations in the dialogue. The medieval begins at the beginning. If, like the geometer, we draw a line *AB* to represent the total time during which all events, explained and represented, must occur, and then mark on this line the portion or portions shown on the stage, that portion which constitutes the Greek play appears as a mere point at the end of the line; those which make up the medieval type of play are strung out clear across it. Some do not belong on the line at all, being irrelevant, but for the sake of simplicity we may disregard them.

We can illustrate this medieval method by Shakespeare. Though some dramatists of his time, like Ben Jonson, were influenced by Renaissance reverence for the classics, the medieval tradition was dominant in the theater, and Shakespeare worked almost wholly within it. From medieval love of brutal horrors realistically enacted come his occasional scenes of violence and torture, such as the blinding of Gloucester in *Lear;* from medieval love of startling effects, his many melodramatic coups. (The example of Seneca no doubt contributed here by giving a pseudo-classical sanction to horrors.) The medieval division of mankind into spiritual sheep and goats influenced even his characterization, at its best so universally true and profound, in the direction of a goodness or badness more absolute and simple than we find in life—the goodness of Cordelia, the badness of Iago. And what concerns us at this time, his formal construction, is medieval in its episodes, subplots, frequent changes of scene, disregard of the so-called unities of time and place, comic diversions amid tragedy, and early point of attack.

If we take *Antony and Cleopatra* for illustration, the line *AB* will represent about ten years, historically speaking, though of course the total time is a matter of vague indifference to a spectator. There are thirty-eight scenes in the play.[6] We shall number each in sequence from one to thirty-eight, disregarding the act divisions. The first scene, as we noted in the last chapter under "Plot," opens very close to *A*, which is the beginning of the love affair. We shall space the scene numbers across the line roughly to suggest their relative spacing across the ten years. Our graphic representation will show how slowly the story unfolds at first and how huddled and close-packed the scenes follow one another toward the end.

A *1, 2–4, 5, 6, 7, 8–10, 11–12, 13, 14–15, 16, 17, 18, 19–38* *B*

Of course this play, with its thirty-four named parts (not to mention supernumeraries) and its thirty-eight scenes, is notable for its looseness of construction, but for this very reason it is an excellent illustration of the medieval mode. We may give to this method of playwriting a descriptive name—"the drama of extension."

In contrast, the Greek may be called "the drama of concentration." It is perhaps best illustrated by *Oedipus the King*. Here the source of the ancestral curse which finally works itself out upon the hero and his children is ultimately the unlucky deed of Oedipus' great-grandfather Cadmus

[6] According to the Oxford edition; in others there are forty-two.

in slaying a dragon sacred to Ares. But if we arbitrarily begin it with the hero's birth and the oracle that foretells his murder of his father—which is as far back as we need to carry the story for the purposes of the play—we nevertheless require a time line of many years. Yet the represented events of the tragedy all occur on a single day, thus:

The tragedy

A——————————————————————————↓B

A scene analysis of *Oedipus* may be helpful to those who wish to study it in detail. It must be remembered that the choral interludes, like our "curtains," were conventional breaks in the action, which, when convenient, might indicate the passing of considerably more time than that required for singing them. Even in this most closely knit of Greek tragedies the analysis shows that in actuality the events could hardly all happen between sunrise and sunset. However, what signifies in a play is not the time its events would require in life, but the time they seem to take in the theater, and in *Oedipus* they give the impression of following immediately one after another.

1. PROLOGUE[7] (Oedipus, Creon, the priest)
   Parodos (first chorus). An hour? Tiresias had to be sent for twice before appearing in 2.

2. FIRST EPISODE (Oedipus, Tiresias)
   First stasimon (second chorus). A half-hour? Creon had heard about Oedipus' accusation before appearing in 3.

[7] The terms "prologue," "episode," and "exodos" are the Greek names for what we now would call the first, intermediate, and last acts. The "parodos" or "parode" is the "entering ode." The "stasima" are the "standing odes." We would call them all, simply, odes.

3. SECOND EPISODE (Oedipus, Creon, Jocasta)
   Second stasimon. A long time. See under "third stasimon."
4. THIRD EPISODE (Oedipus, Corinthian shepherd, Jocasta)
   Third stasimon. The Theban shepherd, summoned in the second episode, has come from the farthest border of the kingdom.
5. FOURTH EPISODE (Oedipus, Theban shepherd)
   Fourth stasimon. Elapsed time?
6. EXODOS (Oedipus, Creon, messenger)

The drama of extension has comparatively little need to relate events, because it shows them, but the drama of concentration must explain all that has preceded its point of attack. This task was made easier for Sophocles since his audience already knew the story of Oedipus. The modern playwright can seldom use so familiar a tale, and usually starts with the problem of enlightening blank ignorance. When Ibsen wrote dramas of concentration like *Ghosts, Rosmersholm,* or *John Gabriel Borkman,* he had to explain many complex and even subtly psychological events which had occurred before the rise of the first curtain. Furthermore, he denied himself the assistance not merely of so naïve a device as the Euripidean prologue, but also the explanatory soliloquy, like Richard III's, and even, generally speaking, such relatively realistic expository devices as the revealing gossip of two servants. As far as possible he set out to tell us of the past in an apparently natural and accidental way through the casual conversation of his characters during the progress of the action itself. His success in this very difficult task is one of the marvels of dramatic art. But even his genius could not always make his exposition wholly clear to an audience on first hearing. *Rosmersholm* and *The Master Builder* are good illustrations of this difficulty.

Once this difficulty is surmounted, however, the drama of concentration gains time to develop the highest points of the plot fully. It is like the fifth act of a Shakespearean tragedy expanded to fill the whole evening. Since it must merely refer to much that the drama of extension shows, it requires in general more attentiveness and quickness of perception from the audience. It is difficult to get it under way, but once it is well begun it moves with greater ease and power. By needing comparatively few characters and little physical action it is better able to throw its emphasis undistracted upon the central conflict. It leaves the strongest impression of unity and, at its best, of artistic power fully exercised.

On the other hand, the relative diffuseness of the drama of extension may be compensated by its greater possibilities of variety. In it the imagination is freer, and the selection and elimination of material inevitable in every drama are less exacting; the probabilities are therefore more easily preserved, and opportunities for dramatic contrast and parallelism may be seized. Above all, the dramatist can show character developing over considerable periods of time. Because Shakespeare is the only one of the great tragedists to use the medieval mode, he is the only one to dramatize the changes in the soul of a Lear or a Macbeth.

The comparative merits of the two modes have never been better discussed than by Dryden in his *Essay of Dramatick Poesie* (1668). In this literary debate the speakers are concerned immediately with a comparison of contemporary

French and English tragedy (Corneille versus Shakespeare and Fletcher), but their remarks apply to all plays of the two general types. In favor of the drama of concentration one speaker says, "There is no theatre in the world has any thing so absurd as the English tragi-comedy; . . . here a course of mirth, there another of sadness and passion, and a third of honour and a duel: thus, in two hours and a half, we run through all the fits of Bedlam." To this the advocate of the drama of extension replies, "Our variety, if well ordered, will afford a greater pleasure to the audience." He finds the declamations of French tragedy tedious in the extreme, like so many sermons timed by the hourglass. "If we are to be blamed for shewing too much of the action, the French are as faulty for discovering too little of it: a mean betwixt both should be observed by every judicious writer, so as the audience may neither be left unsatisfied by not seeing what is beautiful, or shocked by beholding what is either incredible or undecent."

The two modes may be considered as opposite poles of dramaturgy. When we are inclined to romantic effects, the medieval pleases us by its wealth of variety—a variety unfenced, like the open country over which fancy can go vagabonding. Youth is especially inclined to enjoy such formlessness. Also, when forms harden into formalism, as in the eighteenth century, it is necessary to break them in order to infuse new life into art. On the other hand, the classic mode pleases us by its success within fixed limits, its unity in variety; and when romantic liberty degenerates into license, as among Shakespeare's successors or in the nineteenth century, men feel the need of discipline. Individually also, as we grow older, we are normally moved more and more by the virtues of restraint and control. Indeed, with our recognition that society itself progresses in the long run only through orderly processes, we appreciate classic art the more as we mature.

Thus we see that the two dramatic modes are merely manifestations of polar social attitudes between which society oscillates from age to age. Each is felt to be "right" for its time because it is needed; but when the need passes, the forms created by the need cease to have a vital function. Racine created beautifully within the narrow fences of the Rules, but his successors, except, at moments, Voltaire, were "correctly" dull and pompous without power. The revolutionary changes of the eighteenth century, as they concerned the drama, were led by Diderot with his plea for greater realism, and by Lessing with his attacks on French classicism and praise of Shakespeare. Lessing encouraged Goethe and Schiller to pioneer for the romantics. The Revolution interrupted the movement in France, and it did not manifest itself strongly until the 1820's.

Since the romantic view of Shakespeare still persists, we need to point out its mistakes. He was a practical playwright, working in a vital theatrical tradition. In imitating his technique without understanding his theater and without regard for their own theater and its very different needs, the romantics exaggerated the faults of the medieval mode. Hugo, for instance, takes Shakespeare's mixture of moods, along with the dualism of Christian doctrine, as an excuse for juxtaposing the grotesque and the beautiful—Quasimodo and Esmeralda—and giving us noble lackeys and ignoble kings, psychologically inexplicable reversals and melodramatic claptraps. In imitating and admiring Shakespeare the romantics of course claimed him for their own, with the consequence that he is still generally regarded as "romantic" like them. He often deals in highly romantic material, to be sure, but he knew his business as a playwright, he did not limit himself to romance in subject matter, and, above all, he had a profound and unsentimental understanding of men and women. Psychologically, Hugo's plays are compounded of improbabilities, absurdities, and exaggerations: as one critic observed, he "gave his characters a passion apiece, and let them fight it out." Psychologically, Shakespeare's characters are always sanely and soundly drawn, and the greatest of them are incomparable in their essential humanity. When he rises to such heights Shakespeare is no longer with the romantics; he is in the company of Sophocles.

Unity of effect, however, is what concerns us here; and in calling for a freer imaginative treatment the romantics opened the way for more skillful playwrights to gain it, sometimes, outside the classic bounds.

UNITY OF FEELING: THE SYNTHESIS OF INCONGRUITIES

The loose construction and mixed effects of Shakespearean drama do not normally induce a unity of feeling as the drama of concentration does, yet in spite of them his greater plays achieve it, through an emotional rather than a logical synthesis. There are few more incongruous moods than those of low farce and high tragedy, yet the low farce in *Macbeth*—the "knocking at the gate" scene—actually heightens the tragedy, as De Quincey pointed out.

Emotional incongruities may of course occur in either type of drama. In either, the first effect is one of shock and discomfort. If the discord does not express the dominant mood as does the irony of *The Wild Duck,* or is not resolved later into a larger emotional harmony, it will seriously injure the play: thus the murderers' speeches in *Murder in the Cathedral*. But if the incongruity is essential and significant, its effect may even increase the power of the whole. In this it may be compared to the discords in modern music that rouse us to attention, whereas undisturbed harmony would be uninteresting; and when the ugliness leads us on to a harmonic conclusion we are delighted through a feeling of relief and contrast: we have passed through an emotional struggle to a sort of victory.

In all the arts, we find, in recent years, an increasing experimentation with discord or ugliness. Though we often enjoy the peaceful harmony of eighteenth-century art, ours is not a peaceful era, and we expect a modern artist to express its agitation. If a modern composer should try to write like Mozart we would probably find him dull. (In Prokofiev's "Classical" symphony there is surely much more of Prokofiev at his liveliest than there is of Mozart; it has classical *form,* but very modern *feeling*.) Among some modern painters there seems to be a reaction toward formal harmony and representational beauty, but the dominant school has gone in more and more for abstractionist distortions and grotesqueries which, to the untrained eye at least, are generally ugly. (Picasso's "Guernica," for example.) And gradually our taste is affected by these things. It passes through familiar stages: first, shock and abhorrence; then, puzzled interest mixed with dislike; then, interest and unwilling liking; and finally—perhaps—strong favor. If we never arrive at the last stage, nonetheless we find after a time that art with less discord in it seems old-fashioned or insipid.

These violent assaults on our sensibilities involve, of course, the risk that their ugliness or discomfort will be unrelieved. Though a great many earnest aesthetes have become so numbed by them that they do not dare trust to their real feelings but try to like cacophony, formless daubs, and filthy or gruesome fiction, fortunately it is not the aesthetes but the larger public who know what they like that have the final verdict. Ugliness is justified in art only when it is felt to be part of a larger beauty.

We have seen that the drama is more resistant to experiment than other mediums and more dependent on the taste of ordinary people. Hence, dramatic experiments with discord have generally been less numerous and extreme than those in painting, music, the novel, or lyric poetry. The extremes, at least, have not got into the theaters very often, and so remain unknown. And we are concerned here with those that have succeeded both in winning audiences and in moving them to a unity of feeling.

I should like to instance first a play that has formal unity in the classical tradition but very striking disharmony in effects. This is *The Wild Duck* (1884). It is the most puzzling and enigmatic of Ibsens's plays, and probably the majority of its spectators have not felt that its discords are fully resolved. For most it is on the borderline between success and failure—a play that both irritates and moves; a strange mixture of beauty and ugliness. For a few it becomes more fascinating and powerful as they study it in the light of Ibsen's spiritual development.

In his earlier plays the moral idealist in him was dominant, and even as late as *An Enemy of the People* (1882), which immediately preceded *The Wild Duck*, an intransigent idealist is made the hero. But, along with the idealist, Ibsen also had in his nature the disillusioned cynic, ruthlessly analytical and objective. In *The Wild Duck* the cynic suddenly gets the upper hand and turns in ironic scorn on all that the idealist had previously held up for admiration. Brand had gone about among the cottagers making the claim of the Ideal, but in *The Wild Duck* such claims when made by Gregers Werle are both absurd and pernicious. Lona Hessel had declared solemnly that Truth and Freedom were the pillars of society; *The Wild Duck* demonstrates that lies and subservience make the world run smoothly. In *A Doll's House* a "true marriage" is shown to be possible only when based on complete sincerity; but here the marriage of one contented couple is ruined by the discovery of the truth, and the projected marriage of an aging rascal with a clever courtesan promises to be secure and happy on the basis of what the lady herself describes as "complete confidence, entire and unreserved candor on both sides"—a devastatingly ironical distortion of Nora's ideal. In *Ghosts* the sins of the father are visited upon the innocent child; in *The Wild Duck* the father remains prosperous and the child (little Hedwig) is happy in spite of her heredity until her busybody of a half-brother insists on preaching Ideals at her.

In *An Enemy of the People* Doctor Stockmann, the hero, campaigns to drain "the swamp of deception" in society; but here the revelation of truth brings merely the child's futile self-sacrifice and declamatory speechifying from her foster father. Ibsen's spokesman concludes that most men can exist contentedly only on what he calls "life lies."[8]

Such ruthless self-satire, such cruel irony compounded of scornful laughter and pathetic disillusionment, would certainly ruin any ordinary play. Yet in spite of our distress Ibsen beguiles us, partly through his skill of construction, partly through his vivid characterization, partly through the strangely poetic appeal of the setting of the later acts, with its garret that symbolizes the imaginary freedom and actual spiritual slavery of its characters. And when we understand his mood when he wrote it, we are moved to an all-embracing admiration for his honesty and an almost tragic irony—a detached mingling of pity and amusement at these foolish and deluded mortals. I know of no play in which the accomplishment of a unity of feeling is more difficult; its partial success therefore in achieving it is something of a miracle.

Its unity of effect, however, is assisted by its formal unity. Suppose a play has little or none of the latter; can it possibly achieve the former with incongruous material?

The Lower Depths (1902) is probably the greatest of all naturalistic plays. It was written in accordance with the naturalist formula of "a slice of life" without plot, without hero, without dominant theme. If Gorky had been free to speak

[8] For much of this analysis I am indebted to H. J. Weigand's admirable study, *The Modern Ibsen,* already referred to. See also my discussion of Ibsen in chap. ix.

out he probably would have turned it into a violent indictment of the social system in Russia, for he hated injustice and had, as he confesses,[9] a weakness for "the didactic." But he had to write a play that could pass the suspicious Czarist censorship. Hence the "meaning" is doubtful. Stanislavsky, when he produced it, took as a clue to its interpretation the motto, "Freedom at any price." It does not seem to me to demonstrate this; it does show that there remains a spark of spiritual aspiration even in the soul of the outcast at the social bottom, but that this spark remains futile under the conditions in which he exists. Our very difficulty in interpretation proves that dramatically speaking a theme or idea does not unify the play.

There is, to be sure, a formal unity of setting: the people happen to live in the same flophouse. But any other group of down-and-outers might with equal logic be brought together in this way. And our interest is not absorbed by any one character. We are somewhat more interested in Pepel, the thief, perhaps, than in the rest; but I am not sure of this. Though the characters interact to some degree, there is no coherent central action. (The Pepel-Wassilissa-Natasha episode ends with the second act.) For the most part the people affect each other haphazardly; their lives simply run parallel. Luka, the pilgrim, stirs them up for a time, but his significance in the play is uncertain despite numerous theories, and both his arrival and his departure are dramatically adventitious. The play violates all canons of plot, for there is no central character, no dominant motivating force, no inevitable beginning or end. On the contrary it seems to

[9] Preface to *The Judge*.

demonstrate that life will flow on like this endlessly and pointlessly forever.

It seems to demonstrate also that life is an emotional jumble. Its effects include extreme pathos (in the death of Anna), brutality (in the beating of Natasha), and viciousness (in the character of Wassilissa). It is filled with desultory self-confessions that run a gamut from farcical humor to spiritual longing. Gorky has not tried here to impose meaning upon the muddle of existence.

Yet in spite of these things it is a great play. It moves audiences profoundly and leaves them feeling that they have seen a unified work of art.

The secret of this paradox lies, I think, in the harmonizing vision of the author. Most writers of his school, in the novel as well as the drama, fall between two stools. Either they repel us by brutal objectivity or they disgust us by sentimentality. To maintain severe objectivity without inhumanity is extremely difficult, but Gorky does it. He conveys a deep sympathy and understanding for his unfortunate characters, yet he never falters in showing them as they are. He never softens brutal facts out of concern for our sensibilities, as does the Catholic idealist Martínez Sierra, for example, in *A Lily among Thorns*. Neither does he play them up merely to give us a grotesque or horrifying thrill, as do Erskine Caldwell and Jack Kirkland in *Tobacco Road*. It is Gorky's rare balance between compassion and honesty that makes his work unique in its kind. Our feeling of unity comes from his unifying vision of life.

This vision, I feel, is intuitive rather than reasoned. He did not approach his material as a sociological investigator, but as a man who had lived the life he pictures. When he tries to reason about it and give it abstract meaning, as he does in his last plays, he loses the emotional unity without gaining a strong enough intellectual unity to bind their parts together. In *Egor Bulichov* and *Dostigaev,* I think, we are too conscious of the effort of an essentially intuitive genius to force his art along a "party line."

In a way, this intuitive unity might be compared to that of a dream. The discordances of dream material are all harmonized by the prevailing mood of the dreamer, for during sleep his intellect is in abeyance so that he does not perceive them as incongruities, and his emotions are heightened so that he may be profoundly affected by what on waking will seem merely absurd. (In one of my dreams I was moved almost to tears by certain mystic words. When I woke up I found that they were the meaningless syllables "O-ta-po-ta-see.") Something of this spell-like effect a playwright may occasionally achieve with very diverse material, if he writes intuitively and with strong feeling.

Thus with Strindberg's *Dream Play.* Although, as the title indicates, it is a dramatized dream and thus very different in subject matter from Gorky's painstakingly accurate reproduction of waking life, it may be compared with the latter in this respect. Its author was insanely introverted, and all his work is colored by his subjective passions. Thus he was more dominantly intuitive than Gorky. At the same time he had a paranoidal passion for rationalizing his morbid obsessions. Hence he writes of his play, with shrewd psychological insight: "Anything may happen: everything is possible and probable. Time and Space do not exist; on an insignificant groundwork of reality imagination spins and weaves new patterns: a mixture of memories, experiences, unfettered fancies, absurdities and improvisations. The characters are split, doubled and multiplied: they evaporate and are condensed, are diffused and concentrated. But a single consciousness holds sway over them all—that of the dreamer."

"A single consciousness holds sway"—that of Strindberg himself, torn and "bedeviled" by the conflict of its ineradicable psychoses. The play is thus unified out of the very discord of a mind compounded of discordances, and has the emotional oneness of a personality. The oft-repeated cry, "Men are to be pitied," is a suggestion of the dominating mood, not a statement of an intellectual theme.

Most of the expressionists who followed Strindberg's lead, however, failed both emotionally and intellectually to unify their plays. They prevented emotion by being abstract, fantastic, and puzzling, and they prevented any strongly unifying effect from their abstract themes by their incoherence and obscurities. I cited Elmer Rice's *Adding Machine* in chapter iii as a play which prevented identification without the compensations of comedy. In my discussion of Strindberg later on[10] I shall give other examples of their work.

We conclude that though emotion can sometimes fuse the most incongruous material and so give us a total impression which we intuitively feel as single, strong, and moving, such cases must in the nature of things be rare.

These exceptional cases are hard to deal with theoretically, not only because they are anomalies outside the scope of long-honored principles, but also because their unity is

[10] Pp. 341 ff.

entirely subjective and cannot be demonstrated. About total impressions, unsupported by objective evidence, every spectator is free to disagree with every other. If for example my reader does not find *The Lower Depths* emotionally unified, I cannot prove him wrong. This, however, is the difficulty that critics must always face when they leave objective analysis and deal with matters of taste. Hence theorists naturally prefer to deal with objective matters like plot and causal relations. And for most plays the traditional unities are still indispensable tests.

At the same time, the exceptions exist. We should try to distinguish them from those plays which are merely the result of novelty hunting and uninspired experimentation, and to be sufficiently catholic and responsive to accept them for their special merits even when they clash with our preconceived theories of art.

CHAPTER VI

Comedy

HISTORICAL BACKGROUND

GREEK COMEDY grew out of hilarious celebrations honoring the god of wine and fertility, Dionysus. A chorus of men masked and costumed themselves fantastically and indulged in licentious songs, dances, and jokes. Though a long time elapsed between these beginnings and the only survivors of the type, the comedies of Aristophanes, even the latter are in an obviously archaic form. Like contemporary tragedy, probably in imitation of it, they had alternating episodes and songs; unlike it, their episodes were loosely strung together.[1] Though they told a sort of story, it was like that of a modern revue, a mere excuse for fantasy, buffoonery, and satire. The choral lyrics were sometimes grotesque, sometimes serious and even elevated in tone, never sentimental like so many songs in modern "musicals." One of the choruses, called the *parabasis,* was addressed directly to the audience and gave the dramatist a chance to make topical jokes and "cracks" at notables there present, incidentally introducing a little serious political and social criticism under the banter if he wished. One of the episodes, called the *agon* or contest, usually presented two characters in an extended

[1] Some think this "Old Comedy" patterned upon an ancient Dionysian ritual. I use the word "loosely" in a dramatic sense.

comic debate. Each of Aristophanes' plays was built loosely around some topic of serious contemporary concern, like the "subversive" influence of Socrates' teachings or the evils of the prolonged Peloponnesian War. The whole forms a "lyrical burlesque," as Brander Matthews called it, unlike anything else in its peculiar combination of episodic structure, buffoonery and indecency, lyric beauty and satiric violence. Indeed, in the last-named particular it was possible in the ancient world only at Athens in its democratic period, and such license in free speaking has seldom been possible anywhere since. The plays are also hard to match for comic vigor. In spite of their many local allusions that mean nothing to most of us, they can still, after two thousand years, "lay them in the aisles."

Their indecency has troubled many readers, among whom are not merely the puritanical but also the more fastidious. We can say for it at least that it is open, not smirking. It suffers from no unhealthy social suppressions, such as manifest themselves in modern "burlesque" shows. Whether we enjoy it is more a matter of taste than of morals, for it does not incite to vice. Some of it requires a strong stomach, and indeed we would rather keep our modern sanitary habits than return to a state of things in which the excretory joke could again convulse a general audience. But all normal people enjoy sexual jokes when they have point, as Aristophanes' have, and all may benefit by laughing at the grotesque aspects of our physical conduct. It is salutary to perceive the ridiculousness of these things.

Aristophanes followed tradition and his audience's desires in such matters. At the same time, he was a serious moralist.

The Athenians did not confuse conventional sexual behavior with the whole of morality; and neither should we. If we do not, there is no paradox in calling him both indecent and moral. The low jokes helped the dramatist make his serious points without spoiling the fun of the occasion. The serious points—the attacks on militarists, demagogues, sophists, Euripides,—whether justified in our eyes or not, mark the author as a propagandist for what was, to him, civic righteousness.

Though Aristophanes had literary and comic genius, the loose form of his medium and the uncultivated tastes of his audience with respect to comedy prevented his writing what we now call high comedy. Indeed it was not until some three hundred years ago that it appeared.

The centuries that elapsed between Aristophanes and Molière have left us little memorable comedy. This might not be true if later Greek comedy had been preserved, though what we know of it does not indicate that we have lost anything very wonderful. Some long fragments of Menander (342–291 B.C.) have been discovered, and these, together with the adaptations made from him and his fellows by the Romans, Plautus (254 ?–184 B.C.) and Terence (190 ?–159 ? B.C.), give us probably a fair idea of what the Greeks called their "New Comedy."

This was very different from the old. It was partly influenced by Euripides, partly by the growth of urban refinements and tastes, partly by the loss of Athenian independence and dramatic freedom of speech. The chorus had almost disappeared, though not the masks; the coarser buffoonery was subdued and the personal satire eliminated. Instead, the dramatist cultivated plot interest and developed complicated intrigue. If his play were more somber it would be melodrama; if it were more buffoonish it would be farce; it contains elements of both, with occasional touches of romantic sentiment as well. (There was not much romance, since for one thing the semi-Oriental seclusion of respectable Greek women prevented the free mingling of the sexes that fosters it in our modern plays, and, for another, Greek taste was traditionally unromantic.)

The *dramatis personae* were stock characters such as the miserly and lecherous old man, the boastful soldier, the greedy parasite on the lookout for free meals, the clever and intriguing valet-slave, the bawd or slave dealer, the ardent and spendthrift youth, and the girl. The last is of course the object of the youth's desires. In a typical plot she is a slave whom the youth wants to buy. His valet, perhaps assisted by the parasite, engineers an elaborate and improbable intrigue to get the money from the old man, who is the youth's father, and who is also enamored of the girl and hence his son's rival. When, after a variety of mechanically manipulated complications, the fifth act requires that the play end, the discovery is made that the girl is actually the long-lost daughter of the old man's rich friend. Next comes the inevitable "recognition scene" between parent and child, with its "sure-fire" appeal to sentiment—a dramatic effect that Euripides had popularized, and that would still be found effective centuries later. All ends happily with the father's consent to his son's marriage.

Though Plautus and Terence were known to scholars in the Middle Ages, they had no direct influence on popular drama till after the Renaissance. Such comedy as developed in the meantime came from native sources. It was injected into the mysteries and miracle plays, as we see in the familiar scene from the Chester cycle in which Noah's wife, on being invited to enter the ark and abandon her gossips, has a fit of scolding. Somewhat later the French began playing short pieces called *farces,* from which we get the general term. These were dramatized anecdotes or *fabliaux,* usually making fun of a deceived husband. Their audiences found it richly funny if he was not only duped by the wife's lover but also beaten; an added bite was given the sauce if the lover was a priest. (This medieval attitude of amusement at cuckoldom, known as the *esprit gaulois* or broad Gallic humor, has persisted amazingly in France: Sardou actually caused a sensation as late as 1880 because he wrote a comedy, *Divorçons,* in which the husband gets the better of the lover.) These farces had some influence on Molière, and one of them, *Maistre Pierre Pathelin,* is a little masterpiece in its own right.

More important in its influence was the Italian *commedia dell'arte.* This name, "comedy of the [actors'] guild," comedy professionally performed, distinguished the actors of this tradition as professionals or "artists" from the amateurs who had produced the medieval plays. The type is also sometimes called the "comedy of masks" because all the actors except the lovers and the *soubrette* (to use the French term for the pert maidservant) wore half masks (from which our carnival masks are descended), sometimes with long noses and other grotesque features. The actors attained a high degree of proficiency in improvisation, since in advance they were supplied only with the general *scenario* or plan of action for each play, and had to make up their dialogue and business as they played. They naturally prepared themselves by learning large stocks of gags (*lazzi,* as they were called), and high-flown conventional speeches for the more serious passages. Since all the plays had the same stock characters, each actor would specialize in one of these and play it continually. The great similarity of these stock roles to those in Latin comedy suggests an actual unbroken theatrical tradition from Roman times. Among them were the braggart captain, the old man, the plotting valet, the lawyer, the soubrette, and the young lovers. The old man was called, among other names, Pantalone—whence our word "pantaloons," derived from his traditional costume. The valet was known variously by such names as Pulcinella (whence our Punch), Pierrot (his French name), or Harlequin. Columbine was one of the soubrette's names.

The plots varied from farce to melodrama and were generally of a pattern similar to that of Roman comedy, full of improbable intrigue manipulated by the valet around a central love interest, the happy ending of which is held off till the proper moment by misunderstandings and mistaken identity. But this plot was mainly a peg to hang the *lazzi* on. Our circus clowns are remote descendants of those acrobatic buffoons, and may dimly suggest the sort of things they did. They must often have been very funny. We know that they were out for laughs and not very nice about means so long as they got them. Molière's farces—*The Doctor in Spite of Himself,* for instance—combine some features of old French farce with Italian *lazzi.*

Troupes of these Italian comedians wandered throughout Europe and were popular everywhere even though their language was not understood—a fact which suggests that pantomime was the principal source of laughter in their comedy just as it is today in screen comedy. Troupes settled in Paris and played there for many years. Though outside of Italy the species gradually lost favor, and in the eighteenth century quite disappeared, the French *guignol* and English Punch-and-Judy shows have kept the tradition alive in puppetry to this day.

The *commedia dell'arte* had an immense influence upon literary drama. Molière's plays are all affected by his training as an actor in it during his years of barnstorming. The tradition descended directly and through him to Holberg, to Beaumarchais, to Goldoni, and later comedists. And before Molière it affected Lope de Vega in Spain, and in England Ben Jonson and Shakespeare.

On Shakespeare its influence is slight, as is also that of classical comedy (*A Comedy of Errors* was adapted from Plautus). His comic, like his tragic vein, was largely native and medieval; that is to say, the clowning and buffoonery are thoroughly English. These are combined with romantic elements taken from Italian literary sources and elsewhere to form his characteristic "comedies," part farce, part romance, sometimes part melodrama or tragedy. Except for *A Comedy of Errors, The Merry Wives of Windsor,* and *The Taming of the Shrew,* none can be called pure farce; and none of them is a comedy of manners in the modern sense, since he never wrote to satirize society or castigate vice. (Incidental satire there is, but the story interest is always primary.) *The Winter's Tale* is essentially a melodrama with romantic effects and bits of farce; in *Measure for Measure* the mood is more like that of *Ghosts* than of anything we should call comedy. As we have noted earlier,[2] Shakespeare's genius was preëminent in the humanizing of even the most inhumanly caricatured stock figures such as the stage Jew, and the effect of this humanization, reinforced by his lyric charm, was to make audiences identify themselves with the characters. Hence the genuinely comic effects in a Shakespearean comedy are generally confined to the scenes in which the clowns appear, and during the scenes in which the principals take the stage we are rather in the identifying mood of drame. Often our attitude toward the comic characters is a mixture of liking and laughter; it is a mood of humor rather than of pure comedy. We are fond of Falstaff, for instance, and identify ourselves with him, spiritually if not physically, while we laugh at his wit. This humor—this combination of logical incompatibles, sympathy and ridicule—is peculiarly English, for it is rare elsewhere and is recognizable in English literature from Chaucer to Dickens. Shakespeare's comedies, then, are comedies of romance and humor; their effects are not purely comic, and hence we cannot consider them high comedies in the strict sense of the term.

In saying this, of course, I am merely drawing a distinction, not pronouncing judgment. As with drinks, some like their comedies mixed, some straight; we make no invidious comparisons. But there is good reason for the student of the drama to recognize the differences.

[2] P. 93.

Shakespeare's contemporary, Ben Jonson, being a classicist and a satirist, approaches more nearly to pure comedy. But his comedies, like the scenarios of the *commedia dell'arte* that partly influenced them, are often mechanical in motivation, violent in action, and filled with local caricatures. His theory of "humors," indeed, dehumanized his characters by giving them but a single trait apiece.[3] Though this results in objectivity, the objectivity is apt to be too great. Characters that seem too real may spoil our fun by rousing our sympathy, but Jonson's go to the other extreme: they are so unreal that they leave us bored. Though a good actor may vivify a Jonsonian role in the theater even now, his task is a hard one. We no longer recognize the local allusions which amused the dramatist's contemporaries, and the caricature goes so far that it ceases to be caricature because it ceases to remind us of its sources in real people. Though Jonson's plays are often built on comic—or at least satiric—ideas, they lack the humanity and delicacy which since Molière we associate with high comedy.

It is in the major plays of the French master that we find the nearest approach in all the drama of the past to an ideal of high comedy, and we shall need to study them particu-

[3] Jonson's "comedy of humors," as it is called, must not be confused with the "comedy of humor" discussed above. The term "humor," in the Latin original, meant literally a fluid. Ancient physiology taught that there were four bodily humors—bile, black bile, phlegm, and blood; and that a person's "temperament," or mixture of these fluids, was determined by whichever preponderated: thus a person with a preponderance of blood was "sanguine"; of bile, "bilious"; of black bile, "melancholy"; of phlegm, "phlegmatic." In consequence of this theory the custom arose of referring to a person's dominant peculiarity of character as his "humor." Since marked peculiarities are likely to seem funny, the word came to be associated with comic effect. In Jonson a "humor" meant a ruling passion or eccentric trait that could be made ridiculous in the theater.

larly. We shall also pay our respects to later comedists. But having brought the story down to Molière, let us first consider the nature of comedy itself.

THE VARIETIES OF COMIC EFFECT

Though the sources of laughter are of infinite variety, it will be useful to classify the more obvious ones that are important in comedy. They can then be ranged in a scale in accordance with the degree of subtlety or cleverness needed for their appreciation. Thus, we put lowest those that tickle the simplest minds. The upper limit is reached when the quickest and most highly cultivated audience can no longer see the point *at once*. This necessity for an immediate response limits dramatic comedy somewhat as compared to comedy on the page, since the single individual who reads the printed play may be exceptionally keen and always has leisure to figure things out, whereas the stage comedy depends on the keenness of the majority and cannot wait for the slow to catch up. On the other hand, of course, laughter is greatly enhanced by being shared.

Such a scale does not imply that subtler jokes are necessarily better in a moral sense, though brutality and stupidity naturally go together; modern French farce is often clever and sophisticated, and highly corrupt, too. Neither does it imply that a point which is easy for an audience to get is necessarily easy for the author or actor to make. On the contrary, it is difficult to write effective farce, and a first-class comedian must have not only a rare talent, but long and specialized training as well. Nor, finally, does it imply that we should scorn simple effects merely because they are simple. Heaven forbid! Any source of innocent laughter is precious in a world like ours, and that person is indeed unfortunate who cannot share it.

It takes no subtlety to laugh at the shock of indecency or obscenity. Such things have a universal appeal to primitive people. When the laughter depends on shock alone, the joke, if we can call it that, is the result of a visceral rather than a mental response. Hence this sort of thing belongs in a special category at the bottom of our scale. Indeed, it is seldom found in legitimate comedy unless combined with more intellectual appeals to laughter, as in Aristophanes.

Next comes the comedy of the body in physical action: "pratt falls" and custard-pie combats and beatings and the rest of the stock-in-trade of clowns. The silent movies elaborated them as far as they could go in pantomime, which with Charlie Chaplin was pretty far—and high. Here again we must distinguish between the effect by itself and the total result when it is combined with other sources of appeal. Charlie Chaplin's artistry built on clowning, but added such things as social satire and gentle pathos to give his best pictures depth. His earlier ones, done before he began to enrich his clowning with these effects, show how primitive the clowning alone can be. Incidentally, it was often funnier.

Such physical comedy appeals to all normal people from infancy up, but most of all to children, for whom repetition has not staled it and who are untroubled, as many adults are, by sympathetic imagination.

Third come effects that arise from plot: misunderstandings, contretemps, cross purposes, mistaken identity, and so on. It takes a somewhat higher intelligence to enjoy these.

They are not primarily or merely visual, and sometimes even in the theater their intricacies are not easy to follow with all the assistance of the visible and audible actors. Read in the text, they are often hard to disentangle. But we do not rate them high on this account. Like the other two effects, they acquire value when combined with effects of more significant human interest.

A fourth type is verbal. Here are puns and gag lines such as those put repeatedly in the mouths of farce characters. Here also are Shakespearean lines of poetic felicity. The position of this kind of effect therefore varies up or down the scale. In farce it can be pretty low, but people with literary (as distinguished from dramatic) taste often rate it highest of all—this being the reason, no doubt, that Congreve and Oscar Wilde maintain among English comedists the leading places accorded them by literary historians. A more recent example of the comedist who depends on verbal wit is Jean Giraudoux. Almost every speech in his plays involves a novel metaphor or linguistic whimsy. Without these they would be deadly dull. On the other hand, Shaw's comedies would retain their comic paradoxes even if they lost their brilliant dialogue.

Strictly speaking, the verbal appeal in some of these plays is undramatic, but the pleasing is the pleasing, whatever we call it. However, the ideal comedy would combine clever speech with clever plot; and in the theater wit is best when it does just this. The French distinguish three kinds: *mots d'esprit* or witticisms, like Wilde's, which may stand by themselves; *mots de caractère* or remarks that are pointed or funny through revelation of character; and *mots de situa-*

tion or those that point up the drama or comedy in the situation. In serious vein Nora's reply to Helmer is all three at once: when he says that no man sacrifices his honor to a person he loves, she retorts, "That is what millions of women have done." Molière's wit is generally of the second and third kinds; he seldom indulges in what people nowadays call "wisecracks" or in elaborated epigrams, but makes the point from the dramatic situation and character. It does not seem that a character could be better hit off in two lines than that of the viscount whom Célimène describes as "for three-quarters of an hour together spitting into a well to make rings." More dramatic is her dry comment on Alceste's jealous wooing:

> Et du parfait amour mettre l'honneur suprême
> A bien injurier les personnes qu'on aime.

It is impossible to translate this, but what it means is, set the crown on a perfect love by "bawling out" one's beloved. Note that it gains its point from the situation and the characters involved. Again, there is Orgon's besotted praise of Tartuffe's pious scrupulosity:

> Un rien presque suffit pour le scandaliser,
> Jusque-là qu'il se vint l'autre jour accuser
> D'avoir pris une puce en faisant sa prière,
> Et de l'avoir tuée avec trop de colère.

"A mere nothing is enough to shock him—so much so that the other day he blamed himself for having, at his devotions, caught a flea, and for having killed it with too much temper." And there is the mock doctor's immortal answer to those who objected when he had located the heart on the right side: "*Mais nous avons changé tout cela!* (But we have changed all that!)." Here the suggestiveness of the *mot* reaches far beyond the situation itself, touching the whole tribe of doctors and savants—and is as pertinent today as it was then.

All four types of effect thus far mentioned—those of indecency, physical upsets, plotting, and wit—may be found in farce. Before going farther I should like to illustrate them briefly from *The Frogs.* In this best-known of Aristophanes' comedies the principal clown is none other than the god Dionysus himself, in whose honor the play was supposed to be given. He is treated with a peculiarly Greek lack of reverence, being represented as fat, gluttonous, and cowardly. The action begins with his desire to bring a dramatic poet back to earth from Hades, whither all the good ones have gone. (The play was composed shortly after the deaths of Sophocles and Euripides.) In order to brave the dangers of his journey to the underworld he visits Heracles, one of whose most famous exploits was a successful expedition thither, and borrows the latter's club and lion's skin for a disguise. In this ludicrously inappropriate costume he sallies forth accompanied by his slave Xanthias, who totters under enormous bundles of baggage.

The bundles are the excuse for a primitive gag. Every so often, as his master and Heracles are talking, Xanthias interjects with complaints about them: "Nobody thinks of me here with the bundles!" And once the interjection comes with such malicious inappropriateness that from crudity it ascends to high comedy. It is after Heracles has racked his brains trying to remember a single good poet still alive, and he and Dionysus have run through a tentative list of names, rejecting them one after another in a descending scale of merit.

> HERACLES. But then you've Xenocles—
> DIONYSUS. Yes! a plague on him!
> HERACLES. Pythangelus too—
> XANTHIAS. But nobody thinks of me . . .

Here and elsewhere in the play we also have verbal joking in the form of purposely inappropriate quotations from the poets and burlesques of tragic style, made particularly ludicrous in the mouth of the buffoonish Dionysus. Indeed, the agon of the comedy, in which the shades of Aeschylus and Euripides debate their respective literary merits before the god, is a penetrating if biased piece of literary criticism in the form of parody and exaggeraton.

In the second scene, which takes place before Pluto's door, the primitive fun of beatings is combined with the farce of plot complication. The porter Aeacus, at sight of the supposed Heracles, bursts forth into a roaring invective, in mock-tragic style, because Heracles, when visiting Pluto, had stolen the porter's watchdog. When Aeacus leaves, breathing dire threats to summon the police, Dionysus, in abject terror, forces his slave to put on the hero's disguise. Whereat out comes a servingmaid who, thinking Xanthias Heracles, invites him to a feast with her and the other girls. On *her* departure the amorous and gluttonous god again makes his slave change costume. We now expect a third encounter. This time, enter the two proprietresses of an eating-house where the real Heracles had run up an enormous bill for dinner without paying. One of these two females, at sight of the supposed cheat, thrusts her face at the god's and indulges in a prodigious feat of name calling. (This is a special kind of verbal comedy sure to delight a simple-minded audience.) After their exit, a third change of costume follows, with Dionysus once more appearing as a slave. A fourth entrance would now be rather flat if the same trick of reversal were merely repeated; instead, we get a reversal of expectation. Aeacus enters with the police to arrest Heracles. Xanthias, in the hero's role, glibly denies the porter's charges, but magnanimously offers to let them beat up his "slave" if they like. Aeacus thinks this very generous of him, but Dionysus naturally objects, declaring loudly that he is really the master, not the slave, and that furthermore he is not Heracles at all but none other than himself, Dionysus, Jupiter's son. The more reason, Xanthias calmly retorts, for beating him: "If he's immortal he won't mind it."

Farce beatings are always good for laughs, but what follows is a farce beating in literally godlike style. To determine which is which, Aeacus proceeds to give each one a whack, on the theory that the mere mortal will cry out with pain. When he smites Dionysus the latter yells "O dear!" but immediately adds, as though merely quoting verse, "—companions of my youthful years." To the second blow Xanthias cries, "O Jupiter!—that on the Idaean height . . ." Aeacus cannot distinguish god from slave and drags them both off to Pluto and Proserpine, who, being gods, should be able, he thinks, to recognize one of their kind.

The device of repetition with variation, capped by a reversal of expectation, is indispensable in almost all comedy, though seldom as cleverly used as here. Aristophanes makes only enough repetitions of the comic reversal to increase amusement; then the climax is turned by the delightful unexpectedness of the absurd test of godhood. Since the fun in the situation is now exhausted, it must not be prolonged, and the characters are hustled off in a hurry. (The modern stage can use a blackout.)

Two other important kinds of comic effect remain to be considered: those that arise from comic inconsistencies of character, and those that grow out of a comic idea. The former is common in farce but in an elementary form, as in Dionysus' alternations between terror and appetite. It is of a higher sort when the inconsistency is one which the character himself hides or is ignorant of and which we recognize as of a kind we encounter in life. It then depends for effect on the spectator's possession of social experience and observation. It is then an effect of high comedy. It becomes comic irony when it strikes so close to ourselves as to be painful.

An instance may be taken from Sheridan's *Rivals*. Sir Anthony Absolute commands that his son marry a girl sight-unseen and is much incensed when Jack refuses. Later the youth discovers that the girl is actually the one he is already in love with, and so is prepared to make game of his parent. When Sir Anthony again broaches the subject, Jack makes solemn pretense of being all obedience and submission. Expecting insubordination, his father encounters what seems to him spineless acquiescence. With unconscious inconsistency, he is as indignant at the latter as he was at the former.

"O Jack, her lips! . . . her neck! . . ."

"And which is to be mine, sir, the niece, or the aunt?"

"Why, you unfeeling, insensible puppy, I despise you! . . . Odds life! when I ran away with your mother, I would not have touched any thing old or ugly to gain an empire!"

"Not to please your father, sir?"

"To please my father! Zounds! not to please— Oh, my father—odd so! —yes—yes; if my father indeed had desired—that's quite another matter. Though he wa'n't the indulgent father that I am, Jack."

Another instance is Shylock's exclamation "My daughter! O my ducats!" in which love and avarice war with such grotesque poignancy. This is a supreme *mot de caractère*.

The comedy of ideas is not to be expected in ordinary farce that aims merely at laughter, but it is likely to occur incidentally in the farce of highly intelligent and satirically minded writers like Aristophanes. Thus, when Xanthias loudly objects to carrying his bundles all the way to Hades, Dionysus suggests that surely some one of the many dead men who are always traveling thither can help him out. Appropriately at this moment a funeral procession with a corpse on an open bier crosses the orchestra before them.

DIONYSUS [*to the* DEAD MAN]

Would you take any bundles to hell with ye, my good fellow?

DEAD MAN

What are they?

DIONYSUS

These.

DEAD MAN

Then I must have two drachmas.

DIONYSUS

I can't—you must take less.

DEAD MAN

Bearers, move on.

DIONYSUS

No, stop! we shall settle between us—you're so hasty.

DEAD MAN

It's no use arguing; I must have two drachmas.

DIONYSUS

Ninepence!

DEAD MAN

I'd best be alive again at that rate. (*Exit*)[4]

If I may be pardoned for explaining the joke here, I should like to point out that the comedy arises not merely from the unexpectedness of a corpse's haggling over a fee, but from the sharp reflection cast by the dramatist on the universal desire to get the best of a bargain—a desire common not only to men, but to gods and ghosts as well! Such comedy comes only from long observation of life and the ability to laugh at people as they are. So far as it results from reflection it is philosophical, and though comic it may be as profound in its implications as anything in drama.

Satire, except when it is mere ridicule of an individual, is comedy of idea because it involves the comparison between what the dramatist thinks ought to be and what he actually finds in his fellow men. Meredith considers satire too "chill-

[4] Frere's translation.

ing" for high comedy, but he probably had in mind the overly personal type. Molière's comic ideas which Meredith so greatly admires are satirical, but their treatment is so universal that we are lifted above the pettily personal. As Meredith says, the life of these plays is in the idea; its spirit is the spirit of "thoughtful laughter."[5]

To sum up this discussion we may arrange our effects graphically in a scale of increasing subtlety, as follows:

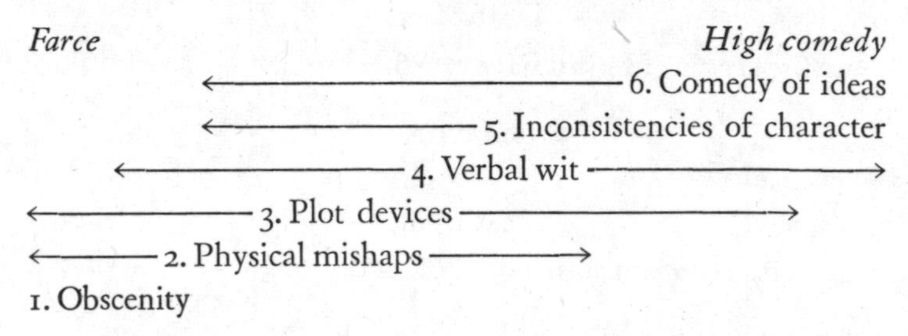

THE NATURE OF COMIC LAUGHTER

A person who attempts to discuss the nature of comedy runs the risk of appearing unintentionally absurd himself. But let us venture.

In the *Poetics* Aristotle suggested that the laughter of comedy is *derision,* and hence that it is caused by a *sense of superiority,* a feeling always grateful to the human ego. Comedy, he says, deals with persons inferior to us: its materials are vices or infirmities that are neither painful nor destructive. In similar vein Hobbes, the seventeenth-century English philosopher, wrote in an oft-quoted passage: "Sudden Glory is the passion which maketh those grimaces called Laughter; and is caused either by some sudden act

[5] *Essay on Comedy.*

of their own, that pleaseth them; or by the apprehension of some deformed thing in another, by comparison whereof they suddenly applaud themselves."[6]

Derision obviously develops into satire. Whenever a dramatist wants to ridicule his fellows he exaggerates their faults or defects so as to excite laughter. If this ridicule has no further justification than the satisfaction of malice, civilized audiences feel compunctions about yielding to it, and when it is too narrowly personal it also lacks general appeal. But if the satire seems to promote social welfare by "castigating manners through laughter," as the Latin tag has it (*castigare ridendo mores*), people feel a moral justification in laughing. Their enjoyment nonetheless rests primarily in their delight in superiority. We all have the impulse of the savage toward glory in the defeat of others even though we are trained to subdue it. When satire offers us a moral justification for gratifying it, the impulse is, as we might say, unblocked.

This point suggests the next theory of laughter, namely, that it is a result of an *emotional release*. Different writers have expressed the idea variously. Kant said that "laughter is an affection arising from a strained expectation being suddenly reduced to nothing."[7] As a general description of what happens when we enjoy a joke or comic episode this seems accurate so far as it goes, except for the word "nothing"; our expectation is often suddenly disappointed in the way anticipated, only to be highly gratified in another way—and then the joke is the more fully relished.

[6] *Leviathan* (1651), Pt. I, chap. vi.
[7] *Critique of Aesthetic Judgement* (Oxford, 1911), p. 199.

Freud emphasized the release of inhibitions, particularly erotic ones.[8] Certainly such release plays a part in laughter at off-color jokes. References to certain intimate matters are taboo in public. People like to think about them, but are embarrassed when they are too plainly spoken of. When an actor breaks the taboo in a fashion such that the spectators can both avoid embarrassment by laughing and also enjoy sexual stimulation, the latter reinforces the former. The obscene joke "simultaneously stimulates in us sexual behavior and modesty,"[9] and thus affords an emotional contrast of high potency. This type of laughter, however, is of limited value in legitimate comedy. If the effect of such jokes is merely obscene it disgusts many, and when they are most funny they involve, as we have seen, other sources of pleasure besides taboo breaking. The best involve a commentary on human nature that demands worldly wisdom if they are to be appreciated. Let me hazard a mild example:

Have you heard of the absent-minded professor whom the police discovered at two o'clock in the morning standing in his pajamas among the syringas in the garden? When asked for an explanation he said that he and his wife had gone to bed but were waked by a car stopping in front of the house. His wife suddenly started up in bed crying, "There comes my husband!" So the professor jumped out of the window.

Modern theorists such as Greig, following a biological approach, trace laughter to the *play instinct*. Max Eastman, in objecting to Kant's view as one-sided, says that laughter

[8] *Wit and Its Relation to the Unconscious* (New York, 1917).

[9] J. Y. T. Greig, *The Psychology of Laughter and Comedy* (New York, 1923), p. 93.

has a positive as well as a negative aspect, and that the positive is an unexpected satisfaction.[10] In a more recent work he urges that the comic is the unpleasant taken playfully.[11]

Henri Bergson, the French philosopher, found comedy in the *mechanization of the living*—the substitution of the artificial for the natural. "We laugh always when a person gives us the impression of a thing."[12] Bergson's instances are drawn largely from Molière and help to illuminate his technique.

Since mechanization where we expect life involves a striking contrast, this theory seems to be really a limited application of the last and most widely accepted theory of the comic, the theory of *contrast* or *incongruity*. According to Schopenhauer, laughter arises from "an incongruity between the real object and its idea."[13] Indeed, a contrast can be found involved in almost every situation that arouses laughter and may be applied to all the theories mentioned except perhaps Freud's (in its simple form) without any denial of the partial truth contained in each of them. I shall therefore try to sum up and reconcile them so far as they apply to stage comedy, making a few additions of my own.

Comedy depends on the existence of a playful mood, and is possible only when the person who laughs is detached, at least momentarily, from the object of his mirth. It arises from the sudden perception of a contrast which if he were in a sober mood he might find painful, but which, as he is in this playful mood, he does not. The contrast is usually

[10] *The Sense of Humor* (New York, 1921), chap. xi.
[11] *Enjoyment of Laughter* (New York, 1936).
[12] *Le Rire* (Paris, 1900), chap. v.
[13] Quoted by James Sully in *An Essay on Laughter* (London, 1902), chap. i.

prepared for by the creation of mistaken expectation—the "build-up." It must be suddenly and strikingly shown, and immediately perceived. The greater the tension of expectation and the more violent the contrast, the stronger the laughter, provided that the playful, detached mood is maintained. The laughter is not dependent on other emotions, but may be reinforced by them, as when the disappointment of expectation yields an unexpected gratification such as a feeling of superiority, or relief from unpleasantness.

A playful mood involves at least momentary indifference to all serious aspects of the subject. "Comedy addresses itself to a mood of aesthetic contemplation which, though it has room for keen penetration, and even for a dim discernment of a serious import in the background of the puppet show, remains on the whole a playful attitude."[14] The actors are, for the moment at least, puppet-like; we are detached from them. Our adult minds are flexible in such matters and can shift quickly from jocularity to sober earnest, and back again; but in itself a joke is not sympathetic. "The laughable is that which excites laughter *at a distance*," as Greig puts it. To use Bergson's admirable phrase, we experience "a momentary anaesthesia of the heart."

Whether or not the object should always have a painful aspect, as Mr. Eastman seems to think, pain at least stimulates us to avoid it and to fall the more readily into a mood of escape. It also affords a strong contrast to the feeling of laughter. Thus the mourner at a funeral, unless overcome by grief, or the less devout churchgoer at a tiresome service, is apt to welcome any trivial diversion from what has be-

[14] Sully, *An Essay on Laughter*, p. 375.

come, for him, the painful solemnity of the occasion. His feelings are squeezed back, and need only a trigger-like touch to be shot off as laughter. Mark Twain illustrated this in his account of Tom Sawyer's beetle and the unfortunate dog in church.

Babies laugh when they are played with, as Mr. Eastman frequently points out; but in the theater we are concerned with adults, who need mental as well as physical tickling. The audience must be intelligent enough to make spontaneous comparisons, and have had enough experience of the objects compared to recognize likenesses and differences between them. A grown-up's greater sympathetic imagination, as well as his familiarity with simple jokes, makes him less easily amused than a child, but he is more than compensated by the richness and variety of amusement in subtler comedy. Great comedy, indeed, stimulates our laughter toward the most profound and delicate of human relationships.

In the theater, comedy cannot wait for the slow-minded to get the point, and would fall flat if too many in the audience were like the Englishman of American legend. There, not merely intelligence and experience but quickness in the "uptake" is essential. In the quotation from Hobbes the word "sudden" was used three times. Tension must be *suddenly* released if it is to cause a laugh.

According to Greig, the tension occurs in expectation of a situation clearly indicated by the preliminaries of the comic episode or story, and is a development of "psychophysical energy" accumulated to meet the situation. When the occasion for this energy is suddenly removed so that we are left without the expected need for it, "the laugh is a channel of escape." The sudden removal is a surprise. "Laughter never occurs except as the sequel to some interruption of behavior."[15]

Each joke or episode that is planned to build up to a big laugh follows the general pattern of a good plot: it begins with a character in a definite situation; an act of will on his part to meet the situation initiates the action; thwarting circumstances cause him to struggle, and this "complication" is developed climactically by repetition of a gag line or piece of business with variations. These repetitions with variations usually permit partial release in laughter, but gradually the tension rises to the breaking point. This is the crisis. At this point a sudden turn dissolves the whole complication unexpectedly and delightfully and—when successful—brings down the house.

This plot in miniature, however, differs from the plot of a drame in that its effectiveness depends on maintaining a certain degree of objectivity. Hence for the comic play *as a whole* an all-embracing plot is less important than it is for a drame. The more playfully we regard the characters, the less do we care what finally happens to them so long as we can laugh at them often. In farce we accept wild improbabilities, from farfetched coincidences and obvious disguises to an ending forced by a *deus ex machina.* Even a great comedy like *Tartuffe,* as we have noted, is little harmed by its use of such a "god from the machine" (in the person of Louis XIV) to untangle the complication. In other words, the comic situations which have arisen throughout

[15] *The Psychology of Laughter and Comedy,* pp. 70, 79.

the play, not its ending, are the justification of its existence. Indeed in this particular play any strictly logical ending would be an "unhappy" one.

More important for ordinary comedy than the entire plot, therefore, are the individual jokes or episodes. If we consider each of these by itself as a miniature plot and represent it by a slowly rising line to indicate climax and by a sharply falling one to indicate the release in laughter, we shall find that the graph of the effect of a comedy will suggest the blade of a saw:

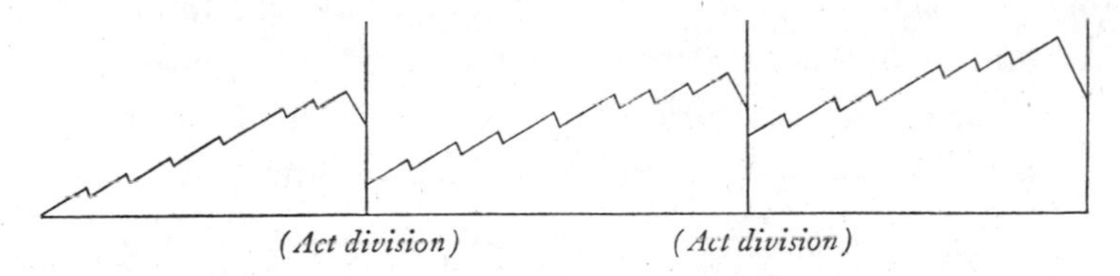

Ordinarily, as is indicated, the gradual rise of the climax of the plot as a whole will make the individual "teeth" climb upward, but they need not do so if there are enough of them, as we often see in Aristophanes or in good musical comedies. Whatever its total shape, the saw will cut if its teeth are sharp.

Since experience is needed for comedy, high comedy appeals most to the worldly-wise. Young people are more responsive than the middle-aged to romantic comedy and, in immediate emotion, to tragedy; they are ordinarily more wrapped up in their personal experiences, more easily moved to sentiment, more ready to hate or sympathize. In particular, they respond so fully to sexual appeals that the mere physical attractiveness of an actor of the other sex will make them incapable of laughing at him. Hence the young lovers in comedy have almost always been played straight. But to appreciate high comedy fully the spectator must know the world and its ways, be disillusioned without bitterness, have lost some of his adolescent romanticism. High comedy can only flourish, as Meredith said, in "a society of cultivated men and women . . . wherein ideas are current, and the perceptions quick."

Sentimentality, especially, is incompatible with a sense for high comedy. Sentimentality may be defined as a readiness for sympathetic identification so quick and uncontrolled by judgment that it acts without regard to justification. The desire to enjoy vicarious emotion is universal and gives rise to justifiable sentiment as well as sentimentality, but the sentimentalist does not discriminate so long as he gets his thrill. Thus the average movie audience will sympathize with a young girl in distress merely because the role is played by a pretty actress, even though the character she represents, objectively considered, deserves a spanking at least. A person with a cultivated taste for high comedy, on the other hand, can regard even pretty young girls objectively enough to know when they deserve sympathy and when they don't. Such persons are naturally rare.

THE HIGH COMEDY OF MOLIÈRE

Molière was fortunate in his audience, for it was worldly and unsentimental enough to fall readily into the comic mood. He was also fortunate in having a society rich in comic contrasts from which to draw his material.

The social structure of Paris in his day was like a mountain peak, with the king at the top, the court just below, and—successively on down—clergy, gentry, burghers, soldiery, servants, and mob. A democratic society is more like a plain. It may be—in many ways it is—preferable both politically and morally, but it does not offer such marked contrasts for comic treatment; it tends to iron out the eccentricities that are the very life of comic characterization. America has, for example, no familiar counterparts to the foppish marquises, the pedants, the pompous quacks, the female bluestockings whom Molière loved to ridicule.

Although women were far from dominating seventeenth-century society, they played an important part in it. Meredith made much of feminine influence in refining society, "without which," as he said, "the senses are barbarous and the Comic Spirit is driven to the gutters." Alas, this remark dates him! If he were writing today he would probably conclude that neither sex has a special aptitude for any virtue, even modesty. In Molière's time, however, ladies went in for elegance and préciosité, and their salons certainly exerted a much-needed refining influence both in manners and style. They also provided a wealth of absurd affectations for the comedist's use.

Such affectations seem absurd because they depart widely from a generally accepted norm of behavior. Unlike the Frenchmen of the seventeenth century, we today are insistent on toning down our speech and polite behavior, and if any large numbers of us should affect the elaborate and artificial manners of Molière's fops and *précieuses,* we would be even readier to ridicule it. But in other matters we possess no widely accepted norm, as Molière's audience did. Social and moral standards are now in such a state of conflict, or even anarchy, that a representative audience will include a number of opposed points of view, so that what will seem absurd to some may offend others, or perhaps rouse their admiration. This makes it difficult for us to write comedy on themes of any fundamental seriousness. In order to share a joke about manners an audience must share a point of view.

On the whole the seventeenth-century Parisians had this common standard. For serious morality they accepted Christianity; for affairs of the heart, the tradition of gallantry; for the conduct of the nobility, the aristocratic tradition of honor; for the cultivated worldling, the classic tradition of moderation and good sense. These codes, or habit patterns, were not entirely consistent with one another, but each in its sphere commanded general consent. Molière had his positive beliefs such as his preference for natural to artificial conduct, and sometimes his *raisonneurs* preach too much; but generally, as is proper for a comedist, he concerned himself with making immoderacy ridiculous. And he could count on having his audience with him. Using the golden mean of social conduct as a norm, he ridiculed extravagance.

Thus he frequently presented triads of characters composed of two who represent opposite excesses and one between them who speaks for moderation. In *The Misanthrope,* for instance, Philinte is the sensible person in whose view Alceste's bumptious plain-speaking is absurd in one direction and Oronte's obsequiousness absurd in the other. Similarly Eliante stands between Célimène's flirtatiousness and Arsinoé's prudery.[16] In *Tartuffe*, Cléante is the reasonable man who attempts to moderate between the hypocrisy of the villain and the pigheaded gullibility of his dupe.

The sensible man of Molière is the exact opposite of the romantic hero developed in the drama of the next century. To Rousseau, the prophet of romanticism, Philinte, who conformed to social usage, was therefore, a despicable hypocrite; and Alceste, who rebelled at white lies, was therefore noble. In Molière's view, on the contrary, to conform in small things was to gain greater freedom in essentials. A code of polite manners simplifies living by lubricating the natural friction of social contacts. I venture to suggest that we Americans would get on more smoothly together if we were generally less ruggedly "democratic" in avoiding polite formulas.

As a practical man of the theater Molière never wrote without regard to the amusement of the ordinary spectator. His great comedies developed naturally from his early farces and always retained some farcical elements. In this there is an exact parallel with Shakespeare's development of his tragedies from melodrama. Both provided amusement for ordinary people as well as for the élite. And in both this is a merit, not a defect, for the drama lives by appealing to what is most universal in human nature.

Yet even ardent classicists reproach Molière for his farce. "If Molière's plays often rise above the realm of mere comedy," writes one, "they have also the tendency to sink below the level of comedy into that of farce. This is their greatest fault." According to this critic, such farce is in-

[16] Michaut, *Les Luttes de Molière*, p. 231.

artistic "because comedy depends for its effect upon illusion, while farce does not. Everything must be sufficiently probable, sufficiently natural to seem real. The law of comedy is realism. In farce, on the contrary, the spectator is under no illusion. . . . The law of farce is, so to speak, an inverted idealism. The methods of comedy and of farce are therefore diametrically opposed, and the slightest touch of farce in comedy is jarring, because it is invariably an interruption to the continuity of the illusion. This fundamental distinction Molière violates continually. At one moment his characters are profoundly human and conform to the standard of reality and nature; in the next instant, they become merely theatrical, are exaggerated into caricatures, and cease to be real in order to be comic."[17]

It will be observed that in this passage Professor Giese takes for granted that "the law of comedy is realism." But Molière's masterpieces are generally acknowledged to be the greatest of comedies, and if we deduce our "law of comedy" from his practice rather than assuming it *a priori,* we must conclude that *the law of all comedy is idealization.* Professor Giese tells us that farce idealizes, and undoubtedly he would accept Aristotle's authority for the idealization of tragic characters: such characters are representative of humanity; superior to the average and therefore admirable; fallible in some particular and therefore like ourselves. But any character is an idealization when it approaches the ideal of its class or type without losing its essential likeness to humanity; and the great characters of comedy are idealizations of qualities suitable to the effects of comedy. A tragic

[17] W. F. Giese, Introduction to *Le Misanthrope* and *L'Avare* (Chicago, 1901).

figure represents the idealization of ennobling traits: it may be more brave, strong-willed, or magnanimous than ordinary persons. A comic figure is made so by the idealization of faults or deformities which, as Aristotle says, are "not painful or destructive": it may be grotesquely cowardly, niggardly, vain, pompous, or cocksure. Comic idealization involves simplification, distortion, exaggeration, such as we see in caricature. It is not realism in any ordinary sense of the term. Its simplifications, and so forth, are less extreme than those of farce; that is all.

To the degree that we are conscious of the idealization, we become detached. I have argued, contrary to Professor Giese, that this detachment is not only desirable in comic plays but actually necessary for laughter. If my view is sound, it follows that farcical effects are useful in high comedy because they aid in maintaining this objectivity. The central action of *Tartuffe,* for example, would be painfully serious if it were so handled as to create an illusion of reality; even as it is, it tends—for spectators with more sentiment than humor—to break down continually into a melodrama, complete with villain, persecuted victims, and regal *deus ex machina.* To prevent such a calamity Molière introduces farce at critical moments. Thus Dorine, the outspoken soubrette, constantly pops in to interrupt emotional scenes with her impudent home truths. An example is the scene in which Mariane pleads with her father not to force her into the hateful marriage with Tartuffe. The prospect is ugly indeed if taken seriously; the young girl is helpless against Orgon's seventeenth-century parental authority, and the villain is repulsive. Sentimental souls in the audience are ready to wipe a sympathetic eye. Orgon decrees, "He *shall* be your husband; I'm resolved upon it!" He is about to add that Mariane's wishes don't matter a straw to him when he is interrupted by Dorine's entrance and breaks off to demand angrily what she is doing there. At once they launch into a farcical word duel. The sentimental souls must put away their handkerchiefs. Mariane will get her Valère in due time, but meanwhile this is not an occasion for tears: this is a comedy.

This is the lesson in dramatic theory that Molière's practice teaches us: *farce and high comedy are allies, both fostering the detached spirit of amused observation, both arch enemies of sentiment and identifying sympathy.* I am happy to have found confirmation of this conclusion in the opinion of one of the greatest comedists now living, Somerset Maugham. He writes: "The great writers of comedy, Shakespeare, Molière, and Bernard Shaw, have never jibbed at the farcical. It is the lifeblood that makes the body of comedy viable."[18]

But the *obviousness* of Molière's technique offends some modern critics and spectators: it strikes them as too mechanical. We may take as an example the carefully engineered lovers' quarrel between Valère and Mariane. The young man is much agitated on hearing of Orgon's plan to marry his beloved to Tartuffe, and rushes to ask her what she is going to do about it. Presumably he is genuinely in love with her; but since this is a comedy, the dramatist chooses to emphasize a less serious motive—his vanity. This leads him to hope that she will flatter him with tears and protes-

[18] *The Summing Up* (New York, 1938), p. 145.

tations of love. But she also has her vanity and wants him to gratify her by pleading his own cause with suitable ardor. To give him the cue for this performance she answers his questions at first noncommittally. He misses the cue because she disappoints his expectations and piques his vanity. Hence he sarcastically commends the proposed marriage. She in turn is piqued and retorts that since he wishes it perhaps she should marry Tartuffe. In a pet at this he rushes for the door, but love conflicts with vanity in him and he pauses on a pretext, hoping that she will give in first and call him back. She on her part hopes that he will give in first. Five times he threatens to go out, and five times comes back. At length the situation is resolved by the interposition of Dorine.

Such a scene as this may not be funny to read, particularly when not visualized in action; but it was written to be acted, and the very obviousness of the comic business makes certain that the audience will get the point and laugh at the incongruity between vanity and love. A less mechanical treatment would run the danger of that identification which is always so easy to arouse when an audience is watching a pair of personable young lovers.

The famous scene of the first act, praised by Meredith for its comic genius, illustrates the same obviousness. Orgon, after a journey, returns home and asks Dorine for news of the family. Madame, she replies, has suffered from fever and headache. But he is obsessed with his new friend and does not listen. "And Tartuffe?" he asks with fatuous solicitude. "Tartuffe!" she snorts, "*He* is getting on famously, fat and greasy!" "The poor man!" exclaims the besotted dupe. Four times this formula is repeated, Orgon using the same words each time in question and exclamation. This is not realism, but caricature, and it carries its point across the footlights unmistakably and unforgettably in thirty lines.

Even in a scene so far removed from mere farce as the encounter of Célimène and Arsinoé in *The Misanthrope* we have a similar mechanism of repetition. The older lady is jealous of the younger and wants to hurt her but masks her desire under an elaborate pretense of friendship. She makes a long and flowery speech which sums up to the effect that Célimène is a vulgar flirt, and ends it with four lines of excessively genteel peroration:

> Madame, je vous crois l'âme trop raisonnable
> Pour ne pas prendre bien cet avis profitable,
> Et pour l'attribuer qu'aux mouvements secrets
> D'un zèle qui m'attache à tous vos intérêts.

"Madame, I think you too reasonable a soul not to take this profitable advice in the right spirit, and to attribute it otherwise than to the secret workings of a zeal that attaches me to all your interests." The forced grandiloquence of the language obviously stresses the absurdity of the contrast between her pretenses and her feelings. She has now had her say, and we of the audience are eager to hear a good comeback.

"I am very much obliged to you," replies Célimène, making a deep curtsy; and she proceeds to mock her visitor's style in an equally long and elaborate reply which sums up to the statement that Arsinoé is a jealous prude. She ends this speech with exactly the same four lines. Spectators are always tickled by an effective rejoinder in such a situation, and here the formal neatness of the *quid pro quo* adds to our delight. Mentally we give her a cheer. Of course, nobody could do it so well in life, but how we wish we could!

The comedy of cattiness is often used today, as in Clare Boothe's *The Women*. But modern women no longer cultivate an elegance so ludicrously at variance with their sometimes unregenerate desire to spit and scratch, and if they feel like cats, they often simply act like them. Hence the comedy in the modern play can hardly be so rich and must certainly forego the charm of Molière's elegant precision. Let me hasten to say that in ordinary relations we surely prefer the candor and absence of affectation in the modern woman! I am considering these qualities solely as a loss for comedy.

In this technique of Molière's there is none of the art that conceals art; on the contrary, the method is intended to draw attention to itself. A modern spectator, reared on realism and desirous of illusion, may, like Professor Giese, be disappointed because he is expecting the wrong kind of effect. To object to such artifice because it is obvious is to overlook the fact that it was intended to be obvious, not to mention the fun which the obviousness accentuates. The fun might still be there without the mechanical technique, but many in the audience might miss the point. Those who are not dull and who feel their intelligence slighted may indeed object, but Molière, the experienced dramatist, was writing for the whole audience. Moreover, such devices, like his farcical episodes, help to maintain objectivity. Finally, though obvious on the printed page, they are brilliantly adapted to the actor on the stage.

But Professor Giese objects to the kind of characterization this method leads to. "It is because his personages are mere types," we read, "that Molière so frequently seeks his comic effects by means not wholly natural. . . . He has been forced to endow his characters with a certain artificiality, making them theatrically and not humanly comic." This observation is entirely sound—except for its censure! Of course the characters are theatrical; they are superbly theatrical. They are idealizations. They are also firmly founded upon human truth. As Meredith remarks, Molière "did not paint in raw realism. He seized his characters firmly for the central purpose of the play, stamped them in the idea, and by slightly raising and softening the object of study . . . generalized upon it so as to make it permanently human."

Perhaps such obvious artifices are unsuited to contemporary comedy; at least they are seldom employed in it, and as a consequence it often loses its comic verve through too much identification. I suggest that this is a weakness even in so splendid a comedy as *The Circle*. Elizabeth and her lover are just a little too charming, the older couple just a little too pathetic. The comedy is there, but so also is serious drama. No doubt many readers will prefer such a mixed effect; certainly we are trained to expect it in our modern art. Nonetheless, it is the less comic the more seriously we take the characters.

At least, Molière's method shows us that obviousness of technique in comedy, unlike other forms of art, is actually a merit so long as it prevents undue identification on the one hand and does not destroy the underlying human interest on the other. The comedist must depart from sober realism; how far shall he go? That is one of many questions in art easy to ask and difficult to answer. They involve a host of considerations: among others, stage tradition, the changing tastes of audiences, the customs of society. At most periods in the history of comedy, exaggeration and stylization could go very far, as we have seen: the play of laughter flourished with grotesque masks, improbabilities of plot, and gross exaggerations of character. Today we are in a tradition that goes to the opposite extreme—and I think we miss a lot of fun.

Molière's practice teaches us something more: a great comedy should be built on a comic idea. This term, "comic idea," is Meredith's, and we should consider Meredith's meaning of it here. "The life of the comedy," he says of *The Misanthrope,* "is in the idea"; and he illustrates this statement by putting the idea in the form of a question regarding the relations of Célimène with Alceste. "Can she abandon the life they [her admirers] make agreeable to her, for a man who will not be guided by the common sense of his class, and who insists on plunging into one extreme . . . to avoid another?"

If I understand this passage, a comic idea is not necessarily a thesis like the idea of a modern propaganda play, not something that can be stated necessarily in a propositional form such as, "Excesses of candor and of dissimulation are social faults deserving of satire." We might deduce such a proposition as this from *The Misanthrope,* but the play itself is entirely in the concrete terms of contrasting character. Alceste is too outspoken, and becomes ridiculous not from being honest but from being both excessively vain of his honesty and inconsistent and unreasonable in his efforts to maintain it. As for Célimène, Meredith writes as though she were the central character, not Alceste, and as though she were without comic fault; but I think Meredith was overly fascinated by witty young ladies. She also deserves satire for her habit of exercising her wit at the expense of her friends, behind their backs. (Consider the long scene in the last act, where this fault of hers is systematically shown up.) But neither character is an abstraction; both are living, though delicately exaggerated, personalities. Thus the basis of *a comic idea is* best thought of as *a comic contrast or clash of character on which the entire plot is built.*

The comic idea will also have its abstract significance, which often tempts the analytically minded student to make more of it than it deserves. A good rule for him is to consider it only as important as it is to an intelligent audience in the theater. Some great comedies, such as Shakespeare's, have no abstract themes, and to look for meanings in them is wasted effort. Granted these qualifications, however, a high comedy, in the strict sense, needs a "core of meaning" as well as character and plot. Though Molière's characters are paramount, their general significance is also important for the thoughtful. In some comedies, like *The Circle,* it is emphasized by the title and needs to be understood by the whole audience. *Jacobowsky and the Colonel* is built on the comic clash of the two main characters; it also symbolizes in them a significant moral conflict. Unfortunately its tone wavers between comedy and drame.

A high comedy thus becomes a criticism of life. And if we generalize on the nature of its social criticism from Molière's example we may suggest that it is written from a philosophy of moderation, kindly but clearsighted disillusionment, detestation of sham; a philosophy that defends human nature, avoids extremes both of sentimentality and cynicism, and rejoices in honesty and good sense.

COMEDY SINCE MOLIÈRE

Molière's spirit was in the classical tradition: it stood for good sense and ridiculed departures from the golden mean. But in the next century a change took place: people grew tired of reasonableness, decorum, and ridicule, and wanted instead warm emotion, imaginative freedom, enthusiasm, and sentiment. In short, to use the familiar term, they grew romantic.

This change in taste was gradual throughout the eighteenth century and did not culminate until the early years of the nineteenth. The overturn in comedy which resulted was but a small part of the general overturning that manifested itself politically as the French Revolution and artistically as the Romantic Movement. These changes were so highly complex that no generalization about even so small a part of them as the evolution of comedy is free from exceptions and qualifications. However, since our interest in this study is analytical rather than historical, we may attempt a simplification of matters here for the sake of brevity and clearness.

Underlying all serious changes in society are changes in men's ethical assumptions and creeds. We can best understand the change in comedy by considering these. Both Christianity and the classical tradition had agreed in considering human nature as bad. The classicist, to be sure, was less severe than the theologian. The latter's view was expressed symbolically in the words of the New England primer:

In Adam's fall
We sinnèd all.

Men are born in sin and foreordained to damnation except when saved by the grace of God: this belief underlies Racine's tragedies. The classicist's view is expressed by Philinte: "Allow some grace to human nature," he tells Alceste. "Let us not examine it with great rigor, but view its faults with a little amiability." But such "grace," unlike Rousseau's, is strictly limited, for Molière does view the faults, and indeed exposes many.

Such an attitude is extremely unflattering to our self-esteem, and whenever men have a strong wish not to believe something they can always find reasons for not believing it. Hence the eighteenth-century revolutionists rationalized a view of human nature that was flattering, and exactly opposite in effect. "Is human nature good, then?" asks Diderot, and answers enthusiastically, "Yes, my friend, very good. Water, air, earth, fire—everything is good in nature; and the whirlwind that rises up toward the end of autumn ... and the volcano ..."[19]

Nature is good; man uncorrupted by artificial society is a part of nature; ergo, man is naturally good. On this basis Rousseau, the chief apostle of nature, made his attack on

[19] *De la Poésie dramatique à M. Grimm;* translation from Clark, *European Theories of the Drama,* p. 289.

Molière. To him Alceste was the man of natural goodness uncorrupted by society, and Philinte, that kindly gentleman, one of those detestable persons "who, so sweet, so moderate, find that everything is always all right because it is to their interest that nothing should be better; . . . who, around a well-furnished table, maintain that it is untrue that the common people are starving; who, with their own pockets well lined, consider it very bad form to declaim in favor of the poor; who, from their well-protected houses, would without complaint watch the whole human race plundered, pillaged, murdered, massacred—it being understood that God has endowed them with a very meritorious sweetness in supporting the ills of others."[20]

This is indeed taking comedy *au grand sérieux!* We can hardly miss in this passage the spirit which thirty years later eventuated in the tribunal and the guillotine; and Philinte was no doubt to Rousseau not so much the object as the excuse for a general attack on the old regime he hated. At all events, when people are generally infected with such sentiments and start applying them to comedy—demanding "social significance" of a revolutionary kind from a drama that is simply amused by men as they happen to be—the comic spirit cannot long survive.

The drama that took its place was still frequently called comedy, but with qualifying adjectives: "sentimental comedy" or *comédie larmoyante* (tearful comedy). It was also given the neutral label *drame.* Though comic scenes were still to be found in these plays, the chief characters were intended to win an audience's admiration and identify-

[20] *Lettre à d'Alembert;* my translation.

ing sympathy. Professor Nettleton puts Steele's *Conscious Lovers* (1722) as the first of the type to appear in England, and tells us that "the distresses of the sentimental Indiana drew tears from General Churchill."[21] As late as 1768 Hugh Kelly's *False Delicacy* "won a theatrical triumph," he writes, because of its genteel sentiments, while *She Stoops to Conquer* was thought indelicate. Goldsmith, indeed, poked fun at the fashion:

> THIRD FELLOW. O damn anything that's *low*. I cannot bear it.
>
> FOURTH FELLOW. The genteel thing is the genteel thing any time, if so be that a gentleman bes in a concatenation accordingly.

Even Sheridan was constrained to include in his *Rivals* the "sentimental" underplot of Faulkland and Julia.

In France, where the forces toward social change were stronger, the new style developed more consistently and fully from mildly sentimental comedies of intrigue by Nivelle de la Chaussée to Diderot's *Fils naturel* (written 1757) and *Père de famille* (written 1758), which may well claim the dubious distinction of being the most sentimental plays ever written. Even Voltaire, who could not bear to be out of any popular fashion no matter how unsuited to his satiric temperament, wrote an adaptation from Richardson's *Pamela* called *Nanine* in which the heroine's trials were calculated to touch the heartstrings.

The histories of drama usually suggest that the vogue for these misnamed comedies soon died out, but what really happened was that they gradually turned into melodrama.

[21] G. H. Nettleton, *English Drama of the Restoration and Eighteenth Century (1642–1780)*, (New York, 1914), p. 163.

As such they flourished down through the nineteenth century and at least as late as 1914. This evolution of sentimental comedy into melodrama, viewed psychologically, is quite natural. At first, when it was a novelty for virtuous protagonists to be displayed for admiration and sympathy, these unwonted and desired sentiments alone sufficed to make the plays popular. But mere sentiment is not enough to sustain interest for long, and audiences soon began to want stronger fare. This was supplied by making the tribulations of the hero and heroine—particularly the heroine—more severe, for which purpose a villain was obviously necessary. Necessarily also, this villain had to be outside the pale, so to speak, in the philosophy of natural goodness. Human nature was good, to be sure, but he was not really human. Indeed, the blacker he was painted the more shining became the virtues of the protagonists by contrast. He was further useful in that toward him spectators might indulge their unregenerate pleasure in hating without losing self-esteem. His machinations made plot building easier and afforded thrills. In the eighteenth century he was usually an aristocrat and thus suggested social significance to the play in which he appeared. As time went on, the anemic comic elements diminished in these plays, the mood darkened, and the villain's machinations became paramount. Finally, though sentimentality remained lush and comic relief was usually provided, the primary dramatic appeal became the thrills of the intrigue.

Down to the days of *Nellie the Beautiful Cloak Model* this melodramatic pattern persisted with amazing popularity. But the First World War seems to have put an end to the tradition except in the movies. Owen Davis, author of *Nellie,* tells us about it himself in his amusing account of his long experience as a playwright. In 1905, he says, a play of his was refused production on the ground that the heroine, having "made a slip" in her youth, would shock an audience. Twenty years later an actress to whom he offered it turned it down again for the contrary reason that the situation didn't seem "worth making such a fuss about."[22] The old sentiments no longer move us, and melodrama must seek other, usually more violent and cruel, patterns.

The nineteenth century was the heyday of sentimentality, and hence the dark age of comedy. Farce there was, to be sure, but England at least, from Sheridan to Oscar Wilde, produced not a single comedy of lasting vigor. Even in France, where the influence of Molière continued strong through the life of his plays in the repertory of the Comédie Française and in the schools, sentimentality makes the greatest comedist of the age, Augier, at times a bit too mid-Victorian (if we may misapply that term) for our taste. The heroine of his masterpiece, *The Son-in-Law of M. Poirier,* seems to us too noble to be true, and elsewhere even his heroes partake of the pious nineteenth-century taste for superhuman virtue.

Now that we have emerged from that "age of innocence," we look back at times with nostalgia for its illusions and still unshaken faiths, but in our appreciation of comedy, at least, we are the gainers by our disillusionment since we have become sufficiently hard-headed and unsentimental to appreciate the spirit of Molière and his kin. On a low plane,

[22] *I'd Like to Do It Again* (New York, 1931), p. 133.

our change of taste is indicated by the success of so-called sophisticated comedies compounded of sex and snobbishness. On a high plane, Bernard Shaw has won audiences to approach social problems intelligently and in a comic spirit. Shaw himself has had a good deal to do with hastening this change, but even he must have failed in the attempt if he had been born a generation earlier.

A rather common criticism of Shaw has been that he is not really a dramatist because his characters "talk Shaw" too much and act themselves too little. The criticism is usually exaggerated, but we may grant it some truth. Here, as on other aesthetic issues, I think we should conform our theory to facts. All his comedies are worth hearing and some of them are masterpieces. We may conclude from them that even to make characters debate their author's social theories will not prevent a play from becoming a comic masterpiece when these characters talk with the wit and pertinence of Shaw's; and I can really see no good reason why we should not enjoy such debate in the theater as well as elsewhere. It may not forward the plot, but plot has less importance in comedy than in drame. Especially in Shaw's comedies the plot in the usual sense, or what one critic calls the "material action,"[23] is subordinated to the "intellectual action," or "logical development of an idea." The discussions of the characters are designed not so much to change their material relationships as to illustrate the central theme. Hence Shaw is often careless of the former and indulges freely in carelessly managed entrances and exits, coincidences, and

[23] Augustin Hamon, *The Twentieth Century Molière: Bernard Shaw* (New York, 1916), pp. 133 ff.

even fantastic occurrences, whenever these freedoms permit him to reinforce his point. Since such freedoms are usually funny, we gladly allow them, even as we do in farce. What has troubled many of his critics is, I think, the incongruous combination in him of preacher and clown. Plays that preach alone are familiar enough, and so are plays of mere buffoonery; but Shaw's plays are unique in bringing together both qualities, and both in superlative degree.

If, therefore, his discussions become at times undramatic in the narrow sense, they do nevertheless involve direct conflict of ideas, which in itself has strong dramatic interest for some of us at least and promotes a detachment that is suitable to high comedy. But it must be amusing (sometimes even Shaw fails to make it so); and it is best when it also forms part of the central action. Hence I should not object to Shaw's critics if, instead of saying that he is not a dramatist when he does such things, they should say rather that he is less successful in comedy when he fails to develop his abstract paradoxes through comic plot. His best comedies are full of comic incident and character contrast; they also have the rare virtue of making us think as well as laugh.

Under present conditions, if wars and revolutions spare us, we might hope for even greater comedies than Molière's or Shaw's, so far as they depend on an audience's readiness to appreciate them, were it not that more than detachment and wit are needed. Molière and his audience shared definite ethical assumptions, but a modern comedist cannot depend on common acceptance of any ethical principle whatsoever. Not merely our received opinions, but our deeper faiths also, have been stripped from us so that we live in a state of moral nudity. If most of us continue to act within the law, we do so rather from expediency than conviction. The writers of comedy themselves have been partly responsible for this state of things. Shaw, for example, has usually employed a destructive formula. Taking some conventional sentiment such as that children should honor their parents, or that martial valor is admirable, he has built his plays to make this sentiment ridiculous. (Shaw has had positive doctrines also—among others, his Fabian socialism, his faith in the "life force," his praise of the superman,—but these are much more effectively urged by his prefaces than by his plays.) Destructive criticism was needed when Ibsen set Shaw the example by turning it against the stuffy traditions of his time, but it has a pretty chilly effect now when our chief need is a rag or two of faith to keep off the winds of despair.

High comedy depends on a stable and cultivated audience, used to intellectual freedom and heir to a long stage tradition. Now that the generation of Maugham and Shaw is passing, and the richly humane civilizations of France and England have undergone such destruction as will take at least a generation to recover from, we alone still possess unharmed the conditions to keep it alive. Unfortunately, our metropolitan society is urban rather than urbane; it is permeated with furious partisans and libertines on principle, as well as the merely frivolous; it is ridden by commercialism; and it is without strong traditions or convictions. Yet it is free, intelligent, lively, and disillusioned, and it has, as a matter of fact, responded favorably to at least one writer of high comedy—S. N. Behrman.

In play after play Mr. Behrman has adhered steadfastly to the comedy of ideas, on behalf of a civilized creed of tolerance, intelligent self-control, and objectivity. In this creed he has gone directly counter to some of the strongest elements in our society. To the radical revolutionist such an attitude seems that of a reactionary enjoying the fruits of unjust privilege; to the earnest religionist it seems superficial; to the "practical" American it seems passive and effete; to the "liberal" heir to the romantic tradition of expansiveness, intolerably restrictive; to the touchily democratic, snobbish. Without agreeing to such extreme views, no doubt Mr. Behrman himself would admit its limitations as a guide to the solution of life's fundamental problems. But it is a creed proper to a writer of high comedy, and—I hazard the fine old word—to a gentleman. How rare are those today who are genuinely tolerant, controlled, intelligent, and objective—how rare, and of how great value!

His difficulties in maintaining his creed against such prevailing attitudes in a time of crisis are not only wittily but wisely presented in *No Time for Comedy,* a play with a title that is a comment on our age and with a hero who evidently expresses the author's apology and defense. A typical reaction to it was that of a newspaper columnist who said it was "undramatic" and "trivial."

In calling it undramatic this critic meant that it lacks action. People who make this frequent charge overlook the fact that speech is action—the principal form of action—when it forwards the plot, and that in Mr. Behrman's plays it pretty consistently develops the central and dramatic clash of character, and, through character, the conflicting ethical points of view which constitute the meaning of his comic ideas. He has action; the trouble is really that it is not made comic enough. He has wit, but he develops character too realistically, without the amount of comic emphasis and exaggeration which a comic treatment demands. We identify ourselves with the characters so much that we cannot fully appreciate them as objects of comic contrast. Thus his comedy is constantly verging on drame without the force and intensity necessary to sustain it as drame. Here is a situation where Molière's example might well have been of better use than that of English drawing-room comedy.

The themes of high comedy are certainly not trivial. But to some it may seem that an era which has seen the horrors of Nazi prison camps and American atomic bombs is indeed no time for comedy. Viewed thus, no era is a time for comedy: not the era of the vicious Peloponnesian War when Aristophanes wrote; not the era of Elizabeth or of Louis XIV. But viewed more deeply, high comedy is needed particularly in time of peril. It helps men to maintain their serenity, treasure their civilization, and smile in the face of danger; for its basis is a moral one.

In this, high comedy and high tragedy are alike.

CHAPTER VII

Melodrama and Tragedy

THE THREE ERAS OF GREAT TRAGEDY

JUST AS THE terms "farce" and "high comedy" are useful to indicate plays of low and high comic appeal, so are "melodrama" and "tragedy" in treating drame.

The ordinary condition of drame is melodrama, just as the ordinary condition of comedy is farce. Audiences most easily appreciate them; mediocre playwrights and actors write and play them. The natural conditions of the theater thus tend to their mediocre level, and it requires the positive effort of an artist, or exceptional circumstances, to lift a play above it. Indeed, if we judge by history, tragedy and high comedy are possible only when genius is born in a peculiarly favorable environment. In comedy this combination has occurred but once, possibly twice. In tragedy it has occurred only three times: in ancient Athens during the fifth century before Christ, in Elizabethan England, and in the Paris of Louis XIV; and for these three eras there are only six dramatists who are ranked as supreme, Aeschylus, Sophocles, Euripides, Shakespeare, Corneille, and Racine. Even of these six some would question two or three, and of the works of those unquestioned, critics rank but a few as supreme tragedies. Any list of these masterpieces would excite debate if it should go beyond a dozen or so. The list that follows is therefore only tentatively a classic canon of tragedy.

Aeschylus: (1–3) The Oresteian trilogy–*Agamemnon, The Libation Bearers, The Eumenides;* (4) *Prometheus Bound.*

Sophocles: (5) *Antigone,* (6) *Electra,* (7) *Oedipus the King.*

Euripides: (8) *Medea,* (9) *Hippolytus,* (10) *The Trojan Women,* (11) *The Bacchae.*

In judging the works of the Greek tragedists we are limited to the extant plays, and since from Euripides there survive eighteen or nineteen to seven each from the others, the number listed is perhaps disproportionate to the merit of his work as a whole in comparison with theirs. I do not include dramas like *Alcestis* or *Iphigenia among the Taurians,* because their tone and happy endings place them among tragicomedies or romantic comedies. Viewed for sensationalism, *Medea* and *The Bacchae* might be classed with the poet's most melodramatic works along with *Electra* and *Orestes.* In strange imaginative power they are among supreme works of genius. I have called *The Trojan Women* a "pathodrama"; it is without plot, concerned wholly with hopeless suffering. Yet a recent presentation before us who have seen two wars far more terrible than the Trojan, proved profoundly moving and tragically beautiful.

Shakespeare: (12) *Romeo and Juliet,* (13) *Julius Caesar,* (14) *Hamlet,* (15) *Othello,* (16) *Lear,* (17) *Macbeth.*

Corneille: (18) *The Cid,* (19) *Horace* or *Polyeucte.*

Some critics, not Frenchmen, would omit both Corneille and Racine. In particular, *The Cid* is technically a tragicomedy, but its elevated treatment, vast importance to French dramatic history, and enduring popularity in France perhaps justify its inclusion. Certainly if we include its author at all it must go in.

Racine: (20) *Andromache,* (21) *Phèdre,* (22) *Athalie.*

I list no tragedies since Racine. Not Goethe's; see my previous discussion (in chap. ii, pp. 67–69). Nor Schiller's, for, nobly idealistic poet that he was, I cannot find in him dramatic qualities of the first rank. He was overly fond of rhetoric, sentimentality, melodrama, and preaching. His characters tend to become the puppets needed to illustrate his abstract ideas, rather than living men and women. His favorite theme of romantic young idealism destroyed by the wickedness of aged tyranny was too personal to him; he could not treat it with mature objectivity and hence raise it to the universal level of great tragedy. In short, I am repelled by his *Sturm und Drang* romanticism. Perhaps I do him injustice. It needs a German critic, at least, to appreciate his merits fully.

Since Schiller, Ibsen of course ranks first, and if we were to include any of his plays the first would be *Ghosts,* followed by either *Hedda Gabler* or *Rosmersholm* or *The Master Builder.* My reasons for omitting him will be offered in the following chapters. The rank of contemporaries cannot yet be determined, and there is little likelihood that any of them will prove to belong in this class.

Some twenty-odd supreme tragedies in two and a half

millenniums! Vary the list here and there as critics might, it could hardly be much longer; it could easily be shorter.

Why is great tragedy so rare? We may be able to answer this question in part if we inquire briefly into the historic facts that concern its composition.

Greek tragedy arose in religious exercises, and at its height retained a religious tone. Its connection with the worship of Dionysus is important for us only because religion gave it an atmosphere of elevated seriousness.

How it arose is a matter of speculation and controversy among scholars. Professor Gilbert Murray believes it to have begun as a sort of passion play representing the death and resurrection of a god of fertility who like the plant is reborn in the seed and like the year is reborn in the spring. Other scholars find his theory unsubstantiated.[1] Sir William Ridgeway argued that it arose as a result of ancestor worship and was at first a ritual commemoration at the tomb of a hero, during which his exploits, particularly that one which brought about his death, were enacted.[2] This theory has the advantage that it accounts for the calamitous ending of what is now considered to be typical tragedy. But as a matter of fact the Greeks did not apply the term tragedy solely to plays that ended in calamity, but to all serious plays acted in the tragic contests, some of which were what we would now call tragicomedies or even melodramas. The modern meaning of the word seems to have arisen after Aristotle had argued that only those plays were truly tragic

[1] See A. W. Pickard-Cambridge, *Dithyramb, Tragedy and Comedy* (Oxford, 1927), pp. 185–208.

[2] *The Origin of Tragedy with Special Reference to the Greek Tragedians* (Cambridge, Eng., 1910).

which aroused the emotions of pity and fear. In any case, Sir William's theory has not met with much scholarly approval.[3]

The whole matter of origins is obscure, and in this connection unimportant. About all that seems generally agreed upon is that tragedy developed from the activities of a chorus of men, apparently masked, who sang and danced in honor of the god. Possibly the word tragedy (τραγῳδία from τραγῳδός, goat-singer) was given to this performance because the chorus contested for a goat as a prize. (Other explanations are that the chorus were costumed as goats; that a goat was sacrificed as part of the ritual.)[4] Possibly the songs which the chorus sang in the earliest stage were narrative and elegiac, and it was only by slow degrees that dramatic presentation developed in the frame of the choral odes. The leader of the chorus was perhaps at first the narrator. Then his function may have been transferred to an "answerer" (ὑποκριτής). When Aeschylus added a second speaker the two could become actors in our sense of the word, because then it was possible to build up dramatic conflict between them. Aeschylus' early plays show clearly that he only gradually became aware of the dramatic possibilities of his innovation. And after Sophocles added a third actor[5] it was possible to write complex dramatic actions and to reduce the chorus to "supers." When Aeschylus began writing, as his *Suppliants* shows, tragedy was still half lyric and the chorus

[3] See Pickard-Cambridge, pp. 174–185.

[4] See Roy C. Flickinger, *The Greek Theatre and Its Drama* (4th ed.; Chicago, 1936), pp. 13–14.

[5] The so-called "rule of three actors" seems to mean that not more than three *characters* should speak in any one episode. The older view was that only three actors were allowed to each poet for the acting of his tragedies, and that these three actors had to double to play all the roles. See Kelley Rees, *The So-Called Rule of Three Actors in the Classical Greek Drama* (Chicago, 1908).

important. Before Euripides ended his career the chorus had become, in some plays, dramatically superfluous. It was traditional, however, and was not eliminated until much later.

Tragedy was elaborately conventional. From their entrance following the prologue until the end of the play it required the presence of the chorus, who, like the actors, wore masks and special costumes. It required the alternation of odes and episodes. The odes were sung and chanted with instrumental accompaniment and mimetic dancing. The episodes were acted. Murders might not be enacted visibly, but might be heard and frequently were narrated in great detail. (The reason, most likely, is that violence was taboo in the precincts of the god where the plays were performed.[6] Probably squeamishness had little to do with it; the Greeks were ruthless enough on occasion. Again, it was probably not that visible murders would seem unconvincing to the audience, for the audience accepted extremely unrealistic effects without demur. It was permissible to enact suicide; the hero of *Ajax* falls on his sword.) The action proper was ordinarily limited to the events of a single day. Dialectal forms from the Doric were used in the language of the odes. All parts of the play were in verse. The meters of the odes might vary, but they had to be arranged in strophes and antistrophes. The verse of the dialogue is occasionally in trochaic tetrameter, ordinarily in iambic trimeter, which so far as number of syllables is concerned resembles the Alexandrine or six-accent line of modern verse. The Athenian audience seems to have had a keen ear for verse effects. Although we cannot now be sure what all of these were, in

[6] See Flickinger, p. 129.

the more elaborate meters of the odes, we know that they were highly developed. The refinements of Greek artistic workmanship which we can see visibly in their sculpture and architecture were surely exercised no less upon their poetry; and they had the advantage of a language unrivaled in its combination of sonority, flexibility, and expressiveness.

The themes of the tragedies were normally of an elevated character and the treatment gravely dignified, but there was no such rigid insistence upon decorum as was demanded in French neoclassic practice; on the contrary, there are occasional touches of gruesome horror, grotesque fancy, or comedy, and Euripides in particular edged tragedy more and more toward realism. The conventions of the form resulted in broad, stately, idealized effects; there was no realism in the modern sense even in Euripides. We miss particularly the detailed characterization which we enjoy so much in Shakespeare. In this respect the taste of the Greeks was the opposite of ours. They came at the beginnings of culture when classification was new and general types therefore interesting and impressive. We, on the contrary, have had so much of abstractions and classifications in our general education, and are so bored by commonplace stock characters in our theater, that in our poetry we thirst for the specific and unhackneyed. Though Greek poetry could be beautifully concrete, as we see in the exquisite fragments of Sappho,[7] in drama the taste was for broad, simple

[7] Thus: Ἕσπερε, πάντα φέρων, ὄσα φαίνολις ἐσκέδας' αὔως,
φέρεις ὄιν, φέρεις αἶγα, φέρεις τ' ἄπυ μάτερι παῖδα.

"Evening, bringing all things that bright Dawn scattered, you bring the sheep, you bring the goat, you bring back to its mother the child." (The translation loses all the beauty of sound, of course.) This seems to me matchless in its suggestion of profound human emotion by means of the simplest concrete details.

characterization that would represent human nature in its nobler and more universal aspects. And Clytemnestra, Oedipus, Orestes are none the less human to us because they lack specific individualizing traits. They are individualized along the broad lines of dominant motivation, and the lines are just. The tendency toward realism that Euripides started did not go very far in his plays.

The appeals to the spectators were various. Under the bright sun there were the visual appeals—elaborate colored costumes, stately processions and intricate dance evolutions, and, beginning with Sophocles, some sort of scenery, probably suggestive or symbolic rather than representational. Appealing to the ear were the accompanying music and the effects of the intricate and varied verse rhythms. There was the lyric appeal of the odes. Above all, and binding the whole together in organic unity, was the dramatic interest. No really popular form of stage presentation since then has rivaled the Greek in this synthesis of arts.

Especially notable was its unforced propriety in dealing with the brutal and horrible. The Greeks even at the height of their culture constituted a small and unsafe island of civilization in a sea of barbarism. Their legends abound in barbaric incident. Yet these crudities were humanized and rationalized by the poets, so that the plays generally move us by pity and admiration rather than by melodramatic thrills. Even Euripides is restrained in such matters when compared with his imitator Seneca or with most of the Elizabethans.

Yet already we see in him a relaxation. The extraordinary equilibrium of forces which Sophocles best exemplifies, and which constitutes Greek classicism—its combination of moderation with power, of formal unity and symmetry with pleasing variety, of lofty general themes with the concrete vividness of personality, its "fit details strictly combined in view of a large general result, nobly conceived,"—this was like the moment of quiet at the top of a wave. But it has occurred only once in the history of mankind.

The practical Romans imported the superior Greek culture wholesale and gave up their own rudimentary native art for an ardent imitation, which like most imitations resulted generally in cheapening and vulgarization, and like all imitations lacked the vital impulse of the original. The only Roman tragedies that have survived are those attributed to Seneca (4? B.C.–65 A.D.). Several utilize the same general plots as are found in the extant Greek tragedies; thus we can compare them directly. The author seized every opportunity for rhetoric and sensationalism. He delighted in gruesome narratives, ghosts, necromancy, and on-stage violence and horror. In these plays Stoic contempt for the world degenerates into brutal callousness. Yet they are much less dramatic than the Greek, for their fatalism makes of the protagonists proud but passive victims who indulge in inflated harangues instead of acting.

By Seneca's time the form of tragedy had become fixed in five acts. The chorus was an irrelevant and archaic survival, being brought on the stage or sent off as suited the needs of the dramatist, and called upon, at intermission time, for conventional songs.

Seneca's "tragedies" have small intrinsic merit except as a storehouse of sententious Latin tags and moral aphorisms, many of which got into Renaissance plays by translation. They would warrant little attention from the student of drama had they not been immensely influential in the Renaissance. To the poets of the sixteenth and seventeenth centuries Latin was a much more familiar language than Greek, and Seneca's taste more congenial. His Stoic scorn of fortune was not hard to tune to the surviving medieval tradition of contempt for the world; his Stoic pride, to the new impulse toward extravagant individualism. His showy rhetoric was much more impressive than was Greek poetry to the sixteenth-century devotees of linguistic stunts, whose taste had not passed beyond the stage of obviousness. His brutality was more exciting than the Greeks' humane restraint.

Senecan influence was stronger on the Continent than in England, where the medieval tradition was less affected by the Renaissance, and dramaturgy until after the accession of Charles II in 1660 was dominantly medieval. In England the Renaissance spirit was chiefly seen in a glorification of the individual hero. In Elizabethan plays he is represented as a natural man with supernatural energy and will who followed the promptings of his lusts regardless of consequences. The lusts for knowledge and for power are particularly prominent in Shakespeare's forerunner Marlowe; and Shakespeare's own heroes, though more representative of man's nature and more complex than Tamberlaine and Doctor Faustus, are far removed from the commonplace protagonists of typical modern plays. Each is a superior man with a ruling passion or special weakness which in the peculiar circumstances of the play leads him to his doom—pride in Coriolanus, impetuosity in Lear, ambition in Macbeth, guilelessness in Othello, introspection, perhaps, in Hamlet. (I put the last tentatively, not wishing to be involved in the perennial "Hamlet question.") Each is heroic in the magnitude of this quality which is at once his strength, or part of his strength, and his weakness in these special conditions. Each is a distinct personality, and is known to a familiar student even by such small characteristics as habitual turns of phrase or mannerisms—as Hamlet's trick of repetition: "Very like—very like"; "Words, words, words."

Shakespeare lacks the pious spirit underlying Greek tragedy. He was a worldling, in love with the variety of life, profoundly moved by its mysteries but unconcerned to solve them. He is unlike the Greeks in being the poet of the individual, not the type. He was not, like them, controlled by a traditional form with strict limitations and requirements, but freely indulged in whim, extravagance, Gothic mixtures of effect, and loose plots and complications. He sought the detail, where the Greek was content with the general quality. His range of thought and imagination is far wider, but his point of view is less sure and serene (if we except Euripides). The contrast between Greek tragedy and Shakespearean is one of civilizations as well as individual genius.

At times critics have summed up this contrast by the terms classical and romantic. Like all names for complexes of values, these are useful when understood, but extremely vague; and in this connection they are likely to suggest more or less than the truth. Vastly different as the two types of tragedy are in many respects, their underlying likeness is more important. Shakespeare was romantic on the surface, but his underlying view of life was sane, moderate, and profound. Though his characters are sometimes passionate or unhinged, he himself is never so. He saw them in the round and in their proper relations to the world. His sanity is not the small-visioned sanity of a mediocre mind, but the wide-horizoned sanity of the most universal genius the world has known. Like the romantics, he touched the extremes of experience, but unlike them, as Irving Babbitt used to say, he filled all the space between.

We have already noted how hard it is for English-speaking students, reared on Shakespeare, to appreciate the French classical tragedies, which were so much more influenced by Seneca and the Greeks. The consequence is unfortunate, for Pierre Corneille (1606–1684) and Jean Racine (1639–1699) are more neglected than any other dramatists of anything like similar importance. Of course it is impossible to translate them adequately, and hard even to suggest their literary merits; yet it is much to be regretted that few have tried to do so. Popular-priced editions of their plays are unavailable. The plays themselves are almost never performed in our theater. And even professional students of the drama tend to regard Corneille and Racine as men who live by reputation rather than by merit.[8] Hence a few more observations may be justified if they help at least to suggest what it is that Frenchmen admire in them.

French classical tragedy is written in Alexandrine verse

[8] "What the French call the elegance, the restraint, the grand perspective of Racine's poetic line is . . . still mainly bombast and pomposity. Nor does the subject matter of his plays—the brutal loves and hates, poisonings and revenges—take on a nobler aspect when they are seen as realistic portrayals . . . rather than as the exaggerations of an overstimulated artistic mind." From a review (*Theatre Arts* magazine, August, 1940, pp. 613–614) of A. F. B. Clark's *Jean Racine*.

of twelve syllables, and since French lacks the strong stress that marks the feet in English verse these lines require rime to indicate their ending. The rime scheme is uniformly an alternation of couplets with "masculine" and "feminine" endings. (The latter differ from the former in being supplied by words ending in mute *e*.) This verse seems artificial to us and its effect at first monotonous and nerveless. But we are really not in a position to judge it. To native listeners it is full of vigor and subtle beauty—and they ought to know. Its difficulties are certainly an artistic challenge to the poet, and to overcome them successfully is to give trained listeners an added pleasure.

Italian theorists bequeathed to the French a set of interpretations of Aristotle, Horace, and ancient tragedy which we know as the "Rules." Tragedy was to have five acts; a single, simple, highly unified plot; an action confined to a single day and place; characters of high station and dignity. It must maintain at all times fit decorum—which meant not only a general grandeur and dignity and the avoidance of comedy, but even the avoidance of such things as the actual representation of physical violence or plebeian objects. (Great offense was caused by the slap that one character in *The Cid* gives another. As late as 1792 a French adaptation of Othello substituted a headband and dagger for the handkerchief and pillow.)

In spite of a few players of superior taste such as Molière, Baron, and Adrienne Lecouvreur, the conventional manner of acting these plays required a strutting, statuesque posture and a chanting or bellowing delivery. Down to the middle of the eighteenth century, spectators sat on either side of the stage itself, crowding against the actors and rendering scenery almost valueless, with the consequence that the physical conditions of performance reinforced the tendency toward declamation and narration. The Comédie Française, the national theater that grew from Molière's troupe, had a monopoly of tragedy in the capital and imposed its authority not only throughout France but all over continental Europe. As late as 1830 the romantic rebels in France were trying to break down this tradition at its source in the interests of a greater freedom and realism such as the secondary theaters in Paris, as well as the English stage, enjoyed.

It is no wonder that we find the limitations of neoclassic tragedy stifling and artificial. But these are the defects of its qualities, and we should concern ourselves chiefly with the latter. This tragedy is clear, coherent, well-constructed. Its style has an admirable purity and eloquence, sometimes exquisite charm and noble power—qualities which even foreigners can often appreciate if they study it. Like the plots of the Greeks and of Shakespeare, its plots are often about barbarous and violent deeds and passions: in using such material it keeps good company. The only pertinent objection to such subject matter would be that it is badly used. We certainly cannot say that it abused it by showing too much; on the contrary, it could not show very much on its stage and sought carefully to avoid anything that would merely shock. (The same cannot be said for Shakespeare.) If as a consequence it failed to arouse the interest of the average spectator that Shakespeare's melodrama excites (and even his greatest tragedies have much melodrama in them), it had in compensation one very great merit: it turned instead to psychological struggle and clash of will, which became the more dramatically impressive because the forced simplicity of the represented action permitted concentration on them. (Some of Corneille's minor plays are as melodramatic as he could make them within the Rules, but I am considering the major ones.) At its best this tragedy is not only dignified; it is noble. Its concentration gave it the power of a single effect, and because of the difficulties of the form the success of the dramatist when he overcame them is the more delightful. "It is drama itself, stripped to the bones," writes A. F. B. Clark in his study of Racine;[9] "it is the conflict of wills and passions, so intense and rapid that it has neither time nor attention for description, mediation, lyricism, or even physical action unless these features spring naturally from its own being."

This seeming simplicity of Racine is deceptive. "He enlarges on a set of obvious sentiments and well-known topics with considerable elegance of language and copiousness of declamation, but there is scarcely one stroke of original genius, nor anything like imagination, in his writings."[10] So wrote Hazlitt, the romantic admirer of Shakespeare; and many lesser Anglo-Saxon critics would like to be as rashly condemnatory. But surely it is a triumph of controlled imagination to express the highest tragic emotion by what seem the simplest and least theatrical means and in conformity with the most rigid of dramaturgic rules. As a matter of fact, our modern conception of the imagination is still dominated by romantic theory, which tended to find it only in

[9] *Jean Racine* (Cambridge, Mass., 1939), p. 29.
[10] *The Plain Speaker,* 1826.

what is strange, wonderful, fantastic, and unreal. This view is unjustified either artistically or psychologically. Imagination is our combining and constructing power. It is not hard to exercise it in a dream world where the poet makes his own rules; and the results of such "fanciful invention"—as Dr. Johnson called it—are so striking to the uncritical that in popular usage such things only are considered imaginative. Yet the mechanical inventor shows great imagination in adapting real forces and materials so as to make them actually work for his ends; the scientist shows it in constructing a theory that fits the facts: fancy here is bounded by the nature of things as they are. The poet shows it in the highest degree when he works out real problems of human psychology within a rigid formal framework without loss of emotional force or stylistic beauty—as Racine does. Imagination is at its height, in fact, when it triumphs over such difficulties. The poet himself spoke out on this point. "There are some," he wrote in his preface to *Bérénice,* "who think that this simplicity is a mark of lack of invention. They forget that on the contrary all invention consists in making something of nothing, and that all this multitude of incidents has always been the refuge of poets who felt their genius lacking in enough abundance and force to hold their audience through five acts by a simple action sustained by the violence of the passions, the beauty of the sentiments, and the elegance of the expression."

The sentiments of these plays are foreign to our ways, and hence of limited effectiveness for us; yet we ought to give them their due. Corneille's love of *gloire* or heroic honor makes his characters seem now inhumanly insistent on what we would term a mere code of conduct, as when Horace slays his own sister for failing in patriotism. We may grant that this Roman hero is monstrous, and many of Corneille's contemporaries thought so too; yet it is possible that we tend too far in the direction of unprincipled behavior and spineless acquiescence. At least to the French, such characters are simply exaggerations of a noble ideal and give Corneille at his best a supreme elevation. And Racine's combination of stylistic elegance with austere classical form should not conceal from us the subtlety of his psychological analysis and the tragic power of the passions that he exhibits. Of all the great dramatists he is probably the least readily appreciated by the novice, and the most appreciated by the connoisseur.

The three eras we have now surveyed were so complex and so different from one another that any suggestions to account for the development of tragedy from like conditions in them must be merely tentative. However, in each era the drama was produced in a capital city, the center of an expanding and prospering state which was filled with men who faced life with optimism and engaged in it with energy. When Athens lost its independence, its tragedy became mere convention. When the adventurous Elizabethans were succeeded by the Puritans, all plays were banned; and with Charles II drama returned to the theater sophisticated and mannered. After Louis XIV, the "Sun King," came the aristocratic decline. Each great era was an age of expansion, and with the subsequent age of concentration satire flourished but tragic literature grew sterile. After Shakespeare, Dryden; after Racine, Voltaire.

In each era, also, though the ancient pieties of the race were losing hold on advanced thinkers, they still strongly influenced the moral views of the dramatists and dominated their audiences. The eras were not weakened by skepticism. "In the periods when great tragedy has been written, two things seem to have been necessary: first, a conventional pattern of belief and behavior, and second, an acute consciousness of how that conventional pattern can be violated."[11] In other words, religion was neither so dominating or formalized as to stifle inquiry nor so enfeebled as to be incapable of controlling general agreement about right and wrong. Audiences therefore could respond strongly to ethical appeals based on this agreement, and at the same time be moved by dramatic situations that challenged too simple interpretations of it.

In each era the artist was born to a vital dramatic tradition and found available for his use a vital theater. In each, literary concerns had not yet so overridden the theatrical as to make the dramatist more concerned for readers than spectators. In each, a vigorous popular taste not only for dramatic action but also for fine acting, fine verse, heroic style, and grand effects, had not yet been deadened by repetition or perverted by satire.

In short, the ages of great tragedy were brief points in the development of unified and vigorous national cultures, midway between primitive naïveté and sophisticated disillusionment.

If the conditions described are needed for the production

[11] Theodore Spencer, *Shakespeare and the Nature of Man* (New York, 1942), p. 50.

of great tragedy, it is unlikely to appear again in the predictable future. Not all the conditions, perhaps, are necessary; it would certainly be unwise to conclude sweepingly that, for instance, since tragedy depends on religion, and since the future belongs to science, therefore tragedy is dead. Such syllogisms are too simple. I shall postpone discussing this point. At least we may agree that in order to write a great tragedy it is not enough for a dramatist to have the will and the gift. He needs also the audience and the atmosphere. As Arnold would put it, the power of the man must be fostered by the power of the moment.

Tragedy, like high comedy, is a rare bloom; and the ordinary garden variety of theatrical product is farce and melodrama. We have urged the value of the former in contributing to high comedy, and in like manner melodrama is the foundation on which great tragedy is built. It is therefore advisable to study it more fully. It also needs study because, unlike farce, it is not always easily distinguishable from the superior sort of drama. We need to recognize it for itself and to realize the qualities that make the exceptional play rise above it.

THE DRAMA OF THRILLS

The term melodrama is a combination of the Greek words for song and drama, and is therefore literally a synonym for opera. It was at first used in this sense in Italy and France, and still is in Germany, where it designates operas that combine declamation with instrumental accompaniment. Its present meaning in French and English derives from theatrical history in Paris at the close of the eighteenth century.

During the old regime the Comédie Française and the Italian comedians held the monopoly of legitimate drama, and to perform plays other producers were forced to evasions. Since they were permitted to show acrobatics, song, dance, and pantomime, two ingenious managers developed comedies and drames out of these ingredients. One of these men, a certain Audinot, a former actor and playwright, began with puppet shows, progressed to child actors, and then, for adult performers, evolved under the curious name of *pantomime dialoguée* (dialogued pantomime) what were, in effect if not legally, plays. Performed for vulgar audiences, they were either farcical or crudely sensational.

In 1791 a decree of the revolutionary government gave liberty to all the theaters, but authors, actors, and audiences were so fully habituated to the use of music, dance, and pantomime that these continued to be used extensively even after normal dialogue had been introduced. The new liberty made the absurd term *pantomime dialoguée* unnecessary, and the word *mélodrame,* already familiar in its operatic sense, was appropriated to label these still operatic shows. But since their most notable feature was not music but sensationalism, sensationalism was what people soon learned to associate with the word—as they have ever since. When the first typical Parisian *mélodrame* was adapted for the London stage in 1802,[12] the word was imported with it.

In this general sense, melodrama is the most universal type of drama—the equilibrium, as we noted earlier, at which drame tends to settle. But many tragedies have had

[12] *A Tale of Mystery,* adapted by Thomas Holcroft from *Coelina,* by Pixerécourt, the leading French melodramatist. It was played at Covent Garden.

sensational elements. Aeschylus frightened the superstitious Athenians by introducing a chorus of Furies with snakes in their hair. Euripides skated frequently over melodramatic abysses, and Seneca plunged into them. Since Shakespeare's audience retained the medieval taste for realistic tortures and gory deaths, he often satisfied it, along with giving other thrills, and hence his tragedies can be enjoyed solely as melodrama. Corneille was at times as melodramatic as he dared: in a play like *Rodogune* he dared much. Racine, like Sophocles, based his plays on sensational stories; and if neither showed many horrors on the stage, both carefully told about them through messengers' speeches. After Racine, his successors Crébillon and Voltaire, in spite of their confinement to the Rules, managed, the one crudely, the other with refinements, to be surprisingly sensational both in narration and in presentation.

Uncritical spectators, who throughout theatrical history have been the mainstay of melodrama, want simply to lose themselves in the story and to enjoy a vicarious satisfaction of their desires. But their desires are various and often conflicting; and as the playwright cannot gratify all, he selects those that are most easily and suitably gratified.

Most obvious and important of these is the lust for thrills. The playwright's art here lies in a melodramatic golden mean between no response and painful response. Because the spectator identifies himself with the hero he is agitated when the hero is in danger, but because he knows the danger to be imaginary he can bear a generous amount of violence and gore. Individuals vary in their sensibility to such things, and fashions in horror, as in other matters, change from generation to generation. When ghosts were generally believed in, ghosts were effective on the stage. We laugh now at the melodramas of Boucicault because of their improbabilities, high-flown style, and sentimentality. Our grandchildren will probably laugh at our thrillers. (We do, ourselves. *Arsenic and Old Lace* makes howlingly funny such effects as are to the same audiences melodramatically thrilling in plays like *Ladies in Retirement,* mentioned earlier.)

When the thrill is the thing, physical action usually dominates over character. It is this fact that most definers of melodrama have emphasized. Brander Matthews observed that "we are accustomed to consider tragedy and comedy nobler than melodrama and farce, because in the former the characters themselves seem to create the situations of the plot and to dominate its structure; whereas in the latter it is obvious rather that the situations have evoked the characters."[13] According to William Archer, "Melodrama is illogical and sometimes irrational tragedy. It subordinates character to situation, consistency to impressiveness. It aims at startling, not at convincing, and is little concerned with causes so long as it attains effects."[14] And, says George P. Baker, "throughout the ages, the great public, cultivated as well as uncultivated, have cared for action first, then, as aids to a better understanding of the action of the story, for characterization and dialogue. Now, for more than a century, the play of mere action has been so popular that it has been recognized as a special form, namely, melodrama."[15]

[13] *The Development of the Drama* (New York, 1906), p. 75.
[14] *About the Theatre* (London, 1886).
[15] *Dramatic Technique* (Boston, 1919), p. 20.

In the search for sensations, event is piled on event, comic relief is used for contrast to heighten subsequent horrors, and backstage thunder rolls. Since the thrill is the object, any trick is legitimate if it works.

Brander Matthews said that in high comedy or tragedy character dominates plot, and in farce and melodrama the reverse is true.[16] If he meant by his word "dominates" that one element is superior to the other in the audience's interest, no doubt he is correct in general: Tartuffe as a person is more interesting to us than the plot of the play. But if, as is more likely, Matthews intended by "dominates" some such meaning as "controls" or "determines the nature or outcome of," then I can think of a good many exceptions to his generalization. Here are four:

Tragedy: *Oedipus the King*. (In the legendary plot "fate" determines the outcome.)

High comedy: *Tartuffe*. (Plot manipulation determines the events, much as in ordinary farce.)

Melodrama: *The Dream Doctor* [by H.-R. Lenormand]. (Character becomes a Nemesis.)

Farce: *The Man Who Came to Dinner* [by Hart and Kaufman]. (Character—or caricature, if you prefer—is the source of what plot there is.)

Furthermore, we must not forget that fundamentally both character and plot are aspects of a unity which is character in action.

The real test by which to distinguish farce or melodrama from high comedy or tragedy is the kind of emotion evoked.

[16] *A Study of the Drama* (Boston, 1910), p. 121.

A melodrama evokes thrills, and if thrills are the principal effect of a play it is a melodrama. Modern psychological melodramas, developed out of Freudianism, can evoke thrills through character. Lenormand's "hero," in *The Dream Doctor,* is a psychoanalyst who goes about seducing women by fishing up their suppressed desires, and who himself suffers from a subliminal conflict which in the end destroys him. In spite of pseudo-scientific and ethical pretensions the play is obviously a thriller. *Rain* is another and more familiar example.

What we mean by "thrills" is perhaps clear enough without definition, but it may be helpful to examine them in some detail. To do so in an orderly manner we may consider them under four heads: (1) thrills of surprise, (2) thrills of superstition, (3) thrills of cruelty, and (4) thrills of identification.

Thrilling surprises have been a subordinate element in many tragedies. Aeschylus, for example, liked the spectacular,[17] as when he showed the Furies with snaky wigs, or when, in *Prometheus Bound,* he called for the nailing of the Titan to a rock and for a catastrophe in which both Titan and rock should apparently be swallowed up by an earthquake. (It would be interesting to know how he expected to produce the earthquake effect on the solid floor of the Athenian theater. Did he utilize the slope of the hill which falls away behind?) Euripides was notorious for letting down gods by the "machine." His *Phoenissae,* as one critic puts it, would make a "very good cinema."[18] Shakespeare's frequent use of spectacle and plot surprise is obvious.

[17] For my reasons for classifying spectacle under surprise, see p. 135.

[18] Kitto, *Greek Tragedy,* p. 366.

In the nineteenth century, when playwrights specialized in melodrama for its own sake, the developments of modern machinery and lighting gave them much greater means of stage surprise. Pixerécourt, for example, called upon the machinist for an eruption of Mount Vesuvius. (The stage direction reads: "The theater is entirely inundated by this sea of bitumen and lava"!)[19] Edward Fitzball anticipated O'Neill by a century when he showed a four-roomed house on the stage with all interiors visible.[20] London stages were called upon to supply conflagrations, floods of water, and real horses galloping on treadmills. Boucicault worked up his plays to his "sensation scenes."[21] Mechanical ingenuity mounted ever higher through the century, and the mind grows dizzy at the thought of the heights it might have attained had not the advent of the movies made such efforts vain.

Melodramatists have always sought surprise through plot. A typical example is in Douglas Jerrold's *Black-Ey'd Susan* (1829), when the hero is saved from punishment for having struck down his villainous captain, Crosstree, by the opportune discovery that his discharge from the navy antedates the blow. Even Aristotle praised such an effect. "In the *Cresphontes* Merope is about to slay her son, but, recognizing who he is, spares his life." In such a coup, he notes with approval, "there is . . . nothing to shock us, while the discovery produces a startling effect." We would now consider it both trite and melodramatic.

[19] *La Tête de mort ou les ruines de Pompeïa* (Gaîté Theater, 1827).

[20] In *Jonathan Bradford; or, The Murder of the Road-side Inn* (1833).

[21] See W. J. Lawrence, "Sensation Scenes," *Gentleman's Magazine*, Vol. XXXVII (1886), pp. 400–406.

The shiver of superstition is another effect now considered peculiarly melodramatic, but it was not so viewed by the Greeks or the Elizabethans. The supernatural, if it grows out of genuine religious faith and a searching "into the mystery of existence," is proper to the highest drama. "When a writer has penetrated to the very verge of human existence, he must confront the question, what lies beyond? And it is in some aspect of the supernatural that he will find whatever answer he chooses to give."[22] Such answers, however, are not the concern of melodrama, and though we may agree that Aeschylus used ghosts and furies in order to question the universe, his successors, with rare exceptions, used them simply to raise gooseflesh. The tradition of "whining ghosts" stems from the Greeks through Seneca to the Renaissance; and its latter end was often even less sensational than ridiculous, as we see in the "Gothic" pieces of "Monk" Lewis and Papa Dumas early in the nineteenth century, which peopled the stage with spooks, demons, vampires, and ghouls. They were as candid as the Fat Boy in *Pickwick* in wanting to make their audience's flesh creep, and their audience must have been singularly susceptible if they succeeded.

The spinal shiver of superstition shares with the thrill of surprise the disability that repetition dulls it; and it has the further disadvantage that the stronger the effects sought the greater is the danger that the audience will disbelieve them and even laugh at them. The management of them is a ticklish business. Shakespeare, for instance, runs a great

[22] C. E. Whitmore, *The Supernatural in Tragedy* (Cambridge, Eng., 1915), p. 356.

risk in the scene where the ghost in a sepulchral voice calls out "Swear!" to his son from various points under the stage. The dramatist partly forestalls ridicule from the audience by making Hamlet joke about it. The result is a queer mixture of dread and absurdity; it might easily have been merely absurd.

Again, the growth of scientific skepticism has made us incredulous about the older superstitions. No doubt we thrill to new ones that we do not recognize as such. We are the more ready to do so if they have a coloring of scientific authority; thus, audiences a few years ago were impressed by psychoanalytical melodramas, and will be more willing to accept one based on telepathy because of recent laboratory experiments with "extrasensory perception." On the whole, however, we are harder to scare than our ancestors were.

For borderline cases like Lenormand's plays the test should be whether the dramatist is sincerely and profoundly questioning "what lies beyond" or is merely trying to provoke the spinal shiver. If a play is of the latter kind the dramatist will naturally parade religion or Fate or insanity or Evil or some other abstraction of dreadful power that may fool or at least befuddle the intellects of the spectators so that, for the time being, skepticism will not destroy illusion. Lillo's *Fatal Curiosity* (1736), for instance, crudely mysticized Fate, as we now see clearly. It is more difficult to see so clearly into recent plays. Are Maeterlinck's early ones mere romantic mood-mongering, or are they symbolic expressions of profundities? Is Andreiev's *Black Maskers* Poe-inspired madness, or is it significant allegory? What of

Franz Werfel's *Bockgesang* (*Goat Song*), behind the fantastic symbolism of which one seems to hear mutterings about Nietzschean-Dionysian ecstasy, Freudian suppressions, the rights of the Natural Man, and the Spirit of Revolution? It is certainly melodramatic; but we wonder if it is not something more. Again, consider such plays as call upon traditional reverence for Christian symbols and themes, like *The Servant in the House* or *Days without End*. The closer we are to a play, the harder it is to decide such problems; considering the appeal of the box office to the playwright, and the rarity of profound meditation on ultimate matters among persons associated with the theater, it may perhaps be wise to hold doubtful plays guilty until proved innocent.

We might add a word in favor of honest thrillers like *Dracula* or *The Bat* that make no false appeals to reverence and faith, and a word of regret that we are become so hard to scare. Few playlovers, I imagine, but have a soft spot in their affections for the theatrical concoctions that curdled their blood in their salad days.

A third kind of thrill is that of cruelty. We have already quoted Emile Faguet's theory that our pleasure at tragedy is a barbarous one.[23] Not that we are savages; we merely have savage tastes, and enjoy the spectacle of others' sufferings only to a certain degree. The degree has varied widely at different times. The Elizabethans seem to have thoroughly relished the raw head and bloody bones sort of thing that we find in *Titus Andronicus,* whereas eighteenth-century French audiences were too sensitive to bear seeing

[23] P. 132.

Othello smother Desdemona with so vulgar an object as a pillow. At present, taste tends toward the "hard-boiled," the dramatists in this respect following in the wake of the "hard-boiled" novelists. They have to keep at some distance behind, to be sure, because the vividness of actual presentation would make the rapes and murders and perversions impossibly distressing, or positively ridiculous. Such ridiculousness is the chief effect of *Tobacco Road,* making it enormously successful—but as a rowdy farce, not a drame. Its characters never rise to a human level, and hence call forth no identifying emotion.

I cannot agree that this pleasure in cruelty accounts for the primary appeal of melodrama, any more than for that of tragedy. Thus I think that Ludwig Lewisohn presents but one side of the picture when he tells us that "war, hunting, and persecution are the constant diversions of the primitive mind. And these that mind seeks in the gross mimicry of melodrama."[24] The man-hunt after the villain, he thinks, turns an audience into a mob. Such things do happen, and I should not quarrel with Mr. Lewisohn were he not so sweeping in his conclusion; but the very force of hatred that makes the villain-chase so pleasurable is ordinarily drawn from the audience's sympathy for the victim and indicates a crude sense of justice: melodrama has its Simon Legrees, but also its Uncle Toms.

At times melodrama may appeal primarily to sadistic lust, but by and large it depends mainly on the thrills of identification arising from sympathy for hero and heroine.

[24] *The Drama and the Stage* (New York, 1922), essay "On Sentimental Comedy and Melodrama."

This takes its force from both of our basic biological instincts, that of self-preservation and that of reproduction. On the one hand it serves our egocentric desires for power and success, and on the other our sexual instincts for love and children, along with all the complex sentiments and loyalties which these entail. The male in the audience gets vicarious glory from the hero's prowess; the female, from the heroine's loveliness. For both, the perfect mate of daydreams is embodied in the stage character. It takes a more sophisticated audience to be much interested in characters as individuals; to the ordinary spectator at a melodrama the hero or heroine is rather an object of desire than a character.

Desire may easily become lust; but though melodrama has often gone far in pandering to a thirst for blood, it has seldom lent much sauce to sexual appetite. Christianity has of course opposed such excesses. Anthropology reminds us that sexual taboos are universal and presumably arise from biologic necessity. In comedy, it is true, a playwright like Aristophanes can go far; but people seldom accept a serious representation of man as rutting animal. The very Aristophanes who rocked his audiences with bawdy jokes blamed Euripides for exhibiting on the stage a woman in love.

As for popular melodrama of the last century, "Vice is vice on the Boulevard," wrote Thackeray in his *Paris Sketch-Book;* "and it is fine to hear the audience, as a tyrant king roars out cruel sentences of death, or a bereaved mother pleads for the life of her child, making their remarks on the circumstances of the scene. 'Ah, le gredin!' growls an indignant countryman. 'Quel monstre!' says a grisette, in a fury. You see very fat old men crying like babies; and, like babies, sucking sticks of barley-sugar." Even today, when the so-called burlesque show descends seemingly as low as possible in indecency, the intention of its comedians is to make their obscenity funny, and the movie melodramas that are often thrown on the screen between these stage shows are by contrast startlingly moral.

People can, however, acquire a taste for depravity in drame as well as in comedy. In the 1830's the aged king of melodrama, Pixerécourt, was fearfully shocked by the horrific romantic plays of Dumas. "Formerly one chose solely what was good, but in these modern plays," he wrote, "one finds nothing but monstrous crimes that revolt morality and modesty. Always and everywhere adultery, rape, incest, parricide, prostitution, the most shameless vices, each dirtier, more disgusting than the other."[25] Yet, two generations later, some romantics had become so sophisticated that in comparison Dumas seems innocent. These later writers delighted in perverse and barbaric passions, and their artistic justification for such subject matter was that it was depicted in language the lurid colors of which were then considered the ultimate brushwork of an aesthetical literary style. Thus were formed Wilde's *Salomé,* Hugo von Hofmannsthal's *Elektra* (scenario for Strauss's opera), and D'Annunzio's plays of lust and blood. The first is not Biblical, nor the second Greek; they both, together with the Italian poet's dramas, are literary melodramas of a sort that can appeal greatly only to aesthetes who, like Baudelaire, have trained their noses to enjoy a scent of decay.

In matters of sex the great public has been restrained by

[25] *Théâtre choisi* (Nancy, 1841–1842), Vol. IV, p. 499; translated.

its moral sense, but it has had no such check upon its weakness for sentimentality. We have called sentimentality an indulgence in soft emotions for their own sake irrespective of justification. The typical sentimentalist is satisfied with a mere show of moral sanction as a green light permitting him to go ahead. A heroine who deserves all her trials seems to him wholly sympathetic if the author provides her with a superficial good quality or two, such as an amiable manner, or shows her passionately in love. And by the same sign, a villain who may to dispassionate judgment appear more sinned against than sinning is to the sentimentalist a hissing and a reproach because he is rude, unsympathetic, or merely intelligent. It is not that the sentimentalist desires injustice or any other evil; his dilated heart is on the side of the angels. The trouble is entirely with his head.

In a larger view we may profitably regard sentimentalism as not really antagonistic to the lust for more brutal thrills, but as merely the pink section of that emotional spectrum across the whole range of which the feelings play when unchecked. Tears for Uncle Tom stimulate lust for Legree's blood, and vice versa. In this instance there is justification for both sensations, but often there is not. We hear that during the French Revolution the populace would weep freely over the imaginary woes of innocent victims in the theater, and then return refreshed to enjoy seeing real victims lose their heads under the guillotine. Such apparently contradictory emotions may be mutually stimulating, particularly when enjoyed for the sake of the thrill.

With a thoroughly sentimental audience, such as supported the melodramas of the nineteenth century, a happy ending (for hero and heroine) is a *sine qua non*. When the New English Dictionary states that the name melodrama "now denotes a dramatic piece characterized by sensational incidents and violent appeals to the emotions, but with a happy ending," the definition considers only this nineteenth-century tradition. A happy ending is not essential to a melodrama that has no sympathetic hero or heroine and that centers its exploitation of passion in cruelty and lust. At such a show the spectator cares nothing for the characters, and, once blooded, feels that the more gore the better. But it is nonetheless a melodrama.

THE TEST OF LOGIC AND THE TEST OF EMOTION

"Illogical and sometimes irrational tragedy" is what William Archer called melodrama, and Brunetière made "an interior logic" a criterion for tragedy.[26] But a melodramatist is not averse from logic; he simply disregards it if he can get a thrill more easily without it and if he is sure that the spectators won't mind. Archer put his finger on the point when he said that melodrama "subordinates . . . consistency to impressiveness." A logical melodrama is still a melodrama. It seems to me that *Rain,* for example, is as logical as most accepted tragedies, and more so than some. Contrariwise, tragedies are not always the severely logical affairs that Brunetière implies. Though Aristotle praised *Oedipus the King* as a model of tragic construction, yet he pointed

[26] "Mélodrame ou tragédie?" *Revue des Deux Mondes,* January 15, 1904. See also A. H. Thorndike, *Tragedy* (Boston, 1908), pp. 3–4; Clayton Hamilton, *The Theory of the Theatre* (New York, 1939), p. 73.

out the improbability that Jocasta should never have told Oedipus how his father met his death.[27] Shakespeare was notoriously careless of details, as in his reworking of the earlier Hamlet play, and even neglected to provide adequate motivation for important characters such as Hamlet and Iago. No doubt Brunetière had primarily in mind Racine, whose simple plots and concentrated treatment most clearly exemplify his principle.

Chance, in particular, lies outside the ordinary logic of cause and effect, and it is frequent in Shakespeare as well as in melodrama. When coincidence is fetched far to disentangle a knotty plot, we properly condemn it; but we must condemn Euripides for it as well as the ordinary melodramatist. Furthermore, a certain amount of chance is justifiable under a broader meaning of the word logic, because chance exists in life. As A. C. Bradley reminds us, the "operation of accident is a fact, and a prominent fact, of human life. To exclude it *wholly* from tragedy therefore, would be, we may say, to fail in truth. And besides, it is not merely a fact. That men may start a course of events but can neither calculate nor control it, is a *tragic* fact. Any *large* admission of chance into the tragic sequence would certainly weaken, and might destroy, the sense of the causal connection of character, deed, and catastrophe."[28] Clayton Hamilton, indeed, perhaps with his tongue in his cheek, has praised melodrama for showing "the persistency of chance in the serious concerns of life."[29] But this is straining

[27] Of this, Sarcey remarked: "All I can say to you, O pointed critic, is that if they had explained themselves earlier it would have been a shame because then there would have been no play, and the play is admirable."

[28] *Shakespearean Tragedy* (2d ed.; New York, 1932), p. 15.

[29] *The Theory of the Theatre*, p. 88.

a paradox. What we object to in a poor melodrama is not so much its use of chance as the obviousness with which it uses it to botch the plot together.

If by logic we mean accord with probability and causal sequence, we can hardly use it as a test to distinguish tragedy from melodrama. If, however, we mean by it penetration below the surface of life, or something of the sort, as is suggested by Brunetière in his adjective "interior" (*une logique intérieure*), the word merely tells us that tragedies are more profound than melodramas—a fact we knew already.

A critic of the present discussion has suggested that perhaps the real distinction between tragedy and melodrama lies in their relative truth of characterization. "The progress from melodrama toward tragedy, from farce toward comedy," she observes, "is marked by the degree of reality which the author has succeeded in giving to his characters. And melodrama and farce are inferior to tragedy and comedy mainly because in them character interest is reduced to the minimum. After all, has any representation of life which has not given us at least one memorable character been ranked permanently with great literature?"[30]

The English-speaking student in particular feels sympathy with this view because Shakespeare was the supreme creator of character. But in a play character seldom exists apart from plot and is known by action. Furthermore, I question whether "the degree of reality" of a characteriza-

[30] Clara F. McIntyre, "The Word 'Universality' as applied to Drama," *Publications of the Modern Language Association*, September, 1929, p. 928: a comment on my article, "Melodrama and Tragedy," which appeared in the same quarterly a year earlier and which I have used as a basis for parts of this chapter.

tion is any more adequate than logic as a criterion. What does one mean by the phrase? Degree of photographic likeness? If so, the characters in a naturalistic play like *The Lower Depths,* or even *Dead End,* should be superior to the broad, simple, generalized types of Aeschylus. Depth of penetration? The deeper penetration of tragedy is admitted. Moreover, I can only repeat that many modern melodramas produce thrills by their exploration of the dark mysteries of abnormal or perverted character. Is not the preacher in *Rain* well characterized?

I think that we of the present day exaggerate the importance of characterization as a separate element to be admired or decried by and for itself. It is the total action that counts in drama, and the total action may be profoundly moving and yet use the simplest and most obvious traits of character. Greek tragedy alone is sufficient evidence of this contention. What we of the Shakespearean-Dickensian tradition have been trained to relish is the individualizing physical features, mental traits, and mannerisms that so often in fiction give the reader the effect of a lifelike portrait: Falstaff is fat and witty; Polonius is a sententious statesman "declining into dotage"; Mr. Micawber is always waiting for "something to turn up," and so on. Yet these traits and mannerisms are the mere surface signs of a character, and unless we see also the motives that drive him we have but the sketchiest notion of his nature. They are often vivid and amusing, and indeed are constantly employed in farce to amuse, but in themselves they do not constitute full characterization. On the contrary, what profoundly moves us in a seriously drawn character is not those traits which differentiate him from all other men, but the desires and strivings which he shares with them. It is not that Othello is a Moor or a soldier or a man of eloquent speech that arouses our compassion, but that he suffers, and erroneously, the pangs of jealousy. Though Shakespeare individualized him vividly, the tragedy arises from the universal passion that racks him. The Greek tragedists centered their art on such universal passions, neglecting the individualizing details, with results grandly tragic.

In judging a play we should first concern ourselves with its total emotional effect upon us, and only afterward examine its elements or construction.[31] It was in terms of total effect that Aristotle defined tragedy when he said that it aroused pity and fear. But a melodrama also excites these emotions, and tragedy excites others at times of greater importance. "The word φοβος," Professor Thorndike remarks, "... hardly indicates the emotions of admiration, awe, hate, horror, terror, despair, and dismay, which belong to tragedy, and modern tragedy has appealed more largely than classical to pity and sympathy."[32] And as these emotions depend on identification, and as identification is likely to be more complete for a naïve spectator of a melodrama, such a person will experience them more fully than the cultivated witness of tragedy. I have suggested that tragedy when fully successful in the theater gives the spectator the same identifying thrills as melodrama.

But it does more, and herein lies the real difference between the two. *A tragedy also generates in the more*

[31] See, in chap. ii, "The Process of Criticism," pp. 41 ff.

[32] *Tragedy,* chap. i.

thoughtful spectator overtones of reflective emotion. A play that is merely melodrama to the unthinking may be tragedy to the thoughtful.

Herein the thoughtful spectator finds a compensation for the comparative incompleteness of his identification. Since he shares the imaginary experiences of the protagonist and at the same time preserves "aesthetic distance," he is able to reflect as well as feel. And the consequence of his reflection is often a perception of depths of meaning and value beyond the grasp of simpler minds. But this perception is not coldly intellectual; it is a result of emotion and a cause of further emotion.

Thus we may say that a tragedy arouses a second order of emotional response which is peculiar to it. The spirit of the observer, elevated by the action on the stage, seeks to harmonize its emotion with past experience and with its habitual sentiments and faiths; it faces ultimate terrors of existence and, in facing them, to some degree reconciles them to the rest of life; by this effort it lifts the particular events into the realm of the universal, and at moments feels the awe that comes from glimpsing fundamental mysteries. Tragic experience is obviously complex and involved to an extraordinary degree, and no doubt other influences work to raise or lower our state of mind: beauty of the language, excellence of the acting, and so on. However, if this analysis is correct, the central quality that distinguishes a tragedy from a melodrama is that it moves us to *the impassioned contemplation of ultimates.*

To a person thus reflecting as well as feeling, emotions become generalized. "Tears haunt the world: man's fortunes touch the heart."[33] Pity is not merely a response to the suffering of another, but pity that such things can be. Fear is not mere anxiety for the hero, but for all men. "The true tragic emotion of fear," writes Butcher, "attaches itself not to this or that particular incident, but to the general course of the action, it is for us an image of human destiny. We are thrilled with awe at the tragic issues thus unfolded, and with a sense of the inevitableness of the result. In the awe so inspired the emotions of fear and pity are blended." As a result, the spectator "forgets his own petty sufferings. He quits the narrow sphere of the individual. He identifies himself with the fate of mankind."[34] In Shakespearean tragedy, Bradley points out, is developed the sense of waste—waste of the best and most precious in humanity. "We seem to have before us a type of the mystery of the whole world, the tragic fact which extends far beyond the limits of tragedy."[35]

In recent times there has been a tendency to carry this philosophical pity well past that nice balance the maintenance of which made possible the perfection of classic tragedy. Ludwig Lewisohn, for example,[36] thinks that tragedy has only in our advanced age attained a proper measure of pity, since we have got rid of the mistaken attempt to

[33] J. Wight Duff's translation of Vergil's line, *Sunt lacrimae rerum et mentem mortalia tangunt,* in *Roman Satire: Its Outlook on Social Life* (Berkeley, 1936).

[34] S. H. Butcher, *Aristotle's Theory of Poetry and Fine Art* (London, 1895), pp. 243, 246. If this is what the much debated doctrine of "katharsis" means, I am for it; but I cannot think that it does, in spite of fine-drawn modern interpretations. I can find little that is helpful to this study in the famous notion of Arisotle's that tragedy "purges" us of pity and fear, and have therefore omitted discussion of it.

[35] *Shakespearean Tragedy,* p. 23.

[36] *The Drama and the Stage,* essay entitled "A Note on Tragedy."

explain our woes as retribution for sin. Modern thought sees men erring, he suggests, but not sinning. In the future, "guilt and punishment will be definitely banished to melodrama, where they belong. Tragedy will seek increasingly to understand our failures and our sorrows." Ethical drama being thus relegated to the masses who still cling to the notion of moral responsibility, for the enlightened classes tragedy will produce a katharsis after the manner of a Turkish bath. Behind such views lies a deterministic philosophy, derived from late nineteenth-century science, which sees man as merely the sport of "heartless, witless nature," "idle, rocking forces," or the like.

This is one extreme. The other is to consider only those plays truly tragic that show the workings of the moral law through sin and retribution. This view was prevalent during the nineteenth century, and stupid applications of it by moralistic critics no doubt account in part for the violence of Mr. Lewisohn's reaction. A recent statement of this position by an excellent critic is that of Prosser Hall Frye, who argues the superiority of Greek to Shakespearean tragedy on the ground that the former has a clearer ethical attitude.[37] The truth, I think, lies between these extremes. I shall discuss the second in the next section of this chapter in connection with "poetic justice." Meanwhile, the first demands further consideration.

To deny responsibility is to deny freedom of the will. And even if it be true that human acts are entirely automatic, audiences in a theater never judge them so, since, as was noted earlier, we are all partisans there.

[37] *Romance and Tragedy* (Boston, 1922).

So far as Mr. Lewisohn opposes flat and indiscriminate moral praise and condemnation in the handling of dramatic character, there is much to be said for his position. Men are often mistaken rather than sinful; chance may bring them to unmerited misfortune; human motives are usually mixtures of self-seeking and altruism; and so on. We can agree also that modern writers have done well to enlarge our understanding of motives and conditions so that we sympathize more widely and condemn less readily than our ancestors.

It does not follow, however, that (as Mme. de Staël's saying is popularly misquoted) to understand all is to pardon all. There are acts that we should not and the vast majority of us do not pardon: acts that result from deliberate choice of evil. And this assertion stands even if we maintain that such a choice is ultimately determined, for its consequences are just as calamitous in the one case as in the other. Looking at morals as a biological matter, evil is whatever endangers life, and hate of it a natural expression of the instinct for survival; supine acquiescence in it, a sort of suicide. Traditional morality may of course become mere prejudice in a person who has not tested it. Furthermore, when a tradition has endured for centuries, as our Christian morality has, a time is bound to come when it will be widely attacked. Such a time is the present. In a time of transition or revolution in ethics such as ours, audiences cannot respond unanimously in admiration or condemnation. But that everybody has moral standards of some sort, and responds to a drama in accordance with them, is to be observed at any play.

Not only that; we ought indeed to respond. To preserve

ourselves we must fight evil, and to fight well we need the stimulus of hate. Even the medieval saint who had taught himself to hate no man hated the Devil. In the theater we should reserve our love and our hate for objects that deserve them. Exactly such discrimination makes a superior audience, and when a play is written so as to rouse the right emotion it becomes a superior play. Utter villains are of course proper only to vulgar melodramas, but saying that does not imply that we should not detest villainy wherever we find it. We may even favor and disapprove different qualities in a single person at once, but we cannot and should not be impartial and detached.

Perhaps I need to dwell a moment more on this point because certain thinkers today make much of the virtue of detachment or disinterestedness, and some cite the scientist's disinterested pursuit of truth as the model attitude for us all. Through such detachment alone, they tell us, can we see things as they are without the distortion of personal feeling. We may agree that for science the elimination of prejudice is necessary. We may admit that something of this detachment aids in the appreciation of certain types of comedy which call for thoughtful laughter. But science seeks mere knowledge; it has nothing to say about the uses we should put our knowledge to. When we come to choose and act, desire and emotion drive us. What we need for conduct is not absence of feeling but the right feelings.

It seems to me, therefore, that this talk about disinterestedness involves an ambiguity. Ideal disinterestedness in pure science is cold intellectual activity. Ideal disinterestedness in matters of conduct, and hence in our attitudes toward arts which, like the drama, deal in problems of conduct, ought to be based on the fullest knowledge and intelligence possible, but motivated and made efficient by a love of righteousness and a hatred of evil. It is "disinterestedness" still, because it rises above petty egotistical feeling; it becomes generalized and philosophic. Without feeling, it cannot rise at all.

Modern drama makes more careful and subtle discriminations than drama of the past, for our study of the human mind and its motives has taught us many things that our ancestors did not know. But such insight as we have gained should not result in either that cold impartiality which the admirers of science would accept, or in an indiscriminating and sentimental pity for all alike.

Tragedy differs from melodrama not in being more logical or more successful in creating character for its own sake, but in leading us to universalized emotion based on ethical sentiments. This emotion is brought into being immediately by our identification with the actors on the stage and is then generalized to apply to all mankind.

POETIC JUSTICE VERSUS ADMIRATION

A good tragedy leads us to love or hate the right persons, but by presentation, not preaching. Its morality thus consists in rousing the right attitudes. Many people have not been satisfied with this, however; they have demanded that it also apportion rewards and punishments according to merit. In other words, they want "poetic justice."

This demand goes back as far as Plato, who believed that the just man should be happy in life and hence should be shown to be happy in fiction. "You compel your poets to say that the good man, if he be temperate and just, is fortunate and happy; and this whether he be great and strong or small and weak, and whether he be rich or poor; and, on the other hand, if he have a wealth passing that of Cinyras or Midas, and be unjust, he is wretched and lives in misery. As the poet says, and with truth: I sing not, I care not about him who accomplishes all noble things, not having justice; let him who 'draws near and stretches out his hand against his enemies be a just man.' But if he be unjust, I would not have him 'look calmly upon bloody death,' nor 'surpass in swiftness the Thracian Boreas'; and let no other thing that is called good ever be his."[38]

Aristotle differed from his master in this as in other matters, and I think that nothing in the *Poetics* shows his extraordinary critical discernment more fully. His doctrine of the "tragic flaw" suggests that an error or frailty of the protagonist is a cause of his downfall. Thus Oedipus, as Sophocles represents him, comes to grief in an immediate sense because of his own impetuosity. But the tragic flaw is *not* tragic guilt. Oedipus' impetuosity and regal will are kingly attributes and actually the means of advancing him and the state; he falls, ultimately, through the will of the gods. Indeed, if he were entirely to blame we could not pity him, but would rather rejoice. And Aristotle is very explicit on this point. We should feel pity, he believes, at a tragedy; and we do not pity the bad man. The hero must be neither utterly bad nor utterly good, but "like ourselves"—a char-

[38] *Laws* II, 660–661; Jowett's translation. For the reference I am indebted to M. A. Quinlan, *Poetic Justice in the Drama* (Notre Dame, Ind., 1912), which may be consulted for a full discussion of this subject.

acter, that is, with whom we can identify ourselves. The tragic flaw is a weakness in an otherwise noble hero. Aristotle's idea regarding it seems to have been that it was a means of making the hero "human," not a justification for his downfall. Tragedies that apportion rewards and punishments, he considered of "second rank," accounted best by some only "because of the weakness of the spectators."[39] Thus, without ignoring the importance of the moral sentiments, he judged the drama first and foremost as a work of art.

Until very recently he has been the rare exception among critics, who for the most part have felt obliged to pay at least lip service to didacticism. Horace's tag about poetry's function—that it should "instruct, or please, or both"—is a politic way of evading controversy by observing that there is much to be said on both sides; it amply justifies the moral apologue. Christian writers of the Middle Ages naturally sought the moral in all fiction, and some of them tried to rationalize their fondness for pagan poetry by inventing, for non-Christian works, suitable allegorical interpretations. Renaissance critics generally felt impelled to favor poetic justice, and by the seventeenth century the doctrine was traditional; hence, Rymer could write of *Othello,* "Our Poet against all Justice and Reason, against all Law, Humanity and Nature, in a barbarous arbitrary way, excites and makes havoc of his subjects, Hab-nab, as they come to hand."[40] Though Dr. Johnson accepted the doctrine in his famous preface to Shakespeare, he argued against it in his life of Addison. But Mr. Quinlan discovers demands for it as late

[39] *Poetics* XIII. [40] Quoted in Quinlan, *Poetic Justice in the Drama,* chap. iii.

as W. T. Price's *Technique of the Drama* (1892). The view is still deeply imbedded in our traditional thought about art, reinforced as it is by our natural desire for "happy"—this is, just—endings. And that despite the violent reaction against it of the artsakists, which has been so widely successful among aesthetes and intellectuals.[41]

If the doctrine had been based on the example of great tragedy, it could never have been so firmly maintained, for great tragedies seldom administer poetic justice. Perhaps *Macbeth* is a case of simple crime and retribution; and Racine, as we have noted,[42] even took pride in punishing his Phèdre. But in other tragedies, like *Prometheus Bound, Agamemnon, The Bacchae,* and *Julius Caesar,* the heroes scarcely deserve the dire fates that befall them, and protagonists like Oedipus, Antigone, Othello, and Lear suffer beyond all desert. Furthermore, the villainess in *Medea*—if it be considered a great tragedy—triumphantly escapes the punishment of her hideous crimes.

Injustice is all too common in life, and tragedy is true to life in showing it. Moreover, tragedy is actually more powerfully affecting exactly when it shows it. It thus sets up a clash of feeling between our desires for justice and our realization that justice is not a law of nature. We are confronted by the mystery of evil, and experience what Mr. Frye calls the "tragic qualm"—"a sort of moral dizziness," "a sudden and appalling recognition of our desperate plight in a universe apparently indiscriminate of good and evil as of happiness and misery."[43]

---

[41] See p. 75.
[42] See pp. 73–74.
[43] *Romance and Tragedy,* p. 148.

Mr. Frye thinks that the tragedy of Aeschylus and Sophocles (not Euripides) allays this qualm by presuming a moral universe and ascribing the calamity to violation of the moral law. He thinks that this is what Aristotle meant by *katharsis*. He ranks Shakespeare beneath the Greeks for failure to impose the moral law on his characters. Other critics, while not generally agreeing with Mr. Frye's valuations of the Greeks and Shakespeare on these grounds, have often agreed with him in finding in Aeschylus and Sophocles this assumption of a moral universe, and seeing in their plays the workings of retribution. Some give grounds for Mr. Frye's conclusions, and Aeschylus in particular was concerned with such ideas; yet I can only feel that the conclusions are too definite and sweeping. I do not think that even Aeschylus was at all sure about the moral law of the universe. Like all earnestly religious spirits, he wanted to believe in it; but his tragedies gain their peculiar poignancy, like the Book of Job, because of the extraordinary difficulty he finds in reconciling divine justice with the facts of human life. Tragedy attains its power over us because it represents the human lot as we see it on earth, not as we hope or wish it to be. It has never offered the consolation of heavenly justice in the next world, even when written by believers. For the drama, death is the end; "the rest is silence."

Most of us today cannot believe that justice exists in nature, and as a consequence we do not demand it in poetry. How, then, does it happen that great tragedy that does not show it inspirits us instead of depressing us?

Some critics, indeed, seem to think that it does not inspirit us; or that, if the great tragedies of the past still do, it is because of the no longer credible assumption in them of a moral order which is vindicated in the hero's fate and which thereby reconciles us with it. Tragedy is impossible in the future, they think, because this assumption is no longer possible. Thus Joseph Wood Krutch, who foretells the extinction of tragedy because it is dependent on an anthropocentric view of the universe. It is the "tragic fallacy," he says, to fancy that one's "passions are important . . . throughout all time and all space."[44]

Mr. Krutch's conclusions are based on the assumption that an audience gets pleasure at a tragedy from seeing a moral order vindicated in the hero's death. This assumption, as I have tried to show, is very difficult to justify by the great tragedies, and much better fits nineteenth-century melodrama, with its man-hunt after the villain. On the contrary, it is exactly because the hero does not deserve his fate that we are moved to pity him and fear for ourselves and the world. Mr. Frye disparaged Euripides and Shakespeare for not vindicating the moral order; on the contrary, Euripides was to Aristotle the "most tragic" of the poets—and Shakespeare is to us. We must surely look elsewhere for an explanation of the feeling of spiritual glory that great tragedies give us.

We are of course elevated by such effects as beauty of verse and plotting, but these may exist in plays that are not at all tragic. They do not explain the central paradox of tragedy—our delight in the spectacle of a hero defeated.

The source of this delight is, I believe, that, though he

[44] "The Tragic Fallacy," in *The Modern Temper* (New York, 1929).

is defeated, virtue is vindicated. We admire him. This admiration, not pity, is the strongest immediate emotion; and we are inspirited because *the hero gains a spiritual victory in spite of a physical defeat.* Instead of his fall's being a punishment for violation of a moral order in the universe, it is a vindication of a moral order in man in spite of the universe.

Not all tragedies, to be sure, clearly demonstrate this formula; and in any case, like most critical generalizations, it is likely to oversimplify. None of Euripides' greater plays fits it. Medea, the witch, the infanticide, is made to triumph over one of the legendary heroes of Greek saga, and the latter is represented as a detestable egotist. This is a victory of greater evil over less. Hippolytus is less an agent than a victim, less a hero than a prig. Pentheus (in *The Bacchae*) is so unheroic as to evidence the impulses of a Peeping Tom, and he suffers the frightful vengeance of Dionysus for no worse crime than such doubts about the gods and their morality as his creator had himself often expressed through his characters in earlier plays. What did Euripides mean by this extraordinary and terrible play? That is one of the fascinating unsolved problems of dramatic criticism. This at least is certain: he did not show his protagonist winning a spiritual victory over death.

Shakespeare's heroes, in his great tragedies, are often less than heroic in some of their characteristics, since they are represented with much realism; but they redeem themselves in defeat. Thus Othello and Lear. And they all, even Macbeth, have spiritual stature. Racine's greatest protagonists, however, are victims of passion, not moral heroines.

Andromaque cares for nothing but her child; Hermione loses every moral and rational restraint in her jealous passion for Pyrrhus; Phèdre struggles against guilty passion but succumbs; Athalie is—the daughter of Jezebel. And Ibsen, as we shall see in the next chapter,[45] turned heroism to subtle ridicule in his later plays.

In earlier versions of this discussion my impulse to demonstrate a single theory of tragedy led me to overlook such exceptions. I now confess to having indulged in rationalization. But in this matter I have not sinned alone. Among theorists on tragedy there has often been a good deal more overwrought discourse than careful assessment of facts. This is natural. Tragedy is one of the most exalted achievements of the human spirit, and critics, who must spend much of their time in censure, find it pleasant to praise, for once, indiscriminately.

The facts, regarding Euripides, seem to be these: he makes us suspect a hidden irony and disillusioned pessimism even in his most inspired work. The splendor of his verse, his pathos, his powerful theatricality, and the richness of his imagination lead us to wish for exalted resolutions to his plays, but he frustrates our wishes, almost as if with perverse intention. Even the specialists do not know how to take him, or if they think they do, disagree violently with each other. He does not fit the pattern of tragedy set by his predecessors. Yet Aristotle called him "most tragic" of the poets; and many modern scholars, notably Gilbert Murray, admire him above his predecessors. The explanation for this admiration, I believe, is that his skeptical dis-

---

[45] Pp. 295 ff.

illusionment fits the spirit of our day. (He repelled the romantics a century ago.) In spirit he is closer to Ibsen than to Sophocles. And he is profoundly serious about the moral problems he raises. He could not solve them, but he refused to lie about them. Like Ibsen he braved the censure, the ridicule, the condemnation of his fellows and persisted throughout a long life in writing the truth as he saw it. There is something heroic about Euripides, after all.

As for Racine, his absorbing interest in female passion, though powerfully dramatic, is if taken alone hardly the stuff of the greatest tragedy. But it is not alone. Racine was reared in the strictest of Catholic sects, and he never, even in his most worldly period, shook off its stern morality. Hence he is never merely fascinated by passion, but always also its judge. His heroines fascinate us romantically by the greatness of their passion and the beauty of the language their creator gives them; but his tragedies are classic in their strict form and objective treatment; they are Christian in their implied morality. He may not offer spiritual victories in his protagonists, but he condemns the evil that causes their defeat.

These exceptions, then, complicate the formula but do not invalidate it. Humanity is elevated, not belittled, by tragedy. And we are justified in calling those tragedies in which there is a victory the normal ones.

Victory both physical and spiritual would not greatly move us; it would constitute a "happy ending." Defeat both physical and spiritual would give us no lift or mitigation and would frustrate the strongest desires aroused by the play. This is in some degree the difficulty with *The Trojan*

Women, and, as I shall indicate later, with many modern tragedies. They may lead us to "the impassioned contemplation of ultimates" and to this extent rise above melodrama; but without admiration the contemplation is depressing.

This admiration is the source of that sense of waste of which Bradley wrote, and offers us some compensation for it. Heroism at least is exalted, though the hero himself fall. Pity of a personal sort thus goes chiefly to minor characters like Ophelia and Desdemona. They are minor, indeed, exactly because they are not heroic like Antigone. The protagonist is made of sterner stuff and we admire him more than we pity him.

At the same time we must also pity him. I think Professor Nicoll overstates himself when he writes: "We do not sympathize with Othello to the extent of feeling pity, because Othello is a force beyond our ken, primitive perhaps, but strong and majestic. We do not weep at the death of Cordelia, because she has a hardness in her nature which forbids our tears."[46] Dr. Johnson will hardly be accused of sentimentality, yet he has recorded his very great distress at Cordelia's death; and I think the experience of few of us in watching Othello's tragedy agrees with Professor Nicoll's.

Though Aristotle does not speak of admiration, he implies that it is central to tragedy when he emphasizes the importance of exalting the tragic hero. The hero must not only be a man like ourselves whom we can pity, but also a man superior to us whom we can admire. Though made "human" by his frailty, he is nevertheless a great man, illustrious in rank and character.

---

[46] *The Theory of Drama* (New York, 1931), p. 120.

This doctrine was narrowly interpreted in the Renaissance as meaning that the hero must at least belong to the peerage. We no longer think that. The essential thing is not the blueness of his blood but the brightness of his soul. Nevertheless, the fall of a man of high station carries with it calamity to many others also and is for that reason more impressive than the fall of a private individual. Moreover, so long as people generally reverenced the nobility, that reverence reinforced their admiration and their sense of high significance in the action. When this aristocratic tradition died as a consequence of the rise of democratic sentiments, the old aristocratic tragedy died with it, but the aesthetic principle that justified its outward exaltation of its heroes is still sound.

Greatness must exist in the tragic hero, and indeed the history of tragedy prior to the eighteenth century shows an insistence on everything that might elevate and dignify him. He did not seem suitable for tragic treatment unless he possessed personal magnitude. This might exist even in wicked figures such as Medea and Macbeth, whom we admire not for their wickedness but for their imperious force of character.

When we speak of heroism, therefore, we should mean it to include all characters that are convincingly typical of man as man, and that are also in some fashion admirable. Thus great tragedy of the classical tradition may inspire us without vindicating an external moral order, because it shows mortals contending nobly against overwhelming odds. It sustains our faith in mankind. It is heroic.

CHAPTER VIII

The Dilemma of Modern Tragedy

HONESTY VERSUS SUBLIMITY

To THE German metaphysical mind, the source of that lift to the spirit which classic tragedy gives has seemed something a good deal more complicated than heroism. Hegel thought tragedy a transcendental reconciliation of opposites. Schopenhauer found it in resignation to loss of individuality and return to the universal Will. Nietzsche turned Schopenhauer's pessimism into a semblance of optimism by defining the spirit of Dionysus as an intoxicated joy in self-annihilation and union with nature. The consequences of such theories, so far as they had any in creative writing, have been rather depressing. Hegelian ideas are seen in Hebbel, whose heroine Clara (in *Maria Magdalena*) is made a sacrificial victim to the necessities of social reform; and, more indirectly, in Ibsen's heavy closet drama, *Emperor and Galilean*. Schopenhauer's pessimism affected Hardy, as is well seen in the latter's long dramatic poem, *The Dynasts,* which he called an "epic-drama," but which has no hero, not even Napoleon, because indeed all its characters, including the emperor, are represented as puppets of a blind, insentient World-Will. Nietzsche's violent assertion of self-will, as opposed to Schopenhauer's gloomy passivity, seems to have influenced Strindberg and O'Neill.

The spirit of the time itself has run counter to the heroic tradition. We may notice several influences that have worked against it. Modern democracy, not to speak of communistic exaltation of the proletariat, is hostile to it. Commercialism has fostered the feeling, in capitalist and "wage slave" alike, that success is measured by the possession of things. And science, however disinterested it may be in the pursuit of truth, has in actuality not only helped to destroy popular traditions that might have nourished a modern spirit of admiration, but has also fostered a wintry air of skepticism, making man appear not an imperfect angel but a highly educated monkey. Psychology in particular has been industriously cutting at the root of heroism—the belief in free will—by exhibiting the mechanisms of conduct. In consequence of the teachings of behaviorism, people sometimes come to think of their acts as no more than "conditioned reflexes" like that of Pavlov's dog which was trained to salivate when he heard a bell rung.

The writer of tragedy is inevitably influenced by these current ideas, and thus finds himself in a dilemma. Unable to believe in greatness, he cannot inspire others. If he would gain elevation, he must falsify his beliefs; if he would express his candid view of life, he must forego the tragic lift. Heroic tragedy was the outcome of a view perhaps pessimistic about things in general but always optimistic about the virtue in individuals. The modern view is pessimistic about everything. As Hardy expressed it in *The Return of the Native,* the prospect most harmonious with the temper of the thinking modern would be a gaunt waste in Thule. Put briefly, the dilemma of the naturist poet is this: *he cannot be both honest and sublime.*

This assertion may be more convincing if illustrated by examples. I shall draw them from other manifestations of the tragic spirit, such as narrative poetry and the novel, as well as from the drama.

I have noted the effect of science. At first thought it might seem that the great romantics of a century ago, who preceded the scientific disillusionment, might have kept the heroic tradition alive. It is true that they inherited it, but in their hands it became not so much heroism as heroics. The romantic tendency was to seek thrills rather than truth and to draw less from human nature than from a literary fashion. *Hernani* and *Ruy Blas,* the most successful romantic plays of serious pretensions, are constructions of claptrap to which Hugo's beautiful and rhetorical verse gives merely a semblance of significance. They can be taken seriously only by abandoning the intelligence, and today seem no more tragic than the plays of the senior Dumas or the *mélodrames* of the boulevard from which Hugo actually learned much of his technique. As melodramas they are still entertaining, to be sure.

Such romantic literature of escape—for that is what it really is—of course did not decrease in popularity with the development of science, but it distinctly lost literary prestige. After the 'sixties and 'seventies the romantic who wanted to be taken seriously had to cope with skepticism and disillusionment. Thus Rostand, writing *Cyrano de*

Bergerac (1897), was careful to preserve the smile of sophistication; he delicately played with pathos and even flirted with comedy. The clever charm of his romantic verse also helped him to make us accept the swagger of his big-nosed hero in the spirit of play. Heroism here is the heroism of a fairy tale.

The ambitious romantic, however, is not content with the role of popular entertainer. Though put on the defensive, he has persisted in attempting the exaltation of tragic art. Maeterlinck, for example, sought to reconcile pessimism with romance by developing a fatalistic "static drama" and throwing over it a Pre-Raphaelite mist of symbolism and suggestive language. With him, as with the other symbolists of the 'nineties, a symbol became less a sign of another object than a stimulant to emotional intoxication and flight from reality; and if we observe his early plays with unfuddled faculties we see that they are rooted in a determinism fatal to the heroic tradition. Though later he grew more optimistic, yet even from *Monna Vanna*, which was inspired by Browning, what the audience receives is exaltation of passion rather than will.

Whereas Maeterlinck tried to preserve romantic values, if not heroism, by reconciling them with science, the great Russians, Tolstoy and Dostoievsky, evaded scientific pessimism by escape into a romanticized Christianity. The result was no less fatal to heroism. As they saw it, the Christian paradox is that the greater the sin the greater the salvation; and they illustrated it by extreme examples. Thus in Tolstoy's *The Power of Darkness* (1886) the leading character is not only a drunkard, a lecher, and a murderer of his own child, but craven, stupid, and weak; yet he wins salvation by public confession. Such a conversion as his seems a mere emotional revulsion rather than a religious regeneration, for it is the result of no discipline of the will. At least, Nikita is no hero. (In saying this I am not disparaging Tolstoy's genius. His character drawing here, as always, is marvelous in its realism and truth. Theoretically, he followed Rousseau[1] in looking for virtue only in the natural man—the Russian peasant, in particular; but when he wrote fiction or drama the artist in him took control and portrayed life as it was in fact rather than in theory.) The greater part of *The Power of Darkness* is Zolaesque in its brutal representation of village life, and thus utterly antiheroic. The ending, in my opinion, is the consequence of a Rousseauistically sentimentalized Christianity which is also unheroic.

The exaltation which the romantic failed to achieve, the realist did not attempt. Ibsen, apart from his great intrinsic importance, which I shall discuss in the next chapter, is interesting in this connection because he shows the transition from the heroic to the antiheroic tradition. His early plays were modeled after Scribe and Schiller and hence were romantically heroic; use of the Norse sagas gave him heroic material. As time went on, he portrayed men more and more as victims rather than shapers of events, and shifted responsibility from the individual to his heredity and environment. This shift from the heroic to the biological view was facilitated by the fact that romanticism had already identified man with nature, and the growing disillusion-

[1] For Tolstoy's debt to Rousseau see George Rapall Noyes, *Tolstoy* (London, 1919), pp. 17 ff.

ment with nature that marked Ibsen's era entailed degradation of man. (Wordsworth, the nature worshiper, sang, in 1798, "Nature never did betray the heart that loved her"; but Tennyson, after a study of geology as well as ardent contemplation of the beauties of the outer world, described nature, in 1850, as "red in tooth and claw.") Though the increasing use of symbolism gives Ibsen's late plays a romantic tone, fundamentally they are studies of mental abormalities which seem almost intended to demonstrate the nonexistence of heroism.[2] The fall of the master builder is indeed a symbol of the falsity of what Shaw called, with inverted commas, "ideals." But Ibsen's antiheroic tendency is seen perhaps most forcefully in the famous tragedy of his middle period.

In *Ghosts* (1881) the formal resemblances to Greek tragedy and the gloomy power of the total effect obscure the fact that this is no longer tragedy in the great tradition. The animus vitalizing the action is Ibsen's desire to attack the false code of morals in the society in which he grew up, of which his heroine is the victim. We can admire the author for his honesty and daring as well as his marvelous dramaturgic skill, but we cannot greatly admire his characters. The only one who might be thought heroic, Mrs. Alving, is pitiful indeed but admirable only in intention, and false to her own convictions—as the author makes a point of showing: "Oh, if I were not such a coward!" At the curtain she is so far from a "spiritual victory" that there remains for her a dilemma which is possibly the cruelest in dramatic literature: killing her son, or sparing him to live a paretic

[2] See, in chap. ix, "Ibsen," pp. 316 ff.

idiot. The contrast between this play and, let us say, *Hamlet,* is plain when we compare Oswald's idiot cry, "The sun—the sun," and the curtain speech of Fortinbras:

> Bear Hamlet, like a soldier, to the stage;
> For he was likely, had he been put on,
> To have proved most royally; and for his passage,
> The soldiers' music and the rights of war
> Speak loudly for him.

The former conveys the bitter irony of disillusion and gives an effect of horror. It is the very mockery of the romantic cliché, "Then came the dawn."

THE TWO ROADS

The elevation that Ibsen achieves in *Ghosts* through beauty of form and atmospheric effect does not carry over to the theme; here he frankly chooses honesty and foregoes sublimity. Few writers since then, or none at all, have been at once as great and as honest. If we observe the literature of the past half century to see how it has met the dilemma of modern tragedy, we shall find perhaps a partial explanation of current literary anarchy and experimentation. Some take refuge in subtle evasions disguised by cleverness of treatment or novelty of material. But those who have not evaded the issue have followed two roads: the road of laughter, which runs by way of irony and satire; and the road of tears and cruelty.

Since the former leads us away from the tragic emotions, it will not long detain us. With effort, a poet can school himself into a detachment of head from heart that enables him to smile at the contrast between his dreams and the reality. His smile may be wry, but it is yet a smile. Thus Pirandello, whose chief effect is the "humor" got from contrasting the flux and illusoriness of life with the permanence and desirability of fiction. Thus Anatole France, who armored his sensibility with artistic detachment and the *esprit gaulois*. Thus Aldous Huxley, who in spite of his earnestness about morality is able to indulge in savage satire of the world by maintaining an attitude of systematic "disinterestedness"; he would like to attain a state of Buddhistic contemplation, but being really a very sensitive and sympathetic person he works off his horror at the evils of humanity by means of diabolical ridicule.

We are here concerned, however, with the tragic attitude. The modern who seeks to gain tragic effects and who cannot admire has no resource but to appeal to pity or to cruelty.

Pathos and horror we find in Hardy, little mitigated by any admiration except what we feel for the author's austere artistry. Rarely, he draws a hero of sorts like Michael Henchard, but it is significant that he ended his novels with *Jude the Obscure*. Galsworthy's habitual irony always bordered on pathos if not sentiment. Even when he presented characters as virile as old Heythorp—better known to playgoers as "Old English"—and the dying patriarch of *Indian Summer of a Forsyte,* the mood is dominantly elegiac. French naturalism was harsher, and at times, as in *Madame Bovary,* overpoweringly ironical. At other times it has been prosaically plodding. *The Old Wives' Tale* of Arnold Bennett is a fine English work of this school, in which we feel the pathos of mere mortality quite apart from anything the very ordinary characters do. (Dramatically speaking, indeed, they don't *do* anything; but since this is a novel, dramatic action is not essential.) In Theodore Dreiser's novels this type of naturalism, though sadly in need of pruning, bore its bitter fruit belatedly. It is characteristic of its spirit that this author used the title, *An American Tragedy,* with reference to the fate of a selfish and stupid young man who drifts into a murder as a consequence of the interaction within him of what Dreiser was wont to call his "chemisms."

Sentimentality was the vice of Victorian literature, and hence was what the last generation sought, above all things, to avoid. Since pathos easily becomes sentimentality, disillusioned writers during the uneasy peace between two world wars frequently cultivated cruelty. The savage latent in us enjoys torture; significantly, the word "sadism" became fashionable in the 'twenties. It was thought a sin to be sentimental, but rather advanced to be tough. What that meant in practice, not in fiction, was demonstrated later by the Nazis. But in the naïve 'twenties D. H. Lawrence won something of a cult with his novels that mysticized sex and violence. In the 'thirties Ernest Hemingway found in crude sexuality and cruelty an escape from the sentimentality in which at an earlier time he would certainly have indulged. Perhaps the one genuine poet of this school is Robinson Jeffers.

Jeffers's long narrative poems spread a more than Thyestean banquet of horrors; we learn with surprise that in private life he is so unwilling to inflict pain that "he never picks a flower wantonly."[3] In his writing he more than compensates for such restraint. *Roan Stallion*, for example, depicts the passion of a Californian Pasiphaë for a horse. *Tamar* deals with incest between brother and sister, includes the ghosts of libidinous ancient Indians, and ends with a fire that, none too soon, burns down the house and the whole mad family. *The Tower beyond Tragedy,* probably because it treats the classic legend of Clytemnestra and Orestes, is perhaps the sanest and most powerful of his poems, yet it also disintegrates at the end into a scene which is typical Jeffers, and as un-Greek as possible: Orestes is mad from having murdered his mother, and Electra offers her body to him to cure him; he, however, refuses and goes off to enter the "tower beyond tragedy," whatever that may be. (The sanest explanation would be that under cover of such mystical language he is, in plain English, about to commit suicide.)

The perversity of theme is partly compensated by elevation of treatment, for Mr. Jeffers has the grand style. I mean this seriously. The grand style, in the eighteenth-century meaning of the term, is seldom even attempted in our prosaic age. In his own way, without noticeable reminiscences of other poets, in long, rhythmical lines, Jeffers gains a truly magnificent elevation of language. He draws upon Greek literature, the Bible, modern psychology, and physical science for references; his power of visual description is great; and one never doubts his sincerity even if at times one wonders about his sanity.

[3] Louis Adamic, *Robinson Jeffers, a Portrait* (University of Washington Chapbooks, No. 27; Seattle, 1929).

A frequently quoted passage from *Roan Stallion* will illustrate at one and the same time his power of style and his point of view.

Humanity is the start of the race; I say
Humanity is the mould to break away from, the crust to break through, the coal to break into fire,
The atom to be split.
Tragedy that breaks man's face and a white fire flies out of it; vision that fools him
Out of his limits, desire that fools him out of his limits, unnatural crime, inhuman science,
Slit eyes in the mask; wild loves that leap over the walls of nature, the wild fence-vaulter science,
Useless intelligence of far stars, dim knowledge of the spinning demons that make an atom,
These break, these pierce, these deify, praising their God shrilly with fierce voices: not in a man's shape
He approves the praise, he that walks lightning-naked on the Pacific, that laces the suns with planets,
The heart of the atom with electrons: what is humanity in this cosmos? For him, the last
Least taint of a trace in the dregs of the solution; for itself, the mould to break away from, the coal
To break into fire, the atom to be split.[4]

Since there is no personal God, but only a fierce and cruel nature—so seems to run his thought,—men should not be content to be men, but should "break out of humanity" by lust, perversion, murder, and madness. The ancient Greeks, who were closer to the violences of barbarism than were Mr.

[4] From *Roan Stallion, Tamar, and Other Poems* (New York, Boni & Liveright, 1925).

Jeffers's generation in their formative years, wanted more civilization, and advised one to "think as a mortal." Mr. Jeffers wants to get rid of a civilization which to him is a crawling mess of evil, and to think as a beast or a god—and between beast and god, in his pantheon, there is really no difference. He is quoted[5] as saying that civilization tends inevitably toward downfall through sexual introversion; and although admitting that to attempt to "break out of humanity" after the fashion described in *Roan Stallion* would be dangerous if "misinterpreted in the mind of a fool or a lunatic," nevertheless he thinks the fault of the civilized person to be that he "regards man exclusively . . . , founding his values, desires, his picture of the universe, all on his own humanity." But what else is there, if we have no faith in God? Only death. And in poem after poem is expressed the longing for the peace and endurance of granite or the grave. The violent destruction of the body is the logical fruition of his creed; denial of human values leads to annihilation of humanity.

In Mr. Jeffers's work we may see how much tragic grandeur can be got out of nihilism. It is significant that to many readers the grandeur of his style is insufficient to prevent the horror of his presumably symbolical but very concretely described incidents from having unfortunate effects. Either one's sensibilities are so harrowed by his word pictures as to find them soon intolerable, or one is gradually induced to laugh—such monstrous fancies become mere nightmare shapes of a disordered imagination.

In Eugene O'Neill we find less extreme tendencies along

[5] By Adamic, in *Robinson Jeffers, a Portrait.*

the same line of development, but generalizations about him are rendered difficult because he is groping and experimental not only in technique, but in thought as well. Because of this difficulty, as well as because of his position as the leading writer of tragic drama in our day, he requires special consideration.

EUGENE O'NEILL

A writer's 'prentice work is likely to be revealing, and O'Neill's is no exception. The one-act play *Thirst,* for example, reveals an imagination absorbed in the violences and brutalities of life. Most of the one-acters in the volume called *The Moon of the Caribbees* have more normal and convincing characters, but about half are built upon abnormal situations involving incipient insanities or morbid passions.

This interest in mental abnormality has not diminished: his plays are studies in psychopathology. *Beyond the Horizon* deals with a weak romantic who takes refuge from harsh reality in daydreams and finally, by a dramatic *non sequitur,* dies of consumption. *Gold* is a melodrama about an insane delusion. *Diff'rent* is the horrible case history of a victim of sex repression—an early example of the author's favorite interpretation of New England puritanism. *The Hairy Ape,* by expressionistic methods borrowed from Strindberg and the Germans, describes a character who, if he is not merely a symbol, is indeed apelike in his mentality, and who develops from incipient to raving madness. With a normal opening *"The First Man"* turns out to be a study of an emotional fixation. *Welded,* a play clearly written under the influence of Strindberg's conception of love as strife,[6] depicts two egotistical introverts tortured by the inevitable conflict between their passion and their uncontrolled temperament. The flames of lust and greed fanned into madness are the materials of *Desire under the Elms*. *The Great God Brown,* beneath its elaborate symbolical machinery, is about a split personality. *The Fountain,* beneath its exotic romanticism, is the story of an *idée fixe*. The plot of *Strange Interlude* might have come from the casebook of Freud. We can hardly judge the hero of *Lazarus Laughed* by human standards since he is not a human being but merely He who Laughs at Death; Caligula and Tiberius, however, are realistic studies of lust, cruelty, and fear. *Dynamo* is a study of religious mania. *Mourning Becomes Electra* turns Greek tragedy into Freudian melodrama; *Days without End,* a weak and hysterical play, is significant only as a confession of the dramatist's need for faith. The obvious exception to this list is the one comedy, *Ah, Wilderness!,* the chief characters in which are sane and wholesome. It is a delightful play, but no one would call it an important one. There is no reason why a play about sane people should not be a strong play, but O'Neill has not yet written one.

Some Americans have developed a sort of patriotic touchiness about the greatest American dramatist. If the foregoing review of his work has irritated it in the reader, I beg him to note that I have been concerned simply to show O'Neill's dependence upon psychopathology. Later, in discussing dramatic poetry, I shall find him less than great in power over words. In neither respect do I deny his power in de-

[6] See, in chap. ix, "Strindberg and Expressionism," pp. 341 ff.

veloping dramatic action, his earnest sincerity, his ingenuity in technical device, his imaginative range, his gift for romantic effects, or the remorseless strength of his character analysis. In other words, I recognize that if he is not a great dramatist he is nearly one. We are too close to him to be sure of our estimate. We may exercise what critical ability we have, however, in judging him.

He has obviously suffered from spiritual frustrations, for these are the themes of all his plays. It would be easy to use a Marxian explanation of them and say that they are due to a bad economic system or something of the sort, but such a method of disposing of a writer does so by ignoring all that is personal in him: it reduces the complex human being, half spirit, half animal, to an abstract unit. Of course economics has affected him; it affects all of us. But men do not live by bread alone. He has hungered and thirsted after righteousness, but he has not been filled. Instead, he has been frustrated by the modern philosophy of nihilism. Endowed with a highly romantic and religious temperament, he has found no acceptable faith to satisfy its needs.

That his temperament is highly romantic is obvious. His early work is almost Conrad-like in atmosphere, and he has filled plays like *"Marco Millions"* with gorgeous settings and strange events. Indeed he is an unquestionable genius in the melodrama of fear and horror, fertile in themes to startle and shock, and skillful in adapting them effectively to the stage. There is a new shiver for the spectator in the gruesome ending of *Mourning Becomes Electra,* when the heroine, instead of committing anything so commonplace as suicide, shuts herself up in the ancestral house that has become a whited sepulcher, there to *live* with her horrible memories. Such a play as *Ile* is not only horrible, but psychologically convincing. *The Emperor Jones* is, in my opinion, the author's masterpiece, perfectly constructed and artistically inevitable. The settings and plot contribute with as inexorable an art as that of Poe to the single effect, and that effect is bound up with a clear problem in character. The theme is the regression of a negro to savagery; and as we watch the succession of weird visions and feel the emotional crescendo of the tom-toms, at the same time we see the disintegration of the negro's mind. The parallel progress of outer and inner events is beautifully executed.

Considering the excellence of such plays of unintellectualized imagination, we may well wish that O'Neill had not tried his wings in the empyrean of philosophy and religion. In spite of his luxuriant fancy, he has never been content to construct a dream world of his own in despair of the real one. He has never stopped trying to find what he wants among things as they are, and as a consequence his visions of beauty or terror are forever being distorted by the lurid light of disillusionment. Thus he has seldom written pure romance. *"Marco Millions"* turns into heavy satire, and *The Fountain* leaves a bitter taste. For the most part, he tries to deal realistically with contemporary life. (Such devices as asides and masks are, in part, attempts to achieve deeper psychological reality by dramatic means.)

It is torture to have visions of beauty which we know do not exist, and at the same time to see human beings as parts of a mechanistic and soulless universe. Lesser men have not been strong enough to face the facts and have been diverted into a seeming reconciliation of their dreams with such a universe by programs of reform. In the depression before the recent war some of them deceived themselves into accepting economic panaceas as though they were religions that could satisfy spiritual hunger by material food. Only a genuine religion can resolve this conflict. O'Neill has written sympathetically of the dispossessed, as in *The Hairy Ape,* but a struggle between "classes" or over economic theories could not really seize the imagination of one who saw so deeply into the struggle of the spirit. At the same time—and this is his misfortune—he could not be sure of any deeper faith.

Time and again he has shown the romantic's characteristic hatred of tradition and restraint; he has expressed it in more than one play by contrasting withered New England spinsters with uninhibited Polynesians. (In this he is part of a long romantic tradition which the French have labeled the *rêve exotique* or dream of far away, usually centered in the South Seas somewhere near Samoa.) Yet he by no means admires the libertine. His rakes as well as his spinsters have uncomfortable New England consciences, and these spoil their fun. Indeed no O'Neill character has a really good time for long. O'Neill himself is far too morally earnest to take anything very lightly. In this fact, of course, lies his power as well as his limitations.

With all his moral earnestness he has no central ethical position by which to judge his characters. He has the aspiration for faith, but not the faith itself. He cannot achieve the exaltation of heroic tragedy, because he cannot wholeheartedly believe in any character or cause. He has powerful desires and antipathies, but no creed. (In saying this I speak without knowing the end of his career: that may find him even in the bosom of Mother Church.) He has great emotional power, but intellectually he is bewildered and fumbling. He finds life a muddle; he leaves it a muddle. He is a typical modern.

Too often, indeed, the muddlement gets into the construction as well as the themes of his plays. *Desire under the Elms,* one of the most nearly tragic, starts as a study of greed, with tough, relentless old Cabot as a worthy protagonist—worthy because, though possessed as he is by lust of possession, he is a man of will. But, halfway through, the play turns off into the more alluring theme of sexual lust; old Cabot gets thrust into the background; and the ending asks us to feel sorry for Eben and Abbie, paramours and infanticides, because they have found spiritual love at last and are ready to take their medicine. This ending, though affecting, is trite and dangerously close to sentimentality, and it does not follow from the premisses. It makes an effective curtain, but the play falls in two.

A similar lack of logic from cause to effect was noted in *Beyond the Horizon,* which has a "tragic" ending only because the hero is gratuitously killed by tuberculosis, and it is again seen in *Anna Christie,* which on the contrary has a "happy" ending[7] in spite of probability. Lack of unity is most striking in *Strange Interlude,* which is held together through its nine acts solely by "unity of the hero"—or heroine, in this case. Of the situations, three or four distinct

[7] This it is for the mass of spectators, in spite of the author's intentions. See Barrett H. Clark, *Eugene O'Neill* (New York, 1927), pp. 63 ff.

plays might have been built. Though the events all concern Nina's "love life," there are several other themes that are too much stressed not to divert our attention to them. Much, for example, is said about "happiness" as the end of life. It is demonstrated that self-sacrifice is often of doubtful value. From Darrell's point of view the blind biological urge to procreation seems to be a modern form of Fate. The most powerful scene is that in which Nina exults over her "three men." Is possessiveness in love the theme, or a woman's need of several sorts of lovers, or the need of several lovers for the same mistress? Again, the play can be thought a study on the theme that what we call insanity is relative to the point of view, for the character with the insane inheritance is the most nearly normal of the lot. The play might, finally, be considered a study in the consequence of meddling with other people's lives. In short, the work is novelistic rather than dramatic—novelistic in its complexity, in its lack of strong central theme, in its length, in its experimentation with the aside to express thoughts, and in its presentation of character as acted upon rather than acting. Nina is the Biological Woman; her fate is in her glands. She is not a genuine heroine, because she does not will.

With a genius for the theater, a powerful imagination and even more powerful emotional force, O'Neill seems unable to canalize his energies into rounded works of tragic art. He suffers the conflict he symbolized in "Dion Anthony," but less between the flesh and the spirit in the medieval sense than between a longing for faith and a despair of it. Yet in one play at least—not to speak of the feeble *Days without End*—he has persuaded himself into a positive affirmation. This is *Lazarus Laughed*. Its symbolist technique forces attention upon the underlying theme. Only Lazarus is unmasked, and he is thus shown visibly free from the illusions of mortality. The rhythmical repetitions and symmetrical groupings of the choruses materialize ethical sympathies and antagonisms. And the theme is stated repeatedly: there is no death.

This sounds clear enough, but unfortunately when we try to understand what it means we are baffled. It cannot be the Christian belief in personal immortality. The resurrection of Lazarus would give ground for such a view were it not obvious that the author has taken over a Christian legend merely as a starting point for his non-Christian allegory. It is non-Christian in its concept of immortality; it is non-Christian also in its morality. The hero is not humble, but arrogant. For him, men are not evil until they shall be redeemed by the grace of God, but are innately good and are perverted simply by fear. (A variation on Rousseau, who thought that men were innately good and were perverted simply by social laws and restraints.) He thus incites men, not to love one another because they are children of a loving God, but to live passionately and instinctively. To be freed from the fear of death means for those who come under Lazarus' spell to go mad with delight in death. (To the Christian it meant living on earth according to the Golden Rule, to suffer in meekness and to forgive evil.) Lazarus makes people laugh with exultation at the prospect of personal annihilation. He cries: "Once as squirming specks we crept from the tides of the sea! Once as quivering flecks of rhythm we beat down the sun. Now we reënter the sun! Cast aside is our pitiable pretense, our immortal egohood, the holy lantern behind which cringed our Fear of the Dark. . . . We will to die!" Like Jeffers, O'Neill here tries to pull himself out of humanity by rhapsodizing over the fact that physically we are a part of evolutionary nature.

Jeffers, however, never laughs about it. Whence does O'Neill derive his mirth?

Perhaps from Nietzsche. I summed up the latter's idea in *The Birth of Tragedy* as "an intoxicated joy in self-annihilation and union with nature." And significantly it is just after he has made an attack on Christianity that Nietzsche urges us to laugh about this annihilation. We must not look for comfort, he tells us, like a Christian.

No! ye should first of all learn the art of earthly comfort, ye should learn to *laugh,* my young friends, if ye are at all determined to remain pessimists: if so, you will perhaps, as laughing ones, eventually send all metaphysical comfortism to the devil—and metaphysics first of all! Or, to say it in the language of that Dionysian ogre, called Zarathustra:

"Lift up your hearts, my brethren, high, higher! And do not forget your legs! Lift up also your legs, ye good dancers—and better still if ye stand also on your heads! . . .

"This crown of the laughter, this rose-garland crown—to you, my brethren, do I cast this crown! Laughing, have I consecrated: ye higher men, *learn,* I pray you—to laugh!"

It indeed needs intoxication—of one Dionysian sort or another—to roar with glee at the necessity of abandoning all hope of immortality beyond the immortality of the electrons that we are composed of. Physically we are made of stardust, which will go on dancing eternally. Apparently we should be delighted at the prospect of dissolving our living complexity back into it.

TRAGEDY AND FAITH

Such ideas do not—for most of us, at least—give a hero spiritual stature, much less a spiritual victory in spite of a physical defeat. And if tragedy depends for its lift mainly on one or the other, tragedy would seem impossible in a time when the poets consider themselves mere parts of an insentient machine. Power over words, skill in dramaturgy, passion, imagination—all are essential for the tragic poet; but they are not enough. He must believe in something spiritual, and his audience must believe in it too.

Spiritually this era is desperate. Science, to be sure, no longer holds to the crude mechanistic materialism of the last century, and sometimes grows almost mystical over the new principles of indeterminacy and relativity. Nonetheless it binds us to physical necessity. If the movements of electrons are indeterminable individually, their effects in the mass are just as predictable as ever; and there is nothing in the new physics, so far as the layman can see, to weaken the iron grip of mechanical law upon the macroscopic world. Furthermore, the consequences of science in the world of industry and commerce have enormously increased our mutual interdependence and our difficulty in coping with the complexities and powers which it has generated. We are forced as individuals to become parts of the vast mechanism of society, and whenever a part of that mechanism gets out of gear, as happens often through the acts of self-seeking and cruel men, we all suffer. Our machines which we so childishly admire bring hell upon us when bad men run them. They have increased our power millions of times—and it is used for evil. Wars used to be isolated phenomena which permitted some men, at least, to lead civilized lives; now they barbarize us all. Even in those who remain physically untouched the capacity for pity becomes anesthetized when wholesale torture and death are the commonplaces of the daily news.

Thus the modern man sees himself not merely a part of the mechanical order of nature, but also a part of a humanly constructed but inhuman machine of social necessity. The personal spirit of the individual grows less and less important because its relative power and freedom decrease from day to day. Yet under these circumstances such is our need for faith and hope that some of us try even to find virtue in the very monster that destroys us spiritually, and succeed in feeling religious ardor for creeds promulgated by tyrants. And not all those creeds were discredited by the defeats of 1945.

We can now see how much the tragedy of the past depended upon humane religion for the maintenance of an atmosphere of spiritual freedom. Dramatists, and indeed all artists, needed to breathe that air in order to live, and needed it none the less that they were usually unaware of it. Now it is failing us.

Though we shrink from our predicament, we ought to face it. This is one thing the great tragic poets all did. And facing it, they found resources of virtue and beauty in man. That is the supreme gift of tragedy to a desperate era: not comfort in hope of heaven or in shifting our moral responsibilities to divine shoulders, but the assurance that our souls can meet anything fate may bring, and that duty is not less binding on us because not established by divine authority. This, indeed, is exactly the lesson that humiliating defeat and the experience of tyranny has taught some younger dramatists, as witness Jean Anouilh's adaptation of *Antigone,* produced under the Occupation.

Such heroism, however, is only for those who will greatly. A war brings out and demonstrates this capacity in many, but even they relax when the battle is over. Unfortunately the spiritual battle of human goodness against human brutishness is never over, and in that fight we can never afford to relax. After World War I we thought we could afford it.

Now, we know better. We no longer think that progress is the inevitable consequence of accumulated things and more and more inventions. Now we know that our inventions may destroy us all. The danger is not in them but in us who use them.

The theologians who once talked about the "old Adam," "original sin," and the general ease with which man slides down to hell, were much more realistic thinkers than the prophets of scientific progress. But if the lesson is unpalatable in terms of ancient Hebrew mythology, it can be applied in terms of modern Freudian mythology with its psychic strife between the "id" and the "superego." Or it can be applied from the plain, concrete findings of physiology, that tell us how the primitive brain of our brutish forebears continues to function in us, only partially overlaid and controlled by the thinking, "human" cortex.

What human nature turns to, when unchecked, ought, in 1946, to be obvious. The medieval triad of lusts sums it up: the lusts of the flesh, the lusts of the mind, the lusts of the will. And in this diabolical trinity the greatest is the last. Our strongest natural impulse is toward power over others, and in any period of anarchy, spiritual or material, such as developed after 1918 in some parts of the world, what invariably dominates the confusion sooner or later is the cruelest and most cunning of its "strong men." The end of anarchy is tyranny.

This is a book about the drama, not about morals or religion? If the evidence we have offered has been sound, great plays are fundamentally concerned with morality and religion, and tragedy has a message directly applicable to the present crisis of civilization. The nobility of the human struggle is the inspiration of tragedy from Aeschylus to Ibsen. And if modern poets can shake off the corruption of nihilism and once more assert the tragic faith, they may again be capable of writing great tragedy. Can there be any brighter beacons amid our darkness?

CHAPTER IX

The Modern Drame

IBSEN

THE MAJORITY of modern drames have not aspired to the height of tragedy. Neither have they sunk so low as primitive melodrama. They are of a middle sort, made to suit a middle-class audience. They have been predominantly bourgeois, like modern society.

For the past hundred years most of these plays have had in the main similar characteristics. They have been neither imaginative nor stupid, neither idealistic nor vicious, morally serious but concerned with local rather than universal issues, and based on limited and often crassly materialistic ethics. They were written for people who still generally worshiped God on Sunday but Mammon the rest of the week.

The younger Dumas, who dominated the French theater during the 'sixties and 'seventies, well represents this bourgeois type. Technically he wrote "well-made plays" which differed from those of Scribe in being adapted for social preaching rather than light entertainment. He supplied witty lines and comic effects to amuse his audiences, and scenes of calculated brutality to shock and thrill them; but generally he built his plots to demonstrate some social thesis.

In order to make sure that no one should miss the point of this thesis, he provided a *raisonneur* who moralized about it as the author's mouthpiece.

His plays were the chief models for younger playwrights. Brieux, for instance, author of *Damaged Goods* and other journalistic preachments, is in the direct line of succession. One sees traces of the tradition in the work of even so carefully objective and artistic a dramatist as Galsworthy. If we allow for changes in subject matter and an increased sense for realism, it is still the pattern followed by most dramatists of serious purpose, including "leftists" who despise the bourgeoisie. On the whole, this type of play preserves a tone of sober realism and depends on strong identification for its effect.

To the student of the drama these conventional plays are much less interesting than the less common ones that experiment with new techniques and effects and so enlarge the scope of dramatic art. We should not, of course, admire novelty just because it is novelty or despise the conventional pattern merely because it is conventional or because the majority of the plays that have used it have been mediocre. So far as it goes it is an excellent pattern. It is the result of centuries of dramatic experience; and considered simply as a pattern and without reference to subject matter it is the norm of dramaturgy, for it requires dramatic economy, classic plotting, and unity of effect. There is no reason why a great dramatist should not still use it, and every reason for believing that few great dramatists will succeed notably with plays that disregard its rules. At the same time, the vigorous imagination and vital themes which we expect of a great dramatist usually stimulate him to original forms of expression, not for novelty's sake (as with a minor playwright) but because his material requires them. And of experiment, for whatever reason, there has been vastly more in recent times than in any other period. It reflects the complexity of the civilization which has produced it.

We noted mixtures of emotional effect in Shakespeare, but mixtures of effect are peculiarly characteristic of the plays that express our confused and complicated era, and it is only natural that many of these plays should run a gamut from farce to tragedy. Thus Sean O'Casey's *Juno and the Paycock,* we are told, brought Dubliners to tears but succeeded in London as farce. And in their efforts to express the variety of modern life, playwrights have tried out every sort of technical device, borrowed from the Oriental stage, revived from ancient drama, or invented.

Contemporary audiences have been so trained by these experiments that few theatergoers are now unpleasantly disturbed by the most unconventional techniques as such, or the most violent mixtures of effect. The conventional pattern is no longer considered the only right way, as it was in the 'nineties when W. T. Price wrote his book on playwriting, or even as late as 1912, when William Archer's *Play-Making* appeared. There is no longer a Sarcey to browbeat writers and public into conformity. If the playwright likes, he can use expressionist puppets and symbols. Or he can call for a bare stage. Or he can pass off a circus clown as a tragic sufferer, as Andreiev does in *He Who Gets Slapped.* Playgoers have become tolerant of methods. All they demand is dramatic results.

They are, however, more difficult to please in the latter respect than their grandfathers were. (I speak here of habitual playgoers and not the movie-trained spectators who unfortunately are the majority except in a few large cities.) They are used to seeing more than one side of a question, and understand something of those subtleties of motivation which psychoanalysts call complexes, transferences, and sublimations. Hence they are less easily satisfied with a manipulated "happy ending" or ill-motivated heroics. They are even hardened to perversions which until recently could only be studied in the Latin of professional monographs, and enjoy seeing them dramatized. (At a performance of Mordaunt Shairp's *The Green Bay Tree* a few years ago, when the young man's final succumbing to homosexuality was symbolized in the scene in which he arranges lilies in a vase, I was interested to hear a sweet, grandmotherly old lady behind me exclaim, "Huh, those flowers ought to be pansies!") But they are not so sure of themselves or of the moral foundations of society, and hence do not respond so readily to simple pieties. They are more sophisticated, but morally they are at sea.

In the bringing about of this greater sophistication among playgoers the influence of the novel must be taken into account. Since the eighteenth century it has been the dominant form of fiction, and has nearly always been far ahead of the drama in reflecting the latest thought concerning human nature and society. It has the scope, flexibility, and range that are needed for exploration; it is not dependent on group approval; it can be bolder than the drama in treating dangerous topics because it does not show things visibly; it is relatively inexpensive to produce. It is thus the medium *par excellence* for experiment. And it is the chief means of educating young people to understand man and society. We generally fail to take it as seriously as it deserves in this respect. Young people read novels not merely for recreation but for vicarious experience through which their views of life are formed. As they grow older, such fiction is likely to grow less interesting to them, either because it no longer tells them new things about human nature or because it no longer seems to tell them the truth. (The same, though on a less sophisticated plane, is to be remarked of the movies.) We may think that our understanding of our fellows is based on actual experience, but much of our actual conduct as well as our ideas about ourselves is modeled on fiction. Since fiction has developed greatly in subtlety, boldness, and psychological penetration in the last fifty years, audiences are far better prepared for these qualities on the stage.

But not all the advance is due to the novelists. Some dramatists also have been pioneers, and fully as subtle, bold, and penetrating. It is these who have brought the drama to enjoy almost the novel's freedom in subject matter and a greatly increased range in technical method and device. Of them, three are paramount: Ibsen, Strindberg, and Chekhov. Others have done some of the things they did, or some things they did not do, but none has had so far-reaching and revolutionary an influence. And as each of the three had a distinctly different approach and method, taken together they present a fairly inclusive picture of the outstanding developments of the modern drame. I wish to note the most significant contributions made by each. And first, Ibsen.

The common notion of those who know of him only casually is that he was chiefly important in developing the problem play, as in *A Doll's House* and *Ghosts*. If this notion were true it would be difficult to explain his superiority to Dumas, who did that and little else. But it is not true. As a matter of fact, he never merely agitated problems; as he himself vehemently declared, he was primarily a poet of human souls.

His technical innovations also are often emphasized above his themes. As the textbooks tell us, he suppressed the aside and the soliloquy; he omitted the first act of mere exposition and developed with extraordinary skill the art of weaving exposition into the forward action; he perfected the constructive artifices of the "well-made play" to such a point that they became fine art; he built plays of "ripe condition" which are the culmination of a long series of events and have the compression and unity of Greek tragedy. He turned the drama inward from conflict of soul with circumstance to conflict of soul with soul, and showed for the first time how dramatic a scene could be in which drab people in suburban households merely sit down and talk it out. He not only found the effective dramatic situation for these spiritual confrontations, but even the *mot de situation* of unforgettable trenchancy. (Pastor Manders. "Just think of it—for a paltry seventy pounds to let oneself be bound in marriage to a fallen woman!" Mrs. Alving. "What about myself, then?—I let myself be bound in marriage to a fallen man.") Finally, in his growing inwardness he delved deeper into the hidden roots of motivation than any other dramatist, and to show these findings he dramatically pioneered the technique of poetic symbolism.

These are great achievements, yet in my opinion they are less fundamental than what he did in treatment of theme and character. He had only a few things to say, but he felt them so profoundly and said them so powerfully that their reiteration in play after play is not monotonous but cumulatively impressive. His work as a whole thus possesses an organic unity arising from these central ideas—a unity which can only be grasped when we have read all his plays and can see them in their mutual relationships, and which, once grasped, enriches and illuminates our understanding of each separate play. This unity was the expression of his own character, and can best be understood by a study of the man himself.

He was a poor boy from a pious Lutheran family in a little provincial Norwegian town. By temperament he was thin-skinned and introverted, imaginative and brooding, bold in thought but too self-conscious and slow to be bold in action. He had a deep love of beauty and a longing for affection, but his own temperament and the harshness of his early environment thwarted any easy satisfaction of these needs which might have taken him out of himself. His mother was a zealous pietist. He never accepted her faith intellectually; but it profoundly affected his character. He seems to have always felt subconscious guilt for having refused it, which would explain his excessive zeal in playwriting. And it trained his will to extreme individualism and self-assertiveness, his conscience to an equally extreme self-searching and doubt, and his imagination to extreme ethical idealism. With the emotional habit pattern of a Protestant preacher of the most evangelical persuasion, but without the preacher's faith, he first tried to find a substitute faith. Failing, he grew disillusioned and bitter, and at length desperate. But all his life he was the moralist, the stern searcher of souls, the searcher—above all—of his own soul. He tells us so.

> What is life? A fighting
> In heart and in brain with Trolls.
> Poetry? that means writing
> Doomsday-accounts of our souls.

But Ibsen was no weak neurasthenic, for with all his gloomy introspection he was very much a man of will and penetrating observation. His will drove him to become a master dramatist and to devote fifty years to writing plays. His observation saw through the pretenses and unconscious hypocrisies in his own nature and in those around him. Thus he saw things in human hearts that few till then had been keen or brave enough to see, and, years before psychologists like Freud, disclosed them, with crushing honesty and objectivity, for those who could read the riddles of his later plays. He hid these esoteric revelations from the casual playgoer because audiences then would not have tolerated them; but with sly subtlety he wove into his plots double meanings and sardonic ambiguities which the initiated could see. His pleasure in this duplicity is recorded frankly in the sculptor Rubek's remarks about his art in *When We Dead Awaken*. (That Rubek speaks for Ibsen as well as himself is, I think, proved by the close parallelism between

Rubek's career and that of his creator—a parallelism so exact that it must have been carefully intended.) Behind my portrait busts, says Rubek, "there is something equivocal, something cryptic. I alone can see it. And it amuses me unspeakably.—On the surface I give them the 'striking likeness,' as they call it, that they all stand and gape at in astonishment—but at bottom they are all respectable, pompous horse faces, and self-opinionated donkey muzzles, and lop-eared, low-browed dog skulls, and fatted swine snouts—and sometimes dull, brutal bull fronts as well."[1]

Such insights are fascinating to the student of psychology, but in themselves do not make drama. They do so only when character is caused to struggle, and struggle to a conclusion. Ibsen's characters do this. He himself fought all his life against his private "Trolls," and his plays get their heat from his own conflict.

This conflict in him arose primarily between two strong and contradictory impulses of his nature: intense ambition, and intense moral earnestness and yearning for love. He never reconciled these impulses in himself, but he objecti-

[1] This aspect of Ibsen's art is explained with amazing thoroughness by H. J. Weigand in *The Modern Ibsen*, already cited. At first I was unconvinced by Professor Weigand's interpretation of such plays as *The Master Builder*. (He suggests, for example, that Hilda Wangel is a sexual pervert with an infantile fixation whose libido can be excited only by narcissistic and sadistic appeals, and who actually experiences an orgasm as the consequence of her exultation in her power over her hero, her vertigo, and her horror, when Solness falls from the tower.) Repeated readings, however, have only strengthened his interpretation, for there are too many points of confirmation for accident, and too few that are contradictory. Ibsen also supplied a conventional interpretation for the crowd to "gape at." Thus *The Master Builder* can be explained as a drama of *hybris* or overweaning ambition and *nemesis* or divine retribution. (It can be interpreted in a third way as a veiled symbolic autobiography.) But *all* the plays from *Pillars of Socitey* on can be interpreted consistently as naturalistic studies in psychology.

fied them in his characters and made them fight to more definite conclusions. Hence his plays are fiercely dramatic. They show us people who will, passionately and with high seriousness, and who struggle unremittingly.

This inner struggle between love and ambition is seen in his juvenile *Catiline* (1849), and in practically all the subsequent plays to the last, *When We Dead Awaken* (1899). Viewed as a whole, as recorded in the plays, it has two phases like a tragic plot: the rising action in which Ibsen strove to find a religious reconciliation, and which culminated in climactic failure; and the falling action, in which he faced the bitterness of his defeat and turned from the poetry of ultimate ideals to the prosaic analysis of particular falsities in the relationships of men and women. This analysis, unsustained by faith, led him gradually to such disillusionment and spiritual desolation that his courage in facing and expressing them dramatically, and his mental power in preserving his sanity and objectivity, are alike extraordinary.

The first phase culminated in his greatest dramatic failure, *Emperor and Galilean* (1873). This enormous work, unlike his later plays, was not written for production, but he put his whole soul into it, for he essayed no less a task than adumbrating a modern religion to supersede and reconcile the best in Greek paganism and Christianity. This ideal religion was called by the philosopher in the play "the third empire." The author succeeded in demonstrating the need of it—he himself was driven to seek it, in the hope of attaining spiritual peace,—but he failed in describing it because he did not really know what it was. His vague glimpses of it on the horizon turned, as he pursued them, into mirages. He could not reconcile free will with fate nor selfish ambition with altruism; neither could he give any of these antinomies up. His failure to found his third empire was the turning point in his career.

Thus he experienced in a peculiarly acute form the typical spiritual sickness of his time—the sickness that comes of loss of faith without a corresponding emotional adjustment. In dramatizing it he served his age in a much more serious way than by improving dramatic technique, for in so doing he objectified and made concrete many a conflict that was felt obscurely by multitudes of people.

The Protestant is a Christian who refuses to acknowledge above his own conscience any final authority but the will of God. So long as he believes in God he submits humbly to His will. But he is trained to the exercise of will more than the exercise of humility, and he runs the danger of rationalizing the prickings of unholy desires as voices from on high. He is, in other words, a spiritual individualist, and thus peculiarly liable to the sin of pride. Ibsen was just such a person, and moreover he no longer believed in God, so that his tendency to exalt his own will was unchecked by submission to divine will. He embodied his ambition, his idealism, and his exaltation of will in his character Brand, whom he referred to as "myself in my best moments."

Brand is a curious sort of preacher who goes about calling on the Norwegian peasants not to repent but to will, and not for the love of God but for the sake of an undefined ideal of unbounded individualism and spiritual anarchy.

This is not Christian doctrine; clearly not, for we have only to compare Brand's cry:

> "Be passion's slave, be pleasure's thrall,—
> But be it utterly, all in all!"

with Dante's line,

> In His will is our peace.

Nor is it Greek paganism, which preached, "Nothing too much; think as a mortal." Brand is rather a pre-Nietzschean "superman," inhumanly scornful of compromise even when compromise will save the lives of his wife and child, and madly insistent on pursuing his ideal regardless of consequences. Yet though Ibsen admired Brand and put much of himself into Brand's character, nevertheless when it came to the crucial point in the play he condemned him. This reversal of ethical attitude is sudden and unprepared for. It is as though the poet was forced in spite of himself to make it at the last moment. But it is unmistakable. At the end of the hero's life, after he has climbed the mountain seeking the symbolic ice church of the glacier, and is about to be overwhelmed by an avalanche, he cries in despair:

> "God, I plunge into death's night,—
> Shall they wholly miss Thy light
> Who unto man's utmost might
> Will'd—?"

And a Voice through the thunder replies:

> "He is the God of Love."

So, despite his scorn and pride and egoism, Ibsen became the poet of love. In play after play he says, in effect, that "the unpardonable sin is to kill the love life in a human soul." He puts these exact words into a character's mouth in *John Gabriel Borkman*. And that play also ends with the protagonist climbing symbolically in the snow, to die of a frozen heart.

To call Ibsen a "poet of love" may seem rather startling at first, for we do not associate his somber plays with the softer emotions. But love manifests itself in many ways, and Ibsen was the poet of love destroyed rather than love fulfilled. Something turned him again and again to this theme. He seems to have been happily married to a devoted and intelligent wife. If there were any incidents in his life that would account for his obsession, he was careful to hide them. But we do know the conflict in his soul, and we can guess the longing for the warmth of happy, uninhibited affection that was hidden behind his shell of peppery egotism. His was an abnormally shy, reserved personality, and exactly because of his inhibitions he was the sort of man to take with tragic seriousness what more normal people take for granted. And who shall say that his seriousness about the supreme value of domestic love was not justified?

We are more impressed at first by his scorn and indignation. Certainly he was no sentimentalist. His Protestant conscience made him rigid in telling the truth as he saw it; and he saw a great deal more of it, as respects the human heart, than most men. But his indignation is the negative expression of his idealism; and even after he gave up the search for a universal ideal he never forsook his faith that unselfish love between man and woman is the only lasting source of happiness.

Though his thought paralleled Nietzsche's throughout *Brand* until the sudden reversal at the end, he differed from the German in being too sane, honest, and good-hearted to follow an inhuman ideal, no matter how strongly he might admire it, when his intuition told him that it must end in spiritual destruction. His tragic protagonists pursue such an ideal in one form or another, with different degrees of intensity, and their downfall is in proportion to the rigor of their pursuit. After Brand come the Emperor Julian, Hialmar Ekdal, Rebecca West, Hedda Gabler, Solness, Borkman, and Rubek. And those who find in Ibsen's themes little that is important for our time might consider what the world has since endured as a consequence of such inhuman ideals of ambition and dominance as Ibsen pictures and condemns.

Love, not egoism, must dominate a life. This is the positive affirmation which Ibsen's plays imply and which they demonstrate with increasing force when the rest of his hopes and aspirations dissolve away in the acids of disillusionment. It is the central meaning of his entire work, and his treatment of it is so elevated, so skillful, and so imaginative that no word less than "poet" is proper for him.

Brand failed because his spiritual pride destroyed his love. Peer Gynt was saved or respited, perhaps, because he retained in his evasive soul some remnants of love for his faithful Solveig. Bernick saved himself not merely by public repentance but by freeing himself from hypocrisy and so becoming capable of genuine love for his wife and son. Love cannot really develop in an atmosphere of make-believe and lies, as Ibsen shows in *A Doll's House*. When love is impossible, the laws of church and state that prevent divorce ought to be broken, as he demonstrates in *Ghosts.* (In both these last-named plays self-fulfillment is only right because it makes possible a true marriage.) The hero of *An Enemy of the People* declares that "he fights best who fights alone," but Dr. Stockmann is strong because he has the love of his wife and daughter to sustain him. And he has this because, unlike his brother, he has never forfeited it through selfish ambition.

The Wild Duck, as we saw earlier, marked a recoil from these affirmations and a second turning point in Ibsen's thought. Such idealistic solutions as he had heretofore worked out are possible for exceptional persons alone. Extreme idealist as he was, he was slow and reluctant to admit this obvious fact, and *The Wild Duck* suggests the bitter disillusionment that he felt in admitting it. To admit it meant that he had no real justification for his indignation, which for some time had given his plays their drive and vigor. Yet admit it he did, and he showed in this play that ordinary mortals must be sustained by "life lies."

After his loss of hope in the "third empire," his art had derived its main force from moral indignation. If ultimates were beyond him, he seems to have felt, at least there could be no doubt about the evil of hypocrisy, cowardice, selfishness, and deceit that pervade society. But finally he came to see that most people are hypocrites or cowards or selfish because they are too weak or stupid to be anything better. He therefore grimly turned to the task of adjusting his ideals to a harsh world of human animals, and to view mankind biologically.

This readjustment was extremely hard because he was so extreme an idealist. For many of us today the view that we are merely animals is so familiar that we grow up adjusted to it, but the peculiar poignancy of most tragic writing of the late nineteenth century, as we see it for instance in Hardy, lies in the discord between the writer's inbred concept of man, Christian in its origin, and his mature intellectual view, forced upon him by contemporary science. Ibsen was less philosophical than Hardy, for, like the born dramatist he was, he thought almost wholly in terms of concrete personalities, but he nonetheless conveyed the torture which this discord caused him.

Indignation has no place in a biological view of man, and the preacher's fire burned out in Ibsen. But with it went the joy that he had felt in combat. He was growing old, and seems to have believed that he had given up the one good thing in life for ambition's sake. The time had passed when he could get a childish gratification from wearing a frock coat weighted with decorations. Famous and honored and rich as he now was, the cold was clutching at his heart. After his final return to Norway, he wrote in 1897 to his old friend the Danish critic, "Here all the sounds are closed, in every acceptation of the word. . . . Oh, dear Brandes, it is not without its consequences that a man lives for twenty-seven years in the wider, emancipated and emancipating spiritual conditions of the great world. Up here, by the fjords, is my native land. But–but–but! Where am I to find my homeland?"

The cold clutched also at the hearts of the protagonists of his last plays. Rosmer is sexually as impotent as an old man, and so is an easy prey to the "sickly conscience" that drives him and Rebecca to suicide. Hedda kills herself as a consequence of having refused and perverted love. *The Master Builder,* from one point of view, is a veiled allegory of Ibsen's career. It shows a man who has denied God and who in gaining his ambition has destroyed his home. In *Little Eyolf* Ibsen sardonically presents a pious fraud, Allmers, who under an impressive cloak of moral sentiments is a sexual recreant, unconsciously incestuous, and a self-absorbed hypocrite. Borkman dies of the cold that follows his sacrifice of love for ambition. And, for a third time, *When We Dead Awaken* repeats the allegory of *Brand;* but Rubek is condemned from the very beginning.

Incidentally, this symbolic climb to the heights obsessed Ibsen's imagination throughout his life. The first clear statement of it, indeed, is found in a narrative poem called "On the Heights," written in 1859 or 1860. The hero of this poem is led by a cold-eyed stranger to desert his mother and sweetheart and live on the mountains where "from above life's line of snow . . . 'twas mine a higher light to attain." The ambivalence of ambition and love in Ibsen's mind at this time is indicated by the strange and ironical ending.

> Parched are the veins where a flood tide ran,
> And I surely find, when my heart I scan,
> All symptoms of petrifaction.

Yet:

> Up here on the fells must be freedom and God,
> Men do but grope, in the valley.

To return, these last plays show love defeated, and therefore fail to give audiences the emotional lift that makes ordinary drama popular and tragedy great. Yet merely to condemn them on this account is to miss Ibsen's peculiar significance to modern drama, for his predicament is in essentials the predicament of every thinking modern who is unsustained by faith, and particularly the predicament of the multitudes who have lost the faith of their fathers without finding another.

Faced with the biological view of man, Ibsen did not snivel or evade, but bravely told the truth, and he never gave up his ideal of human love. If his successors fall short of him, it is not chiefly because they lack his technical skill, though most of them do. His characters *will:* they put up a fight. And they fight for their souls, whereas too often the characters of contemporary dramatists merely scramble to satisfy their biological impulses. He can still teach them more important lessons than tricks of exposition or symbolism, and the chief ones are that the exercise of will is the essence of great drama, and that men become human by loving unselfishly.

CHEKHOV AND NATURALISM

Ibsen's influence on modern drama is so immense and has been exerted in so many ways, technical, thematic, ethical, that it cannot be simply defined. Chekhov, on the other hand, wrote only five major plays, all of which are developed in the same manner and convey much the same emotional effects. He came a generation after Ibsen, yet finished his work before Ibsen died. (His dates are 1860–1904; Ibsen's are 1828–1906.) He can therefore be dealt with more briefly.

In attempting to account for a great writer's originality critics are often tempted to make too much of his personal experiences, but the fact that Chekhov was a practicing physician by profession and a writer rather by avocation seems of primary importance. It means not merely that he was well informed about human beings on the physical side, and richly supplied with intimate glimpses into many lives at moments of crisis and self-revelation, but also that his approach was from the first biological rather than ethical as was Ibsen's, or political, or literary. It is not apparent that he had any such struggle as Ibsen did in adjusting himself to the world of late nineteenth-century thought. Though he came of a pious family he seems not to have been deeply affected by piety or indeed by any general faith or doctrine, but rather to have kept to a view that was skeptical and detached. He wanted to show life, not to preach about it.

It is never to be forgotten in any study of Russian writers that they all lived (and still live) under strict and dangerous censorship. Except for Tolstoy, whose position put him to some degree above the law, they could not say all that they thought. But there is no evidence that Chekhov wanted to. His temperament and training fitted him to be an objective depicter of life—"an impartial witness," as he called it. He therefore came by his naturalism apparently without struggle, intuitively rather than theoretically.

His achievement may not at first seem so wonderful as it was. He had written short stories or sketches of people as he knew them, with much humor and delicacy of understanding and pathos, but with little plot. When he turned to the drama he employed the same methods in the new medium.

He cared little about the techniques which were then expected of a playwright, for he detested the stage as he knew it, with its artifices and midcentury conventions that still repeated outworn romantic tricks in an age of science and skepticism. Either from distaste of the traditions of dramaturgy, or from ignorance of them, he chose to write plays in his own way. The miracle was that these plays, composed in a new and revolutionary manner, were produced and were successes. Chekhov found intuitively the right technique for dramatizing the naturalist's view of life.

Zola had advocated a naturalistic drama, but, when he tried to write it, was unable to avoid the dominating nonnaturalistic traditions of the French theater. Henry Becque, whose *Vultures* (*Les Corbeaux*), 1882, is sometimes called the greatest naturalistic drama of the century, derived his technique mainly from Molière. In Germany, Gerhard Hauptmann began his dramatic career with a painstaking attempt to put the theories of naturalism into practice; but *Before Sunrise* (1889) depends considerably more on plot contrivance and chance than on the scientifically determined causality that naturalistic theory demanded. In Germany also, as in France, older traditions were too strong.

But not so in Russia. There the traditions of the West existed only as importations, and a strong vein of realism had already been brought into the theater by Turgeniev, the novelist, whose play *A Month in the Country* (1854) is novelistic in method, and by the dramatist Ostrovsky. Chekhov had their example to go by, but he also had what was probably more influential in determining his methods—his own practice in writing tales and sketches.

So, calmly, and without seeming to realize that he was doing it, Chekhov deracinated dramaturgic traditions. For example:

1) "A play must have a protagonist." There is none in *The Three Sisters* or *The Cherry Orchard,* in which interest is divided among several characters; there is scarcely one in *Uncle Vanya* or *The Sea Gull,* the leading characters of which are too weak to dominate the action.

2) "A play must have a plot." Since a plot, in the technical sense employed in this book, requires a hero who wills, it follows that Chekhov's plays lack plot. None of his chief characters is an active agent in the traditional sense; all are passive drifters, acted upon by circumstance. Hence the formula of will, struggle, and catastrophe, even with liberal interpretation, does not fit their stories. Of his first long play Chekhov wrote, "Such men as Ivanov do not solve questions, but sink under their burden." This sentence applies to all the rest. Treplev (in *The Sea Gull*) wants to be a dramatist, but stops the performance of his play in a pet because his mother, an influential actress, laughs at it. He loves Nina, but since Nina loves Trigorin and is broken by Trigorin's desertion he can find no way out but suicide. In *The Cherry Orchard* Madame Ranevsky and her family must choose between selling off their estate in building-lots or losing it entirely through foreclosure. They do nothing at all, and the play ends with the sound of the axes cutting at the trees. The three sisters in the play of that name, and their brother, long to escape from their country town and go to Moscow, but none of them does anything about it. Uncle Vanya, bitter at Professor Serebryakov, who for years has

been a parasite upon him, tries to shoot him, but, as might be expected of a Chekhov character, misses. All that comes of this act of hysteria is that the professor hurriedly departs, leaving Vanya to sink back into the old routine. Except for one or two minor characters like Lopahin in *The Cherry Orchard,* all Chekhov's people are ineffectual. (For that matter, even Lopahin can't make up his mind to propose to the girl he loves.) They dream, talk, confess themselves continually in public, drink, flirt a little out of boredom, but never act. The only violence they commit successfully is self-destruction. The plays are studies in frustration.

3) "The dialogue and action must conform to the law of dramatic economy." Nobody in a Chekhov play seems to forward the action, such as it is. On the contrary, each character spends his time in egotistical self-absorption or hopeless yearning. Characteristically the dialogue is not about something to be done or faced, but is rather a series of self-revelatory monologues cut up in alternate speeches. One's interlocutor interrupts momentarily but scarcely disturbs one's train of introspection or reminiscence. These people do not listen; they merely think aloud. As their thoughts flitter from one thing to another, they change the subject without warning. At times they fall silent (a most revolutionary thing for the stage of Chekhov's time). Just as their minds wander on and off the subject, so their bodies wander on and off the stage without apparent dramatic occasion. They seem to be living their inconsequent and will-less lives before us.

4) "A play should have a unity of some kind." These heroless dramas lack unity of action, for there is no central action

strong enough to hold our attention. They also lack a dominating emotion, for nobody in them is ever strongly passionate or even merry. Instead, there is much facile weeping and childlike shifting of mood, as if the characters all suffered from manic-depressive psychoses complicated by mild dementia or neurasthenia. At the end of the first act of *The Sea Gull,* when Masha tells Dorn that she is unfortunate in love, the latter cries, "How hysterical they all are! How hysterical! And what a lot of love.... Oh, the sorcery of the lake! But what can I do, my child? What? What?" He knows no answer. There never is an answer. Instead of a single mood, the plays convey the effect of moodiness.

Do these four items cover the main ways in which Chekhov violates dramatic tradition? They certainly should suggest to anyone unacquainted with his plays that such compositions ought to be failures on the stage. Yet of course they are not failures. When well acted and produced they are extraordinarily moving. Miracle is not too strong a word for Chekhov's achievement.

But they must be perfectly performed. The audience must have a deep identification, a convincing sense of the individual reality of each character. Chekhov's greatest art lies in making each a distinct individual, not merely with such-and-such surface habits and mannerisms, dress, and appearance, but with a definite past that explains him, and definite abilities—or disabilities—and desires. Masha is Dorn's illegitimate daughter; she loves Konstantin hopelessly, takes snuff, dresses in black ("in mourning for my life"), and drinks vodka. Gaev, though aging, is still a spoiled though amiable child, hopelessly ineffectual in consequence, and continually retreating from unpleasant realities into play. (He is always playing billiards in fancy: "Cannon off the red.") Dr. Astrov is a defeated idealist who finds some small outlet for his ideals in cultivating his hobby of reforestation, but who drinks too much in order to forget. Some peculiarities scarcely rise above the gags of farce, as for example Epihodov's awkward mishaps and Charlotta's unexpected tricks of magic. Yet, though they may amuse an audience transiently, they must not be merely farcical; they must seem on the contrary to rise inevitably from real character, and to convey overtones of pathos.

One device that Chekhov uses successfully to gain these pathetic overtones is sound effects. There are constant directions in his plays calling for off-stage singing, ringing of bells, and the like. Stanislavsky was inclined to overdo them in his first enthusiasm, and led Chekhov humorously to say, "In my next play I'll make the stipulation: 'The action takes place in a land which has neither mosquitoes nor crickets nor any other insects which hinder conversations between human beings.' "[2] But, well done, these sounds of the life surrounding the characters lend, even to their trivial actions, a sort of special lyricism and significance.

The seeming aimlessness of the action puts a great burden on the actor, for he must appear not to act but simply to be. Yet all the while, of course, he must really be acting, and acting so perfectly in character, and in such perfect synchronization with his fellows, that the illusion of actuality is never shattered. This drama calls for teamwork or en-

[2] Quoted by V. I. Nemirovitch-Dantchenko, *My Life in the Russian Theatre* (Boston, 1936), p. 162.

semble acting of the highest perfection, and entire subordination of the star's ego to the role.

The Moscow Art Theater learned these difficult arts in trying to play Chekhov, and as a consequence taught the Western world a new way of acting. This influence has been immense, and it continues to grow wherever there are still active groups of serious theater artists. As actors and directors began to appreciate and produce plays in this fashion, dramatists began to imitate Chekhov. There was Clifford Odets, for example, before he went to Hollywood. Even within Chekhov's lifetime his pupil Gorky wrote his one great play, *The Lower Depths,* in the Chekhov manner.

Thus Chekhov achieved the nearest approach to pure naturalism ever likely to be seen in the theater. His success will hardly be duplicated, because it depended on several special conditions which are unlikely to occur together again. First, he himself was objective without inhumanity, skeptical without bitterness, compassionate but at the same time humorous and disillusioned, and above all a very sensitive artist with the tact to avoid the wrong effect and the imagination to throw poetic charm about his action, so that the frustrations of his characters are never merely boring or depressing. Second, he wrote of a society under a tyranny, in which the villainy or heroism of an individual was crushed by the all-pervading weight of governmental oppression. We thus find his pictures of ineffectuality almost tragic because we feel that his men and women could not be otherwise than they were. The tyranny, never mentioned, never seen, but always behind their acts, is the real antagonist; and because of this fact their futilities are pathetic rather than silly or despicable. Third, his plays were produced by a great acting company the directors of which put the fulfillment of the dramatist's intention above every other consideration.

The Soviet regime at first swept away the conditions that made such plays right, for it gave Russians new hopes and outlets in action. They ceased to be dreamers because they had something that they could do. Soviet plays at once became traditional in developing heroic protagonists, struggle, and triumphant denouement. Many of them, indeed, were crudely melodramatic. And it would seem that in any society where there is a sense of freedom and hope, even if illusory, and where there are practical things to be done, plays will be built in the traditional manner.

To some degree such plays can be naturalistic. They can show people in real surroundings, acting from convincing motives, talking in actual dialect, and so on. But the naturalistic theory that fiction should imitate the formlessness, incoherence, and indifference of life cannot be followed when people want positive heroes and purposeful actions on the stage, and when conditions make heroic effort plausible and inspiriting.

At the same time, Chekhov has shown that sometimes naturalistic dramas can achieve the effects of great art. He has thus immeasurably enlarged the scope of serious drama.

STRINDBERG AND EXPRESSIONISM

Though expressionism has already been discussed in other connections,[3] it is so difficult to explain that it needs further

[3] See, in chap. iii, "A Classification of Plays According to Illusion," pp. 88 ff., and, in chap. v, "Unity of Feeling: The Synthesis of Incongruities," pp. 177 ff.

discussion here. (The best course for anyone unacquainted with it is to begin by reading three or four expressionist plays such as those mentioned below.)

The movement had its chief source in Strindberg's plays of the 'nineties, but got its name and flourished mainly in Germany shortly after the First World War, when the defeated nation was in a mood for a drama of disorder. As a fad it lasted only a short time, but it has enlarged the technical equipment of modern drama generally, so that its peculiar devices are often used in new plays without causing much surprise or difficulty.

Since the term loosely covers a great variety of technical experiment, includes thematic elements such as Marxian or pacifistic propaganda, and varies among such styles as allegory, satire, fantasy, would-be tragedy, and farce, no simple formula will adequately fit it. But one fact seems of paramount importance, and that is its effort to represent concretely on the stage what happens inside a character's mind. To do this the expressionists revived traditional devices and developed new ones. They revived asides and soliloquies, for example, but with the difference that theirs are usually incoherent like actual thought. Symbolism also is nothing new, but they used it in startling fashion to indicate mental states, as when the skeleton tree in *From Morn to Midnight* suddenly turns into a human skeleton while the absconding cashier soliloquizes under it. Again, they reverted at times to the technique of the moralities by personifying abstractions in order to express their own revolutionary attitudes; but in keeping with the general spirit of anarchy pervading Germany at the time, these personifications are not clean-cut presentations of moral or political concepts, but are labeled vaguely as, for instance, "The Gentleman in Black" or "The Unknown One."

The element of revolt against things as they are, without any clear idea of what they should be, is present in most of these German plays. Toller's *Man and the Masses* is a familiar example. The author hated war and capitalistic greed, but feared the violence inevitable with revolution and seems to have doubted the justification of any cause which requires bloodshed. He was thus caught in a dilemma. The nightmarish effect of many of these plays can be explained in large part as due to the spiritual distress and frustration of their writers. (In 1939, Toller, a refugee in this country, committed suicide.)

Technically, these effects are gained by some very distinctive methods. The dialogue, for example, tends either toward a telegraphic style of exclamations and cries, or toward long-winded rhetorical harangues like those in Kaiser's *Gas.* The setting does not remain unchanged through orderly constructed acts, but shifts frequently as in dreams. (This is sometimes called "cinema technique," but Strindberg developed it long before the movies.) Distortions and deformations of visual and auditory images are resorted to in order to show reality as seen through a disordered mind. (Of course this could be done more easily on the screen, as in *The Cabinet of Doctor Caligari.*) Though the story may follow a general plot pattern, the motives that actuate the characters are often inadequate or unexplained and their actions are in consequence startling, unexpected, and violent.

This dream quality suggests that expressionism may also be viewed as actually an extension of naturalism. Naturalism began by representing outer reality photographically; in expressionism it sought to represent inner reality. The earlier naturalist wanted to show "a man of flesh and bones on the stage, taken from reality, scientifically analyzed, without one lie."[4] The expressionist tried to show a man's thoughts on the stage, in accordance with the modern psychology that emphasizes the instinctive urges which motivate them, and their flowing incoherence. Though the expressionists lacked Zola's zeal for scientific objectivity, their efforts are in this sense a development of the tendency which Zola championed.

The transition may be noted in Hauptmann. His earliest plays were unremittingly realistic, but in *The Assumption of Hannele* (1893) he mixed realism with vision. A little girl, dying of starvation, ill-treatment, and exposure, is brought into a poorhouse and put to bed. Throughout this introductory scene everything is brutally naturalistic, down to the squalid bickering of the indigents. But then Hannele becomes delirious; and all at once we must shift our point of view entirely, for her dreams are enacted on the stage. The nurse who cares for her is transformed into her dead mother; the schoolmaster, for whom she has an adolescent crush, into the Angel of Death and later into Jesus. Her wishes are symbolically fulfilled. Her fear that she has committed the "unpardonable sin" is assuaged by celestial reassurances; her longing to be admired and to punish the

[4] Zola, "Naturalism on the Stage," in *The Experimental Novel and Other Essays* (trans. by Belle M. Sherman; New York, 1893), pp. 142–143.

girls who despised her at school, by a Cinderella dream; her love for the schoolmaster, by a dream in which he mourns over her bier. Her cruel father is condemned to hang himself by none other than Jesus (the schoolmaster), and she herself is welcomed as a saint into heaven. Though the play was much criticized for sentimentality, it seems to me a very objective portrayal of a child's mind. The dream distortions, substitutions, and wish fulfillments are just such as a girl in Hannele's condition might have; also her very unsaintly vanity—pitiful though it is—and her vindictiveness. Even the language, in its pompous mixture of the Biblical and fairy-tale styles, is the language of a schoolgirl.

The audience of the time was not prepared to appreciate all this, but psychologists and psychoanalysts have since then better educated us. They have also influenced the expressionists, who have utilized at times a good deal of such psychological naturalism. *Hannele* is a sober, loving study of a child's mind; it has no startling incoherences or stylistic tricks, and may even be considered an adaptation of the medieval dream technique. Hence, though it shows how easily a naturalist can slip from the objective to the subjective world, it is not a direct influence on the expressionists. They, no doubt, were more indebted to Ibsen and Maeterlinck for symbolic devices, and to abstractionist painters for visual distortions of outer reality. They certainly owed a great deal to Wedekind.

Frank Wedekind (1864–1918) led a varied, traveled life in such capacities as journalist, press agent, private secretary, and actor. Although he had a strain of heavy Teutonic humor which shows in the grotesque features of his plays, he took himself with intense seriousness. He revolted against what he considered the tame domesticity of Ibsen and Hauptmann, and by reaction from their sober dramaturgy gave his own violent fancies free rein. These fancies were mainly colored by his obsession with sex, which led him to deal dramatically with even the most horrible perversions. The consequence was plays like *Spring's Awakening* (1891), *Earth Spirit* (1895), and *Pandora's Box* (1902).

In the last two plays men and women are represented as mere animals actuated by primal sexual impulses; love is consequently lust, and the relations of the sexes a brutish struggle. Having this point of view, Wedekind naturally scorned subtleties of characterization and delighted to make his creatures talk and act with galvanic abruptness and acrobatic violence. His heroine Lulu, the "earth spirit" of sexual attraction, robs men of their thin clothing of civilization and reduces them to a menagerie of lustful brutes. After she has been the cause of a long series of male deaths by suicide and murder, which are the main matter of the two plays, she herself is finally killed in a London brothel by Jack the Ripper.

Spring's Awakening is less brutal and more pitiful, but technically it is more startling. It is a somber study of adolescents trying to adjust themselves to sex while kept in ignorance by adult prudery. Though audiences were shocked by it at first, German educators actually used it later on as a sort of tract against the "conspiracy of silence." It is important in this context, however, on account of its technique. It is constructed in a series of short, loosely connected scenes, some of which are fairly realistic but others wildly fantastic. These fantastic ones were direct models for the expressionists. For instance, the scene at the school boardroom shows a group of teachers whose actions and speech are mechanized and stylized for crudely satirical purposes, as though they were so many puppet caricatures. And in the final scene at the graveyard the boy suicide arises from his grave with his head under his arm (he had blown it off) to engage in a cynical dialogue about life with a "Masked Man." (This scene is the obvious source for the similar one in *The Adding Machine.*)

The Russian eccentrics, Evreinov and Andreiev, may also have had some slight influence on the German expressionists. Evreinov's *Theater of the Soul* was produced in 1912. In this play the setting is inside the heart of an amorous professor, who himself, in a prologue, explains in lecture style to the audience that he is suffering a conflict of desire for his wife and a dancer. The interior of his heart is appropriately lighted in red; and when at the climax the professor shoots himself, red streamers of blood burst inward from the bullet hole. Andreiev's work is more deeply imaginative, and at times expresses powerfully his profound and bitter pessimism. His plays were not all extravagant in form, but *The Black Maskers* (1908) can match anything in this respect. It seems to have been inspired mainly by Poe's story, "The Masque of the Red Death," and Poe's lyric, "The Haunted Palace," from "The Fall of the House of Usher." The play might be interpreted, as a whole, as a very elaborate expansion of the symbolism of "The Haunted Palace." In that poem the destruction of a fair human spirit through madness is allegorized in terms of a beautiful palace (the human face) through the "two windows" of which travelers could at first observe

> Spirits moving musically
> To a lute's well-tunèd law;

but later

> see
> Vast forms that move fantastically
> To a discordant melody;
> While, like a rapid ghastly river
> Through the pale door,
> A hideous throng rush out forever,
> And laugh—but smile no more.

But in the play this main theme—if this it be—is obscured by all manner of incongruous and inexplicable details. The Duke Lorenzo invites many guests to a masked ball, but the guests are all inhuman, either mockingly like his wife and friends or demonic in shape and conduct. Later the duke meets his double, and one of his two selves kills the other. (Perhaps Poe was again the inspirer, with his "William Wilson"; perhaps Andreiev got the notion from the *Doppelgänger*—ghostly counterparts of living persons—affected by German romanticists.) In general the effect of the play is entirely subjective; it is a dramatized nightmare.

The Life of Man (1906), though a painstakingly obvious allegory, at times takes the audience inside the protagonist's mind by such devices as the weird and silent chorus of phantoms in the closing scene when "Man" dies. *He Who Gets Slapped* (1915), Andreiev's most successful play, though on the surface objective, strongly suggests a subjective interpretation through symbols and enigmatic remarks.

Even if we share the author's reported ignorance of what it all means, we know that it is intended to be more than a mere melodrama about circus clowns and acrobats.

It is, however, from August Strindberg (1849–1912) that expressionism most fully stems.

This extraordinary genius wrote some plays of fairly normal character, but his significant influence has been due to his abnormal ones. These are extremely subjective. Indeed, Mr. V. J. McGill was able to write his long biography, *August Strindberg, the Bedeviled Viking* (1930), almost entirely on the basis of the but slightly veiled autobiography contained in his subject's stories and plays. Such a method of getting information for a life would be wholly indefensible if the subject were almost any other story writer who ever lived, but Strindberg made no bones about the fact that his fiction was drawn directly from experience. Indeed, he wanted people to know it, especially when he was by this means telling off those who had formerly been his friends or wives (he was married three times) and whom he later hated. He got a vindictive satisfaction out of such amiabilities as picturing his first wife, for example (in a transparent disguise of fiction), as an adulteress, a Lesbian, and a "vampire."

Under these circumstances it is amazing that his plays should have been successful, for they violate the general principle that a drama should be objective. This is a principle which we have not discussed before. It requires of the dramatist, more than of any other creator, that he must portray his characters as individuals in their own right, undistorted by his personal passions and prejudices. The main reason for this is that the characters must be impersonated by living actors on a stage and therefore take on a much more definite and separate existence than is necessary in merely written fiction. Furthermore, a play cannot depend on the charm or power of style or subjective fancy as a novel can do. The general validity of the rule is supported by the evidence of literary history. Lyric poets are by definition poets of self-revelation and hence least likely of all literary folk to write good plays. There have been exceptions, like Shakespeare, who was both lyrist and dramatist, but the nineteenth-century romanticists certainly prove the point. Almost all of them tried to write plays and failed, though many of them shone in lyric poetry. On the other hand, successful playwrights avoid mere autobiography in their plays. Their moral judgments, as we have seen, are generally clear and often emphatic, but they keep their private affairs to themselves. Strindberg is the exception. But he does not wholly disprove the rule. Outside of Scandinavia his influence has been little felt in the theater, but mainly through the printed page.

We found that we gained a fuller understanding of Ibsen's plays when we understood his mental conflicts. In drawing upon his personal life, however, Ibsen always rigidly objectified it by embodying it in characters and actions distinct from himself. There are no known autobiographical touches in his characters or plots; at most there are similarities and parallels; even Brand, Dr. Stockmann, and Solness are thoroughly externalized individuals. Strindberg, however, often identified himself in whole or in part with his protagonists, and composed his plots out of his own experience.

His father was a man of good family who years before had taken a waitress as a mistress, and who married her just before the boy was born. Strindberg's childhood was passed in a squalid poverty which forced nine people in the family at one time to herd together in three rooms. His mother was ignorant and neurotic, and preferred another of her sons to August. His futile yearning to win her affection gave him an emotional fixation that he never overcame. At the same time, he recognized her inferiority to his father, who had aristocratic blood and cultivated tastes. But his father was a stern disciplinarian. Thus arose an irreconcilable conflict in the boy: he loved and despised his mother; he hated and admired his father. Freudians would call this an "Oedipus complex." The ambivalence and violent conflict of these passions set up a war in his soul that continued fiercely throughout his life.

School, to his maladjusted temperament, was torture. As he began to mature he developed morbid fears and introversions. His mother died when he was fourteen, and he could not accept the stepmother who soon took her place. His feeling of inferiority led him to extravagant overcompensations of self-assertion. These in turn led him to fits of groveling and despair.

He was always swinging from one extreme to its opposite, as Mr. McGill tells us: from atheism to pietism; from aristocratic snobbery to socialism; from scientific naturalism to Swedenborgian mysticism. Emotionally he was always driven by an unsatisfied and unsatisfiable longing for his mother's love, and hence he continually sought women and idealized them in pursuit, but always after winning them suffered from a disillusionment that turned to hate and scorn. He developed paranoiac suspicions of his wives and his friends, scenting plots, unfaithfulness, and treachery. He dreaded insanity, and for a time was actually insane. (He wrote up this experience, like everything else.) He had megalomaniac ambitions and grandiose fancies about himself. In reaction from these he passed through moods of abject self-abasement. His exacerbated and frenetic temperament allowed him no rest, but drove him to drink and debauchery that aggravated his neuroses.

Yet he lived a long life and wrote and wrote, enormously. No doubt his ability to write up and publish his troubles served as a purge for the poison in his spiritual bowels.

The most familiar of his fifty plays, *The Father* (1887), shows a married couple whose hate of each other is their chief motive for existence. They illustrate his thesis that love between the sexes is strife. The man is a superior being, a scientist as well as a military officer, whereas the woman is ignorant and superstitious. The man acts from principle, the woman from instinct. And it is because of the male's superiority of intellect that he is less stable emotionally than the female. She leads him to suspect that he is not the real father of his daughter, then baits him until he throws a lighted lamp at her. This deed of violence enables her to have him declared insane, and the play ends as his old nurse mothers him like a baby and at the same time slyly slips a straitjacket over his shoulders.

To the public of the time the play was so brutal and outspoken that it was classified on this score with *Ghosts, The Power of Darkness*, and Zola's novels as a piece of thoroughgoing naturalism. Yet none of the plays in this group is strictly in accord with Zola's theories. Tolstoy's comes closest to them in form, but was written for the moral ending. Ibsen's masterpiece was ethical in theme and highly unnaturalistic in construction. And *The Father* is not naturalistic (in the strict Zolaesque sense) either in form or substance. Formally it is a remarkable piece of dramaturgy, being almost flawlessly unified, swift, smooth, and powerful in its onward march of events. Because it makes a strong impression of spontaneity, as though its author had conceived it as a whole like a dream and written it down in the first flow of inspiration, one does not think of it as having been composed, like Ibsen's plays, yet it is built with logical and convincing motivation, strict dramatic economy, and tremendous climactic effect. And in substance it is so clearly autobiographical that it cannot be considered a piece of objective observation such as Zola wanted. I cannot agree with Mr. McGill and other critics that in this work and *Miss Julia* Strindberg created the naturalistic play. On the contrary, its subjectivity foreshadows expressionism.[5]

Zola is reported to have objected to the way in which Laura and the Captain philosophize about themselves. Laura is certainly not naturalistically inarticulate, as we should expect a stupid, ignorant woman to be. And much of the time the Captain is not talking in his own person, but for his author: to an appreciable degree he is the author. Through his mouthpiece Strindberg psychoanalyzes himself: "My mother, who did not want to bring me into the

[5] This is the view of C. E. W. L. Dahlström in *Strindberg's Dramatic Expressionism* (Ann Arbor, 1930).

world because I was born with pain, was my enemy when she deprived my embryonic life of its nourishment and made a weakling of me. My sister was my enemy when she taught me that I was to be obedient to her. The first woman I embraced was my enemy, for she gave me ten years of illness in payment for the love I gave her. My daughter became my enemy when she had to choose between me and you. And you, my wife, you have been my arch-enemy, because you never left me till I lay here lifeless."

To be exact, it is necessary to distinguish two kinds of subjectivity that apply to our problem. One, the kind which has just been illustrated, is the projection of the author's personality into his creations. (In the broadest sense, of course, no author can create except from himself, but the distinction here drawn is between creations which so far as we can tell "live" wholly in and for themselves, like real people, and those which are more or less projections of the personality of the author.) The other subjectivity was discussed earlier as characteristic of the expressionists: it was the projection of the thoughts of a character onto the stage in some concrete manifestation. There is none of this second kind of subjectivity in *The Father*. But the expressionists often indulged in both kinds; and with Strindberg indulgence in the first kind led to an impatience with the restrictions against unlimited self-analysis and autobiography which were imposed by traditional objective methods of the drama, and hence to experiments with new techniques which should free him from these restrictions.

In *The Dance of Death* (1901), a two-part drama, a similar married couple try again to torture each other to death.

This work lacks the earlier play's dramatic strength of construction; it is diffuse, repetitious, and, as Mr. McGill remarks, overlaid with mystical Swedenborgian symbolism. It clearly shows the transition to an overt dramatic presentation of the author's inner life.

This last we find fully developed in *The Dream Play* (which was discussed in chapter v). But the trilogy *Toward Damascus* (1898, 1904) is even more fully expressionistic because the reader cannot be sure on which plane of reality, dream or waking, inner or outer, the action takes place. It is in fact a mixture of nightmare and allegory, with disconcerting touches of realism. Its characters are abstractions called The Stranger, The Lady, The Physician, and so on. The Stranger is Strindberg, and the action, incoherent and allegorical though it is, tells after a fashion his own "journey to Damascus"—his struggle up from insanity and sin to sanity and (at least temporary) peace through religious conversion. Various figures in the play resemble each other, suggesting that they are merely the author in different phases. The critics see the influence of Swedenborg again in the concept of hell as being a place where the damned attain their desires only to find them misery. Following Swedenborg also, Strindberg used natural phenomena symbolically to suggest spiritual significances. The Stranger has powers of telepathy and clairvoyance, in which Strindberg believed. And the stage directions call for expressionistic effects as in *The Dream Play:* symbolic settings and properties, transformations, significant effects of sound and light.

Here for the first time the drama transports us completely inside the mind and shows the "stream of consciousness" without rationalizing it into artificial order and coherence. This was the notable achievement of expressionism, for it enabled a dramatist to deal with the subjective world directly, as the novelist does. The pessimism, anarchy, and madness so common in the movement are at first its most striking characteristics, but they are not inherent in it as a dramatic technique. Because of these plays dramatists can now use this technique for quite different ends.

Scarcely any play is more unlike these Strindbergian nightmares than, for example, Marc Connelly's *The Green Pastures* (1930), with its tender, humorous, and elevated vision of the Biblical tragedy; yet technically it is expressionistic. Its entire action is the Biblical narrative as distorted through the simple minds of Pastor Deshee's class, and consequently has much of the fluidity and free fantasy of dreaming. It is expressionism pruned of its extravagances and eccentricities; but the play could hardly have been written had its author not first tried his hand at such thoroughgoing expressionism as *Beggar on Horseback* (1924, with G. S. Kaufman). Since *The Green Pastures* is surely one of the finest plays of our century, we may conclude that the art of drama has been greatly aided by the extensions of its scope made by Strindberg and his followers.

THE SCOPE OF MODERN DRAME

We find few pure comedies and even fewer pure tragedies among modern plays. Even pure farce is comparatively rare, worse luck; and melodramas are usually disguised by pretensions to serious theme or manner. The majority of plays are mixed in effect, and in this respect mirror our increased psychological subtlety and sophistication, the complexity of our society, and the uncertainty of our attitudes toward human ends. The unsatisfactory word "drame" must stand as a general label for them.

Technically, playwrights have explored what seems to be every avenue toward enhanced dramatic expressiveness. Ibsen perfected the French technique of economical construction, welded it firmly to important themes, and enriched it with poetic symbolism. Chekhov found a way to make dramatic the casualness of ordinary life. And Strindberg brought the stream of consciousness upon the stage.

In subject matter, dramatists have been even more adventurous. Ibsen made the first and most powerful attacks against taboos in bourgeois society, but even Ibsen in his last plays felt constrained to hide his biological view of man behind a conventional disguise. Chekhov's material seems unrevolutionary at first, but it was no mean achievement to move audiences by the soul-searchings and frustrations of little people. Strindberg and the rest of the expressionists boldly treated all manner of things previously considered impossible on the stage.

Besides these men I may now mention a few others who have moved the boundaries outward.

I think Shaw has demonstrated that intellectual discussion is effective in drame as well as in comedy. The last act of *Saint Joan,* for example, which seemed to me when I first read it not only out of tone with the rest of the play but hopelessly undramatic, proved otherwise on the stage. There—at least in the Katherine Cornell–Guthrie McClintic production—it seemed, on the contrary, and very powerfully, with extraordinary ironic poignancy, to enhance the tragic quality and enlarge the significance of the action. It had the effect of a Greek chorus put at the end instead of interspersed. Even such abstract debate as this can be made to contribute to dramatic art.

Lesser dramatists also have done good pioneering. There is the fantastic theater of Lord Dunsany. There are the disillusioned soul-searching and melancholy charm of Schnitzler, last great representative of the dying civilization of Vienna. There is the Freudian melodrama of H.-R. Lenormand. There are D'Annunzio's sadistic eroticism and lush romanticism; there is Martínez Sierra's feminine delicacy; there is Giraudoux's style; there is Hauptmann's Dutch genre painting in *The Beaver Coat*. I name but a few striking examples of the variety to be found. The reader can add to the list.

Before I conclude, I should like to say something more about two other writers of drame whose work seems to me outstanding. They are Pirandello and Jean-Jacques Bernard.

Luigi Pirandello (1867–1936) was a Sicilian, and had what his biographers consider the Sicilian's sudden passionateness. At the same time, he had a marked capacity for restraint and objective observation. Like Ibsen, Wedekind, and Strindberg he suffered from mental conflict, but it took a peculiar form in his case—between the emotional life and that of the intellect. As we see his personality through his writing, it seems as though his capacity for reflection and analysis existed separate from and above the rest of his being, like a disembodied spirit, with something of a spirit's lucidity of vision but with a very human and incessant curiosity. Hence the strange juxtaposition in his plays of a wryly comic detachment with an intense and sometimes almost tragic emotion.

Though he is hardly a great dramatist, he deserves to be recognized as one of the most original. We can trace some of the influences on his work—from the *commedia dell'arte* and from Ibsen, for example—and cite a few other playwrights, such as the contemporary Italian "grotesques" and Shaw, whose plays have similarities of one sort or another; but there is nobody really like him, and probably never will be.

To understand his plays we must begin with his philosophy, because his plays are concrete demonstrations of it. To him life is a short and bad dream in which our hopes and desires are generally frustrated, and in which there is nothing definite or unchanging except the ideal constructions of the mind, especially those recorded in fiction and history. These are permanent, but for each one of us they are unique. In the dream world which outer reality is for Pirandello, what seems real to one person is unreal to another. We are shut up in our subjectivity, and what we think is so, is so for us. Moreover, our desires drive us to interpret outer experience so as to flatter them: we construct the world, as it were, to conform to our wishes. Particularly, we construct a picture of ourselves as we wish to see ourselves; and this ideal "I" is for each of us his private reality, for and by which he lives. But the tragicomic irony of life (which Pirandello called "humor") is that no one else sees this "I"; others see us only according to their own private vision.

We cling to these images of ourselves, which have for us

a sort of permanence in a changing world. Hence to rob a person of his image of himself is to rob him of what makes his life worth living. Also, to think for oneself is to endanger the image; instinct, which builds it, is threatened by intellect, which undermines it. But instinct is often terrible in its dark passions through which the ill-subdued savage rises again, and intellect shrinks from seeing these passions as they are. Men therefore live behind masks, so to speak, so that when they look at themselves in a mirror they may not see themselves as they really are.

Pirandello's plays are elaborately constructed actions designed to bring about a sharp opposition between two or more of these subjective images of life, and to leave the audience puzzled to decide which is true. Reality, in fact, is what you think it. *Right You Are (If You Think So!)*—*Così è (se vi pare)*—is the characteristic title of one of the plays, which he calls a "parable," and which he ingeniously designed to prove the title. Signor Ponza lost his first wife in an earthquake, married again, and now lives in another city with his second wife and the mother of his first. He shuts up his second wife so that she and the old lady cannot meet face to face and can talk only at a distance. He explains that he does this because the old lady had been driven mad by the death of her daughter and now lives in the delusion that his second wife is actually his first. This delusion keeps her happy, but if the two women should meet this happiness might be destroyed. This is his story.

The old lady's is equally plausible—or implausible!—but directly contradictory. According to her, it is not she but Ponza who is insane—insane on this one point only! He is incorrect in thinking that his first wife, her daughter, was killed; it is *he* who has the delusion. He had been prostrated by the catastrophe, and after his recovery would accept his wife only when she pretended to be a different woman and went through the form of marriage a second time. Ponza is now pathologically afraid of losing her as he believes he lost his "first" wife, and so shuts her up for safety.

As all records were lost, no objective facts can be brought in to help one decide who Mrs. Ponza really is. The townsfolk, consumed with curiosity, finally force her to appear before them and declare herself. But her declaration, which concludes the play, only deepens the mystery: "The truth? The truth is simply this. I am the daughter of Signora Frola, and I am the second wife of Signor Ponza. Yes, and—for myself, I am nobody.... Whoever you choose to have me."

In other words, each person's subjective reality is as true as any other's, and objective facts are irrelevant. This is, of course, the dramatization of extreme subjective idealism, toward which Pirandello's philosophical studies in Germany appear to have directed him.

The first effect on an audience is to puzzle and amuse. The conclusion of *Right You Are,* for instance, seems merely a trick ending like that of Frank Stockton's famous story, "The Lady or the Tiger." Pirandello's ingenuities, moreover, force a spectator away from identification into a puzzle-solving state of mind. This might do no great harm if he were provided with a sufficient number of comic effects to keep him amused, but fundamentally Pirandello was too deadly serious to be really comic. Indeed, his passionate feeling sometimes communicates itself to us, strangely enough, in spite of the intellectual hurdles that he sets in its way.

"Henry IV" best illustrates this. The author called it a tragedy, and, in spite of everything, for moments a tragedy it becomes. It is the account of a man whose brain was injured by a fall from a horse in the course of a pageant in which he was acting the role of the eleventh-century German monarch. This accident fixed in his mind the delusion that he actually *was* Henry IV. He is allowed to live in the delusion, being provided a castle and servants trained to play roles appropriate to the emperor's entourage. But in the course of years "Henry" begins to grow sane and to know who he is. At the opening of the play he is visited by a group of people which includes the girl he loved, now a middle-aged woman; his former rival for her, now the woman's lover; her daughter, who resembles her as she had been at the time of the accident twenty years before; "Henry's" nephew, owner of the castle; and a psychiatrist. Their visit is to see whether the madman can be cured. To this end the psychiatrist devises a trick to confront him suddenly with both mother and daughter—his sweetheart as she has become and as she was, so to speak—and thus visualize for him the passage of time. The madman, however, is not mad, and has not been for some time. He has played his role lately from habit rather than necessity. He is now confronted with the choice of returning to the world, which in the twenty years of his confinement has gone on without him, or remaining in his "eternal masquerade," which, because it is history, cannot change. He prefers the latter, desolate though it is. There, at least, his ideal of womanhood

has not become despicable; his youth and hope have not gone forever. In the final scene he embraces the daughter as a salute to the image of his lost love, and kills the rival, who, he suspects, caused the accident in the first place. By this murder he is condemned to play the madman forever.

This summary may not be very clear to a reader who has not read the play, but it is much clearer and simpler than the play itself, which is complicated by a variety of matters not mentioned here and develops its action with tantalizing slowness. (Technically, it is a play of "ripe condition" in the style of Ibsen.) At all events, the summary should suggest at least that *"Henry IV"* does not have the plot of a conventional tragedy. Its ingenious series of contrasts—between the history of eight hundred years ago and the present; between the image of the mother as embodied in the daughter and the mother as she has become; between "Henry's" life as masquerade to others and as real to him—cannot appeal to us with that immediate emotion which is typical of tragedy; rather, they force us to a detachment prolonged through three acts unalleviated by comedy. Yet the queer fact is that in spite of these extraordinary handicaps the play ends on a tragic note.

I said that Pirandello was among the most original of dramatists. Perhaps my reason for that assertion is now evident. What could be less likely to arouse emotions of identification than such jugglings of metaphysical concepts? Yet because his mind worked in this way, because his emotions were genuinely engaged in these concepts, and because he had a genius for manipulating plot and constructing characters to embody and dramatize them, he succeeded. The result is, of course, a highly "impure" type of drama, emotionally speaking, but for this reason it is peculiarly modern. He could not have written so in an age of faith. Though his passionate metaphysics is not a common view even now, his pessimism and irony, his uncertainty of truth, his spiritual self-division, are shared by many thoughtful and sensitive people.

Pirandello has resemblances to the expressionists in his concern with inner experience, but he never uses the expressionist device of representing inner experience on the stage. The nearest he comes to it, perhaps, is in *Six Characters in Search of an Author,* in which these "characters," who had been created only in the imagination of the dramatist, are made to appear in bodily form. They are intentionally given a sort of independent life because they thus illustrate Pirandello's belief that such creations are more "real" and permanent than mere mortals. In this play, furthermore, there are four planes of reality: that of the "characters"; that of the stage director (the setting for the action is the stage of a theater during the rehearsal of another of Pirandello's plays); that of the actors when they attempt to play the roles which the "characters" explain to them; and that of the audience watching the play. These planes are cleverly contrasted and juggled about, but the author keeps each distinct. If we are confused at first, it is because of the complexity of the action, not because of any confusion in it. Unlike the typical expressionist, Pirandello never indulges in vague symbolism or irrationality. His premisses are strange, but on their basis he works out his intellectual demonstration with careful logic. Because of his extreme eccentricity Pirandello is likely in the future to be much more interesting to students than to audiences.

I wish to close this review with mention of a dramatist whose appeal, in contrast to Pirandello's, is normal, and who finds in familiar, simple subjects ample opportunity for subtlety and poetic feeling.

Jean-Jacques Bernard is one of several French dramatists whose work has been done in the main between the two world wars and whose characteristics are in general sober though imaginative realism, delicacy rather than vigor, and quiet rather than bitter disillusionment. Perhaps they illustrate the weakness, from a dramatic standpoint, of a civilization rich in tradition and refinement but deficient temporarily in masculine energy and will.[6] They certainly illustrate the high degree of French civilization. No other country could have produced or encouraged them during two decades after a holocaust of destruction. There was plenty of frivolity in Parisian theaters during those years, to be sure; but there were also audiences for plays that appealed only to the cultivated and perceptive, and theaters, unlike those in New York, that could afford to produce plays for such people alone.

Bernard is not a stylistic ironist like Giraudoux; he is interested in character rather than expression. He does not aspire to Racinean intensity like Paul Raynal, but he has equal psychological penetration with none of Raynal's

[6] The first French dramatic movement to come to notice since the war, "existentialism," calls for terse tragedy of will conflicting against will over moral issues, in the tradition of Corneille and the Greeks! (Anouilh's *Antigone* is an example.) It is too soon to judge this movement, but that it should go so counter to prewar cynicism and abulia is of great interest. See Jean-Paul Sartre, "Forgers of Myths," *Theatre Arts* magazine, June, 1946.

heaviness. He is less concerned with fantasy than Jean Sarment, who shows the influence of Pirandello in form but who lacks Pirandello's earnestness. He is unlike Lenormand in avoiding startling cases of the psychopathic. But he is no less sensitive to mood than Sarment, no less concerned with subtleties of motivation than Lenormand. Perhaps he is most like Charles Vildrac, whose quietly beautiful play, *The Steamship "Tenacity,"* has had some popularity with amateurs in this country.

Bernard gained critical attention some years ago with his theory of the "theater of silence." This is that "the theatre is above all the art of the unexpressed. It is less by replies than by the shock of replies that the deepest sentiments reveal themselves. Beneath the heard dialogue is an underlying dialogue to be rendered sensible."[7] This doctrine, which he would seem to have derived partly from Maeterlinck, is the direct antithesis of the classical theater of overt struggle and rhetoric, but it fits into the tradition of naturalism in seeking to render, on the stage, life as it might be observed. It goes beyond early naturalism, however, in being concerned with externals only as means to dramatizing the inner life of its characters. It has this last aim in common with expressionism, but it uses no extranatural means of dramatizing the life of the soul. We are not told what the characters think and feel, or shown it by elaborate symbols. We guess it, partly through the implications of their words but more through the implications of their silences. Bernard reached new extensions of dramatic expression by his skill

[7] Quoted by F. W. Chandler in *Modern Continental Playwrights* (New York, 1931), p. 247.

in the use of sentences broken off, topics avoided, concern with trivial objects such as a fan or a book, and, above all, noticeable silences when speech is expected. His is the art of nuance.

For subjects, he likes to choose characters who live in some sort of romantic fantasy or dream world, and he places them in situations in which this dream world clashes with reality. They thus undergo a conflict that by its nature is intangible, for the most part hidden, and even at times unrecognized by themselves. In *L'Invitation au voyage* (1924; called *Glamour* in translation) Marie Louise, a sheltered, dreamy wife of an adoring but prosaic manufacturer of shoenails, develops a neurotic crush for a business acquaintance of her husband's merely because he suddenly goes far away to the Argentine, which she pictures as a land of romance. She recovers herself when the man (never brought on the stage) proves on a return visit to be even more prosaic than her husband. The Argentine has rivers and skies like other places, and people like Frenchmen. "He said he was Vice-President of the Buenos Ayres Chamber of Commerce . . . the Buenos Ayres streets all run in a straight line, and that he never went to the theatre—" She had treasured, fetish-like, a Baudelaire and fan as mementos of him. Symbolically, at the close of the play, she puts these away.

The heroine of *Nationale 6* (*National Highway No. 6*) is a sensitive girl who sits at her window imagining romantic qualities and destinations for the motorists who flash by on the main route south. The highway takes a dangerous curve near by, and one day an accident there brings to the house two of these motorists, a young painter and his father, a middle-aged writer of popular romances. The girl promptly falls in love with the painter, but it is the father who is attracted to her. They are detained for some time in the house because of the accident, and the painter does her portrait. She misinterprets his idle chat during a sitting as a declaration, and her father prepares a celebration. The consequence is such embarrassment for both visitors that they hurriedly leave. Two weeks later she gets a postcard from them; her mother reports that the highway is to be moved away from the house to straighten out the curve: the romance is over. Now comes the readjustment. She and her father will raise chickens and rabbits "scientifically." Still romantic, she starts counting her chickens before they are hatched, but at least she is turning to a real occupation. She says that it seems as if she had been on a long journey and had just come home.

The mother in *Le Printemps des autres* (*Others' Springtime*) nearly loses her daughter's love because of her own passion for her son-in-law. It is never mentioned; she herself does not recognize its existence until the end; it is scarcely even symbolized. (When her daughter confesses that the young man and she are in love, in the first act, the mother quietly puts back her compact in her handbag.) The situation is resolved when the mother, finally forced to realize her own feelings, goes away and leaves the young couple alone. The essential drama in this play must all be inferred.

The plays thus far mentioned are gentle, touching, almost sentimental, rather than profoundly moving. There is stronger emotion in *Le Feu qui reprend mal* (*The Fire Slow to Rekindle*), 1921, an early work, which shows a returned soldier's jealousy of an American officer who had been quartered with his wife during the war. His morbid suspicions almost drive the faithful woman to accept a proposal that comes from the American by mail. But gradually the husband's war neurosis heals; he grows to realize her loneliness during the years of separation; the fire begins to burn again.... One critic wrote of it (I translate): "There is the sense of action, of vehement action, essential, decisive." Yet the rival never appears; the real action is beneath the surface.

Finally, there is *Martine* (1922), which, of all Bernard's plays I know, is his masterpiece. Here it is the man who is the romantic, and here as elsewhere the author shows how a person of this temperament evades genuine human relationships and responsibilities by escape to a dream world of wishful thinking. Julien is a well-educated young writer who at the opening has just been discharged from the army and is returning from the service on foot, in early summer, to the village where his grandmother lives. On the way he meets the peasant girl Martine. The summer day, the new freedom, and his artist's sensibility to beauty reinforce the drive of his long-pent sexual longing to throw him into an ecstasy over her naïve charm. He poetizes extravagantly about her, and she blooms in his admiration, taking it all in earnest. But shortly afterward he is visited by his former sweetheart, Jeanne, and immediately forgets Martine. (Jeanne "speaks his language"; she can cap a quotation from Chénier.) He marries Jeanne; Martine reluctantly marries her peasant lover; the wise grandmother dies; Julien leaves the village for good to live in Paris. Jeanne says that they will return once a year in memory of grandmother, on All Souls' Day. The play ends with Martine standing alone where Julien has left her, a peasant housewife shut out forever from her poet's world, murmuring, "On All Souls' Day."

There is sentiment in these plays, and in these brief outlines it may seem far too evident, but the author's attitude toward his sentimentalists is objective and just. Consider the cruelty of the young lovers toward Martine, a cruelty rendered the more poignant by being unconscious, especially Julien's despicable hankering after the old romance in the last scene, when Martine has married and begun to adjust herself to her village life and he insists on renewing all her painful memories.

JULIEN. Has there never been a moment in your life that you think of more ... tenderly ... than this? (*Martine's head droops.*) There has, Martine. Say that you have kept a corner in your heart for that beautiful July when we met upon the highroad. ... I shall never be able to think of it without something going through my heart.

MARTINE (*completely overcome*). Why do you say it? Oh, why do you?

JULIEN. Because I thought you'd forgotten.

MARTINE. I never said anything to you, Monsieur Julien. ... I thought you wanted me to forget. ... Then, what *do* you want?

JULIEN (*hesitatingly*). What do I want? ... Only ... only to know what you still think of ... of ...

MARTINE. What's the use?

JULIEN. Nothing.

MARTINE. Then if it's no use, why do you talk about it now? Aren't you satisfied yet with what you've done to me?[8]

Bernard's treatment is so delicate, sure, and revealing that he makes his simple actions extraordinarily moving. He shows us what naturalism can do when refined of grossness and directed toward the analysis of the souls of civilized people.

The extensions of dramatic boundaries made by writers who fire the big guns are easy to appreciate, but such exquisite refinements as these are likely to be overlooked. They do not draw "big houses"; they are not "smash hits." Under present conditions in this country, where the professional theater is almost entirely confined to one city, and is there a gamble rather than a legitimate business, nothing but a smash hit is considered worth bothering about. (I admit honorable exceptions, but this is the general situation.) We are not concerned here with the economics of the theater, however; we are concerned with the drama as an art. I may be justified, therefore, in closing this chapter with a dramatist whose art has been restrained to tell a simple tale with the deceptive simplicity of highly developed artistry. Without resort to the freakishness of expressionism or the melodrama of the psychoanalytical playwright, he has found means of making inarticulate emotions dramatic.

In this wide field of the modern drame, then, we find rich variety. But the field is wide rather than elevated. It includes many plays that are subtle, clever, fresh in observation, subject, or technique; but it seldom rises to poetry.

---

[8] From *Eight European Plays,* selected by Winifred Katzin (New York, Brentano's, 1927).

CHAPTER X

Drama and Poetry

THE POETRY OF ACTION

ONE IMPORTANT subject remains to be discussed—the relation of drama to poetry. It really involves two rather distinct problems: to what degree the drama is or can be poetry, and what poetic methods in verse-form and diction are best suited to modern tragedy. (I assume that these will be used for plays that aim at tragic effect.)

Is drama poetry? Is an eagle a bird? For many centuries, at least, the second question might well have been the answer to the first. Aristotle, the leading critic among the Greeks who originated the word poetry, deemed tragedy its highest form, ranking epic next, but scarcely mentioning the lyric. He declared that poetry is the "imitation"—or, as we should say, the imaginative representation—of human actions. It is not distinguished from prose by being in verse form (an idea even then current), "as if it were not the imitation that makes the poet, but the verse that entitles them all indiscriminately to the name." The poet, to Aristotle at least, was primarily a maker of plots. And we may infer from his treatment of plot that what he meant by the word *mythos* was not merely the skeleton outline of the events, but the dramatic action itself, viewed in its entirety.

This Greek view that the highest and fullest expression of the poetic impulse was to be made in epic and dramatic forms persisted through the centuries down to the nineteenth of the Christian era.

From Aristotle's distinction between poetry and verse it follows that a novel or a tragedy in prose, if of elevated theme and treatment, is poetry. But since novels and prose tragedies were not written until recent times, and since poetry till recent times had nearly always been written in verse form, the identity of poetry with verse became fixed in people's minds. Even Coleridge, who was in the main a good Aristotelian in his critical theory, declared verse essential to poetic effect, though he hedged a great deal coming to the point.[1] But the "man in the street" has no doubt on the matter: to him, verse = poetry; poetry = verse. This confusion in common usage is unfortunate. Verse is a matter of form; poetry, of spirit. Verse may indeed assist poetic effect, which is about all Coleridge's argument amounts to. But other devices of expression may assist it also; they may even make what any reasonable person would consider poetry, or at least very beautiful and powerfully moving literature, without verse. Thus ancient Hebrew poetry (as in Proverbs, The Song of Solomon, and Ecclesiasticus) employs elaborate parallelism, numbered series, and symbolism.

The rise of romanticism at the beginning of the nineteenth century involved a challenge to many classic views, and particularly to the one that tragedy (epic being seldom written) was the principal poetic form. Romantic poets, as we have seen, were notably unsuccessful in drama and

[1] *Biographia Literaria,* chap. xviii.

notably successful in short lyrics. Romantic critics, moreover, emphasized the expression of feeling as the prime function if not the end of poetry. Wordsworth declared that "all good poetry is the spontaneous overflow of powerful feelings." Poe urged that poems be short, "written solely for the poem's sake" (hence his appeal to later artsakists), and approximate in effect to music—an idea in which Pater followed him. Music has no definable meaning; hence poetry, according to this argument, "should not mean, but be." Hazlitt actually identified poetry with passion: "fear is poetry, hatred is poetry; contempt, jealousy, remorse, admiration, wonder, pity, despair, or madness, are all poetry." If we allow that Hazlitt was carried away by the rhetoric of his passage (he was writing a lecture), we still must admit that for him emotion is paramount, not action. To the romantic, poetry expresses the thrills of the poet's sensibility and is known by the responsive thrills of the reader's. In this spirit A. E. Housman recently described poetry as "more physical than intellectual," recognizable by its capacity to make the skin bristle and run a shiver down the spine.[2]

Thus the practice and theory of the romantic poets has led the public to think that poetry is the sort of verse which does not tell a story or convey a meaning, except incidentally, but which does express emotion—in other words, the lyric. And the narrative art of the last century has not done much to dispel this error. The immense popularity of prose fiction and the intensely prosaic nature of most

[2] The quotations are from (Wordsworth) Preface (1800) to *Lyrical Ballads;* (Poe) "The Poetic Principle" (1850); (Hazlitt) "On Poetry in General," in *Lectures on the English Poets* (1818); and (Housman) *The Name and Nature of Poetry* (London and New York, 1933).

novels, indeed, have helped to maintain it. The leading poets, moreover, failed at playwriting and generally scorned the novel. We have seen[3] how Gautier, the romantic critic, gave up the drama as hopelessly unpoetic after striving in vain against Scribe's popularity. The consequence of these changes is that today, in the average mind, the drama, which was once recognized as the leading form of poetry, is (1) never considered poetry, and (2) often not even considered literature. Barring Shakespeare, of course. But he is the one exception. Among people interested in the theater a play has come to mean merely a "script" or vehicle for the actors, which is likely to fail if handicapped by verse or high-flown language.

The traditional concept of poetry as primarily dramatic narrative is thus practically defunct. How foreign it is to our usage may be indicated by what seems to us the strangeness of Arnold's statement when, going back to Aristotle for his principles, he tells us that the "eternal objects of Poetry" are "actions; human actions."[4] This statement implies that the substance if not the form of a poem is dramatic. But every modern schoolboy knows that, on the contrary, great poetry is such things as Shakespeare's sonnets (not his plays, or at most only excerpts from them), Milton's *Lycidas* (not *Paradise Lost*, or at most only excerpts from it), Gray's *Elegy*, and the shorter verse of the romantics from Wordsworth to Yeats.

Responsible critics also say just about this. Max Eastman, for instance, boldly (or naïvely) undertakes to reverse the plain meaning of the *Poetics*. "Drama was regarded as a

[3] Pp. 62–63. [4] Preface to *Poems* (1853–1854).

division of poetry by Aristotle," he informs us, "simply because prose dramas were unknown to him"! To this critic poetry is what "heightens consciousness," and dramatic effect is contrary to it because "the essence of all high narrative is anticipation, and the essence of poetry is realization, and they are opposed."[5]

In objecting to such an equating of poetry with lyric I have not the slightest desire to disparage great lyrics. God forbid! I simply wish to urge that the term should still be broad enough to include not merely lyrics that "heighten consciousness," but also those other works, representing human actions, which through twenty centuries were universally considered the preëminent forms of poetry.

Actually, of course, people still use the term poet when they speak of Shakespeare, who was unquestionably a dramatist, and they are often willing to apply the name to other dramatists who write successfully in verse. The real problem, however, is not a matter of names but of artistic effect, and the artistic effect of great dramas is clearly different in part from that of great lyrics. Anticipation has something to do with this difference, as we saw in our discussion of suspense; but Mr. Eastman's dictum is far too simple. We might better say that *the great lines of lyric poetry remain great when quoted alone, but the great lines of drama gain their chief power from their dramatic context.*

> While the still morn went out with sandals gray.

> In what distant deeps or skies
> Burnt the fire of thine eyes?

[5] *Enjoyment of Poetry* (New York, 1930), p. 107 and (last quotation) p. 111; *The Literary Mind* (New York, 1931), p. 169.

> The sedge is withered from the lake,
> And no birds sing.
>
> And beauty, making beautiful old rhyme.

Though lovers of lyric poetry will admit that individual lines like these, no matter how beautiful, are insufficient alone, and must be parts of larger wholes, nonetheless such lines are to them "pure poetry"—the magic perfection of literary art.

The drama lover, on the contrary, seldom thinks of lines when he remembers his supreme moments in the theater: he thinks of situations involving action. To mention a few instances at random from my own playgoing, I recall the "Emperor" Jones in the jungle staring horrified at the slave ship and the crocodile god; Anna's death in *The Lower Depths,* as performed by the Moscow Art Theater; the mysterious garret in *The Wild Duck;* Sister Joanna of the Cross, in *The Cradle Song,* kneeling in a passion of tenderness over the basket containing the foundling; the opening of the "Glittering Gate" in Dunsany's play of that name; Hamlet (as acted by Forbes-Robertson) watching the king hawk-like from the feet of Ophelia; the balcony scene in *Romeo and Juliet* (as played by Katherine Cornell and Basil Rathbone); Bessie Burgess with a baby carriage full of loot, in *The Plough and the Stars;* the reconciliation of the Queen and Albert after her jealousy, in *Victoria Regina* (thanks to Helen Hayes!); John Ferguson with the Bible on his lap; a brief interview between a father and his son, in *Our Town;* the last scene between the canon and the schoolmaster in *Shadow and Substance.*

Any drama lover could make his own list—which would naturally differ from this one. Whatever we recall, the impression was made not merely by what was said, still less by the rhythm or phrasing of what was said, but by the total impact of the dramatic action, including the physical setting and the physical presence of the actors. Furthermore, in the theater the rhythm or diction of the words has less power over our emotions than the peculiar resonance and inflection of the actor's voice, which alone for inimitable moments may give an almost unendurable beauty to lines which, on the page, move us but slightly. This is an art of the actor rather than the dramatist, and may at times prove nothing about the values of "script," as when Sarah Bernhardt—according to the current story—moved English audiences to tears by speaking French nonsense in a tragic tone. And if we consider drama as a form of poetry only completely expressed when performed on the stage, we should not exclude the actor's art. We may demand, nevertheless, that the lines themselves be genuinely moving, so as to withstand rereadings and analysis on the printed page. The power of all such separate scenes and effects as I have mentioned, however, is little except in their place in the drama. All the preceding action is needed to give each its peculiar significance.

Are these memorable experiences, not to speak of the total effect of a great play, "poetry"? Obviously they are something other than the poetry of words on a page; they are, if you like, the consequence of a combination of several arts. At the same time, they constitute the central beauty of the drama; and if a play may be called poetry when read, *a for-*

tiori it might be called by that name when experienced as intended, in the theater. It is not the poetry of words alone. *It is the poetry of action.*

Words, however, are primary agents in the total effect; they express fully what the rest of the action conveys imperfectly. In crucial lines the action is, as it were, distilled into its quintessence. Yet even then the words gain their power not from any magical excellence of phrasing or meter, as lines of lyric poetry do, but because they are "right" and "inevitable" in their dramatic context. We are always longing to find adequate words for our personal feelings, but we seldom succeed—at least not until too late. The retort that only comes to us on the stairs when we are leaving—the retort that exemplifies the *esprit d'escalier*—is the *esprit de situation* in drama: there the characters always find the right words in time. Thus Nora is able to reply, when Helmer tells her that no man sacrifices honor for love, "That is what millions of women have done!" Such happy brilliance delights us; it is a sort of wish fulfillment.

Such admirable effects are not limited to what we call wit or repartee. They are often most profound when they are simply and adequately the words the occasion demands. Thus, at the end of the scene in *The Green Pastures* in which "de Lawd" calls Moses away from earth, he speaks four simple words: "Come on, ol' man." In that situation, if I may trust my own experience on seeing and hearing the play, they are among the most moving of words, and culminate a scene of memorable beauty. But they are nothing in themselves. Their beauty is dramatic beauty: it arises (in part) from the pathos of man's mortality and his longing for a life hereafter and for belief in a loving God who will be, toward a faithful servant, like a father toward a son—thoughts which are not talked about in the play, but which are represented and implied by the action. Indeed the very brevity and simplicity of the words are exactly right here: they rouse our imagination to complete their significance.

Often, however, the dramatic line makes a comment on the situation or suggests its significance by symbol. Take the curtain line of *Liliom:* "It is possible, dear—that someone may beat you and beat you and beat you—and not hurt you at all." These words of Julie to her daughter are still almost intolerably moving to me years after I first heard Eva Le Gallienne say them, and after many rereadings. (And though I may be overly sentimental about them, it is not for being uncritical of their author, who, in my opinion, let himself be a poet just once, and for the rest of his career has written rather below than above the level of Noel Coward.) But these lines are little more than nothing in themselves; their emotional force derives from their comment on Liliom in the whole of his relationship to Julie, as we look backward over the play: his overt bullying and brag and toughness; his hidden, shamefaced tenderness; his blundering, ridiculous, but strangely heroic efforts to express his love. After sixteen years of "cleansing fires" the best he can think of doing for the daughter he has never seen is to steal something for her; and when she shrinks from him he slaps her. Yet—it was a star he stole; and she did not feel the blow.

Sometimes, indeed, the line reflects the universal significance of the action and may even stand alone as an aphorism. "Must then a Christ perish in torment in every age to save those that have no imagination?" These words of Cauchon in the epilogue to *Saint Joan* were for me the most memorable moment in the play: they moved me more than Joan's trial. (And no disparagement of Katherine Cornell is intended!) Yet, though they are meaningful, in themselves they would merely interest the mind, not rouse emotion. They derive their power from their place in the total action, as a statement in language of the tragic theme which until then has been shown rather than expressed.

These lines are in prose. Those in verse are no less dependent on the dramatic context. Webster's famous lines are dramatically, not lyrically, beautiful: Bosola's "Look you, the stars shine still"; or Ferdinand's "Cover her face; mine eyes dazzle: she died young." If we have not read *The Duchess of Malfi,* we may find them striking and rhythmical, but never strokes of poetic genius.

Shakespeare is quoted so much that a fresh impression of any of his plays is impossible. A consequence of our study of him in school, on the page, in snippets and quotations, is that we tend often to value his lines for themselves far more than for their dramatic beauty. And this tendency is encouraged by the fact that they are usually beautiful in themselves, like lyric lines, or pregnant with reflective significance. Sometimes, indeed, Shakespeare—unlike Racine—did not confine himself to purely dramatic poetry but yielded to the temptation to write lyrically. Such interpolated lyrical passages in dialogue (not to mention the occasional songs) are frequently very beautiful, and because we know and love them we applaud them in the theater. (Prospero's speech, "We are such stuff as dreams are made on," is an example.) But our pleasure in them does not make them dramatic, and if any less supreme master of language and dramatic interest should attempt them they would be obvious blemishes. Unfortunately for English poetic drama since Shakespeare, they have encouraged lyricism and rhetoric in it at the expense of dramatic beauty.

Intrinsic beauty may enforce dramatic beauty; it should never be a substitute. Too often the way in which Shakespeare is taught obscures this principle. Othello's magnificent self-condemnation is dazzling in its own right, but it is dramatic poetry because it sums up his tragedy and ends in his death:

> I took by the throat the circumcisèd dog,
> And smote him, thus.

And Shakespeare is even more the dramatic poet, I feel, with the touch of homely humanity that in lyric poetry would be bathetic but in its right place in the drama is sublime. Thus Lear's last lines:

> . . . Thou'lt come no more,
> Never, never, never, never, never!
> Pray you, undo this button.

Much confusion over the real nature of dramatic poetry would be avoided if students should keep this principle in mind: its power is derived from the circumstances in which the lines are uttered. "The true poetic drama," wrote Brander Matthews, "must be lifted up into poetry by the haunting beauty of its story, since it cannot be made truly poetic by any merely lyrical decoration."[6] The words become memo-

[6] *A Study of the Drama* (Boston, 1910), pp. 266–267.

rable when they are the lightning-like illumination of the human situation.

It follows, then, that whether they are in verse or prose is comparatively unimportant. Verse and elevated diction enhance dramatic effect when appropriate to the action; they may ruin it when inappropriate, as in the many closet dramas of poets who have failed to put action first.

VERSE IN MODERN TRAGEDY

Verse and elevated diction, we have said, may enhance dramatic effect. In what does their value consist?

"To me," says Maxwell Anderson (and Mr. Anderson is our leading American exponent of poetic drama; his opinions deserve consideration), "it is inescapable that prose is the language of information and poetry the language of emotion." By the word "poetry" here he evidently means verse, or metrical language, for he goes on to say that in "exceptional cases, as in Synge's and O'Casey's plays," prose "can occasionally rise to poetic heights by substituing the unfamiliar speech rhythms of an untutored people for the rhythm of verse." But prose can do this rarely. "Under the strain of an emotion the ordinary prose of our stage breaks down into inarticulateness. Hence the cult of understatement, hence the realistic drama in which the climax is reached in an eloquent gesture or a moment of meaningful silence."[7]

By verse we mean rhythmical language. Rhythm, according to our dictionary, is "regularity of recurrence." In this sense the word is used by musicians, and by people gen-

[7] Preface to *Winterset*, quoted from the *New York Times*, October 6, 1935.

erally; only literary critics indulge in such self-contradictory terms as "prose rhythm" and "free verse." They may if they wish, of course, employ words so as to destroy all definite meaning in them, but presumably even literary critics wish to convey thought when they write. And furthermore the chief theory offered to account for the superiority of verse over prose as the language of emotion rests on its recognizable pattern of recurring effects. This theory is that the regular repetition of accents in English verse, or of long and short quantities in Greek, or of rimes in French, has a hypnotic effect upon the ear. Our feeling of this regularity beneath the surface variety soothes and pleases us, as stroking does a cat. Our critical faculties are quieted, our sensibilities quickened: we think less and feel more.

This effect can be achieved, however, only so far as we are actually conscious of the rhythmical regularity. In primitive times, when verse was chanted to instrumental accompaniment, its rhythm could not be missed. A modern reader accustomed to verse can scan the lines on the page. A skillful public reader can make their meter perceptible to the ear. But modern actors face special difficulties if they try to do the like in the theater, for their first duty is to observe rhetorical stress, which cuts across the verse rhythm and obscures it. Indeed, the stronger the stress on the meaning of the words, the less is it possible to maintain that regularity of recurrence which, according to the theory, hypnotizes us into feeling.

Again, when we talk about verse in English drama, we mean, to all intents and purposes, blank verse. Iambic pentameters can be read so as to be unmistakable, but as read by most modern actors they are hardly distinguishable by ear from prose. Unlike his forerunners of Shakespeare's day, the modern actor is usually concerned to gain, first, an effect of naturalness. Furthermore, since blank verse is without rime, unless the actor pauses slightly at the end of each line a listener cannot tell when it ends. Finally, blank verse is so free with irregularities such as trochees and triple feet that it easily approaches the effect of prose.

Even Shakespeare's verse and prose are likely to sound alike to the ordinary man in the theater. I wonder how many of us, if we had not studied *Macbeth* on the printed page, would know whether the actress who plays Lady Macbeth is speaking verse or prose in her sleepwalking scene.

> Out, damnèd spot! out, I say! One; two:
> Why, then, 't is time to do 't. Hell is murky!
> Fie, my lord, fie! a soldier, and afeard?

I write this as verse, but the text prints it as prose. Yet is it such bad blank verse, so much less regular than much of Shakespeare's intended pentameters? In particular, *is it distinguishable to the ear?* The ear is the only judge of the dramatic power of measured language, for dramatic poetry is meant to be heard, not seen. Most of this famous passage cannot be forced into pentameters; it is, when we examine it, unquestionably prose. Yet is its poetic power the less for that?

If the importance of meter in Shakespeare is less than is often supposed, it is certainly very slight in Mr. Anderson's "verse" plays. Verse can logically be distinguished from prose, as we have said, only by having a recognizable prosodic pattern, but the nearest approach to such a pattern that I can discover in *Winterset* is a blank verse so much less regular than even Shakespeare's at his freest that if it were written in solid prose form a reader could never guess that it was intended to be verse, still less where each line (except the first) should begin.

> This is the glory of earth-born men and women, not to cringe, never to yield, but standing, take defeat implacable and defiant; die unsubmitting. I wish that I'd died so, long ago; before you're old you'll wish that you had died as they have.

Split this up into phrases, and each one is rhythmical by itself, perhaps; at least, it sounds well when delivered eloquently, which I think is what most people who talk of "prose rhythm" really mean. But it has no meter. It might be forced somehow into iambics, perhaps, but the English language, as is well known, naturally falls into iambics, especially in emotional passages; and Mr. Anderson might have come nearer to blank verse if he had not tried to write it at all. Or perhaps he was not trying here. If so, why does he break up his speeches into lines? To please the eye? But a play is written to be heard.

I am not overlooking the effectiveness of such a passage when well delivered; I am merely saying that whatever rhythmical effects it has are discontinuous and irregular, and that therefore they are not, in any exact sense, verse effects. Hence I believe that Mr. Anderson really gets his main heightening effect from his use of unrealistic diction. By this I do not mean merely conventional "poetic diction" after Shakespeare or the nineteenth-century poets, though

Mr. Anderson draws upon these sources frequently enough. I mean words of whatever sort the language provides and audiences understand, when they are unexpected, expressive, and emotionally congruous to the dramatic situation. Thus American colloquialisms, and even scientific terms, may prove poetically heightening in a drama if in their context they are vivid and "right."

Mr. Anderson, or any other poet trying to write a play on a contemporary theme, faces a dilemma here. Shakespearean or Biblical diction carries with it an elevated tone and dignity that are very desirable in a tragedy, but they are too conventional to the listener and too full of unconscious echoes. Modern speech, either colloquial or learned, on the other hand, seems to the hearer unalterably prosaic if not vulgar. Mr. Anderson mixes the two dictions up, and thus startles us into an awareness of the primary value of his words because we come upon them out of their conventional contexts. Sometimes the resulting incongruities are jarring and distasteful, particularly to the ear tuned to classical drama; sometimes, however, they are at least stimulating and fresh, perhaps beautiful.

Let us take examples. Since Trock is a gangster, we expect him to talk the lingo that fiction and the movies (if not experience) have taught us to associate with such gentry. Yet he is made to describe human beings as "these pismires that walk like men." "Pismires"! I am willing to bet that the author got that word, direct or indirect, from the King James version of the Bible. At all events, it is probably the last word that the best authority on American speech (H. L. Mencken, for instance), were he to be hanged for guessing wrong, would think of putting into the mouth of a contemporary "public enemy" just out of the penitentiary.

Again, Trock's henchman Shadow speaks:

> Because, look, chief,
> it's all against science and penology
> for you to get out and begin to cuss that way.

This juxtaposition of words like "penology" with words like "cuss" is, to say the least, unexpected, and it would only be in character if coming from a man of some culture and ironic observation of life. Coming from Shadow, it runs the danger of amusing rather than impressing us. At the same time, it is "heightened" language exactly because it is unexpected. If we cannot accept a gangster who talks like that as a real gangster, but rather feel that the author is talking through his mouth, nonetheless the remark is not verbally commonplace.

Learned and poetic words in several styles fall jumbled and strange from the lips of Mio, the "road boy" who is son of a huckster and has spent his last years bumming.

> Why, girl, the transfiguration on the mount
> was nothing to your face. It lights from within—
> a white chalice holding fire . . .

Or:

> His aromatic virtues, slowly rising
> will circumamb the isle, beyond disguising.
> He clung to life beyond the wont of men.
> Time and his silence drink us all. Amen.

How I hate these identicals [identical rimes]. The French allow them, but the French have no principles anyway. You know, Miriamne, there's really nothing mysterious about human life. It's purely mechanical, like an electric apparatus.

Or:

Fell in with a fisherman's family on the coast. . . . He sang while he fished. Made the pea-green Pacific ring with his bastard Greek chanties. Then I went to Hollywood High School for a while.

Can we really believe that even Hollywood High School, excellent as it may be among high schools, gives the most brilliant of its pupils such command of language and mature range of reference? Can we believe that he picked it up on the road?

We are troubled by such matters in spite of our wish to forget them in the poetic illusion, and hence the obvious difficulty with a play which the author himself called an experiment, recognizing, as he says, that "poetic tragedy has never been successfully written about its own place and time." It was easy for us to accept his employment of unrealistic speech when he put it into the mouths of Elizabeth and Essex, for it is enough like the speech that Shakespeare has made us associate with that period, and we feel it proper for such highborn folk to talk in a high style. We accept unrealistic speech in a play laid in foreign countries where English is not spoken, or in a period long past, since realistic speech in such a play is impossible. It is otherwise when such language comes from characters whom we might meet on the street. We may gladly admit that the author has avoided the commonplace; but he has not solved his problem.

Yet the advantage if not the necessity of heightening language for tragic effect is obvious, and playwrights will certainly want to write tragedies on contemporary themes since the greater immediacy of interest in such themes makes the risk involved in their diction one well worth running. A playwright can overcome the risk if he can make us lose ourselves in the splendor or vividness of the words. The trouble with the diction of *Winterset* is not that Mr. Anderson experimented, but that he did not always succeed in making us lose ourselves. At times, however, I think he was successful. The most notable instance, so far as my impressions are concerned, was not a passage of what is ordinarily considered poetic elevation. It was a speech of Trock's, and since it impressed me first in the theater, not on reading, I feel particularly justified in citing it as pure dramatic poetry.

> They've soaked me once too often
> in that vat of poisoned hell they keep upstate
> to soak men in, and I'm rotten inside, I'm all
> one liquid puke inside where I had lungs
> once.

We do not associate such words as "puke" with poetry because we have been conditioned to expect "poetry" to be always about pretty things, but such an expectation is the result of the sentimentalized, maiden-auntish way in which the arts have been taught to us. Poetry is about real things—when it is real poetry; and this expression is unhackneyed, vivid, and dramatically appropriate. Merely startling language, as we have observed, may be bad if it rouses the incongruous response or the critical faculties. But here Trock's words reveal Trock's background and depravity as no euphemisms could, and startle us into recognizing him as his author conceived him.

This praise is no recommendation of any extended use of Anglo-Saxon monosyllables just to shock the hearer. They are justified only when there is a legitimate dramatic reason for them, and such reasons come the more seldom because these words are so highly charged with emotional electricity. For that very reason they should be hoarded, as it were, and not squandered by the poet, since there are left in our English vocabulary few words to which constant use has left any power to give off sparks.

I think it is generally agreed that language is not Eugene O'Neill's strong point, and that in his more ambitious efforts toward tragedy he usually attains his effects through situation, sometimes in spite of the language. His failure is not for want of effort, for he has obviously labored over his speeches. It is not because he writes in prose; still less because he uses colloquialisms. Neither is it because he has no poetic ear, for his early plays of the sea, and passages in his later ones, prove the contrary. His main trouble, I believe, has come from his development of an excessive anxiety to convey to the audience the abstract meanings of his plays. Each of his later plays is a morality if not an allegory, and he seems so afraid that the listener will not understand its significance that he leaves nothing to the listener's imagination. He uses all manner of devices to emphasize meaning: masks and masklike make-up, symbolic costumes and groupings of actors, symbolic stage sets and formalized plots. The preëminent example of this abstraction is *The Great God Brown,* in which we are asked to accept an empty mask, in one scene, as a substitute for a human being. But the other late plays are full of it. In the mind of anyone acquainted with psychoanalysis, *Mourning Becomes Electra* rouses so much speculation about complexes and perversions that the plays of the trilogy seem more like a series of case histories than tragedies. Beneath the ponderous and obtrusive machinery of the plot scheme almost all human spontaneity and naturalness are squeezed out of the characters and they mouth like marionettes. (At least, for the reader. Good actors can help vivify them.) Such things prevent identification and hence tragic emotion; they foster impersonal moralizing.

So also with his style. Instead of expressing their own emotions in terms of their understanding of them, his characters often deliver sententious moralizings on the situation. These moralizings are plentifully supplied with exclamation points, and prettied up with adjectival posies from the garden of poetic diction, but they remain abstract, undramatic, unpoetic.

> "Your words are meaningless, Lazarus. You are a fool. All laughter is malice, all gods are dead, and life is a sickness."
>
> "So say the race of men, whose lives are long dyings! They evade their fear of death by becoming so sick of life that by the time death comes they are too lifeless to fear it."

> The laughter of Heaven sows earth with a rain of tears, and out of Earth's transfigured birth-pains the laughter of man returns to bless and play again in innumerable dancing gales of flame upon the knees of God.

Contemplate the eternal life of Life! . . . Be exalted by life! Be inspired by death! Be humbly proud! Be proudly grateful! Be immortal because life is immortal. [And so on, and on and on and on.][8]

Thus his intentness on meaning seldom frees the poet in him. One of the greatest powers of dramatic poetry, as of most great poetry of any sort, is the stimulus it gives to the imagination, so that the sensitive listener glimpses depths and complexities and nuances of meaning far beyond his capacity to analyze. To illustrate this point we might take more famous examples, but I should prefer an instance from another contemporary American prose dramatist. In *Our Town* Thornton Wilder almost never falls below poetry, but we may take the scene in which Emily's soul is permitted to return to the past and to her home on the morning of her twelfth birthday. Mr. Webb has remembered a present for her: "Yes, I've got something here." Mrs. Webb says, "Goodness sakes! I hope she likes what I got for her. I hunted hard enough fer it. Child*ren!* Hurry up! Hurry up!" Mr. Webb calls: "Where's my girl? Where's my birthday girl?"

MRS. WEBB. Don't interrupt her now, Charles. You can see her at breakfast. She's slow enough as it is. Hurry up, children! It's seven o'clock. Now, I don't want to call you again.

EMILY (*softly, more in wonder than in grief*). I can't bear it. They're so young and beautiful. Why did they ever have to get old? Mama, I'm here. I'm grown up. I love you all, everything.—

[8] The quotations are from *Lazarus Laughed, The Great God Brown,* and "*Marco Millions*," in *Nine Plays by Eugene O'Neill* (New York, Random House, n. d.).

I can't look at everything hard enough. There's the butternut tree.[9]

Here, if you look for them, are implications as profound as anything in *Lazarus Laughed* concerning life, death, and immortality, but they are implications, not preachments; they lie beneath the surface, where only the imagination can find them. And what is said is simple, homely, not prettied up, but dramatic dialogue made beautiful by its revelation of real people in a real situation full of unspoken love. Many people, not sentimentalists, have been moved to tears by that scene. I see no reason why it should not be called poetry.

In contrast consider the asides, or spoken thoughts, of *Strange Interlude,* which analyze, analyze, and instead of stimulating the imagination stultify it by declaring in effect that the *only* thoughts the characters think, of any importance, are those which they speak aloud.

DARRELL (thinking) [aside]. How much need I tell him? ... Can't tell him the raw truth about her promiscuity ... he isn't built to face reality ... no writer is, outside of his books ... have to tone it down for him ... but not too much!

[aloud]. Nina has been giving way more and more to a morbid longing for martyrdom ... [etc.]

In drama, then, overt verse rhythm seems less important for gaining the elevation of poetry than the right kind of language. Nonetheless, overt verse rhythm written by a poet and delivered by an artist may powerfully move us.

There are difficulties in finding the right meter for

[9] *Our Town* (New York, Coward-McCann, 1938).

modern tragedy. It is generally felt that Shakespearean blank verse cannot be used with the freshness and naturalness that made it right for Shakespeare, and that some other rhythm, perhaps more abrupt and harsh, is needed to express the characteristic moods and speech habits of our time. But this question cannot be answered by theorists; it must wait on the creative genius of the poets themselves.

I should like to suggest, however, that possibly the difficulties believed to exist in blank verse are not actually in the meter as such, but rather in the Shakespearean diction associated with it. It is easy to turn the vulgar tongue into iambic pentameters:

> Look out, the bulls! You guys had better scram!

But as soon as a dramatist seeks to rouse the mood of tragic elevation, memories of *Lear* and *Hamlet* flood upon him. Anderson's unevenness of effect clearly results from an imperfect fusion of his impulse toward "poetic diction" with his impulse toward the genuineness of contemporary speech. Until a dramatic poet succeeds in making the fusion perfect in the white heat of controlled inspiration, we are likely to prefer either the one or the other "straight." Some day our spoken language may prove adequate alone for elevated effect. Meanwhile, traditional poetic speech can still be beautiful in a play when a poet weeds the clichés out of it and uses it to express character in action.

I cannot do better in closing than to illustrate these possibilities of our literary heritage from T. S. Eliot. Mr. Eliot is not so sure in his sense for dramatic action as he is in his sense for lyric expressiveness, as we see in his pretentious and faintly absurd play, *The Family Reunion*.[10] Here is a good deal of merely lyrical poetry the meaning of which at times would certainly be hidden from a theatergoer. Yet in these passages the rhythm and diction cast a hypnotic spell.

The eye is on this house
The eye covers it
There are three together
May the three be separated
May the knot that was tied
Become unknotted
May the crossed bones
In the filled-up wall
Be at last straightened
May the weasel and the otter
Be about their proper business
The eye of the day time
Be diverted from this house
Till the knot is unknotted
The cross is uncrossed
And the crooked is made straight.

But Mr. Eliot can also write dramatic poetry, expressive of a character in a moving situation. Thus the speech of an old lady at the beginning of the play:

... I have nothing to do but watch the days draw out,
Now that I sit in the house from October to June,
And the swallow comes too soon and the spring will be over
And the cuckoo will be gone before I am out again.
O Sun, that was once so warm, O Light that was taken for granted

[10] New York, Harcourt, Brace, 1939.

When I was young and strong, and sun and light unsought for
And the night unfeared and the day expected
And clocks could be trusted, tomorrow assured
And time would not stop in the dark!
Put out the lights. But leave the curtains undrawn.
Make up the fire. Will the spring never come? I am cold.

Nothing could be less eccentric or more simple and conventional than the meter and diction here, yet how fresh it sounds, and how vividly it conveys the state of an aging woman clinging to physical life! Perhaps in passages such as this we see how a modern poet can speak in language that is both dramatically and lyrically beautiful.

Appendix: Toward a Working Library

THE STUDENT with limited funds will want to buy the most useful books first. Here are suggestions for his benefit.

PLAYS

The first necessity is of course the plays themselves, complete, not in condensed versions. Most value for one's money are the anthologies of great plays, of which there are a number. I should begin with one or two of the following:

Clark, B. H. *World Drama* (2 vols.) (1933)
Mantle, Burns. *A Treasury of the Theatre* (1935)
Matthews, Brander. *Chief European Dramatists* (1916)

I should then proceed with other volumes as my interest and means led me, but guided by a regard for the relative importance of the dramatists represented. A special interest in contemporary plays is natural, but for historical or intrinsic importance the following should be considered.

SUPREME DRAMATISTS

Shakespeare	Aeschylus	Racine
Molière	Euripides	Ibsen
Sophocles	Aristophanes	Corneille

ROMAN DRAMATISTS

Historically rather than intrinsically important.

Plautus · Terence · Seneca

ELIZABETHAN DRAMATISTS

Marlowe · Jonson · Webster

Beaumont and Fletcher

SPANISH, SEVENTEENTH CENTURY

Historically of some importance.

Lope de Vega · Calderón

GERMAN, EIGHTEENTH CENTURY

Lessing · Goethe · Schiller

EUROPEAN, NINETEENTH CENTURY

Hugo	Becque	Hauptmann
Scribe (Historical importance only!)	Rostand	Strindberg
	Maeterlinck	Chekhov
Dumas the Younger	Hebbel	

EUROPEAN, TWENTIETH CENTURY

(Among others!)

Gorky	Shaw	O'Neill
Synge	Maugham	Pirandello
O'Casey		

I have amused myself, at times, making lists of the ten best plays of the twentieth century. I offer one of these lists as a tentative selection.

TEN BEST PLAYS, 1900–1940

Chekhov, *The Cherry Orchard*
Shaw, *Saint Joan*
Synge, *The Playboy of the Western World*
Connelly, *The Green Pastures*
Molnar, *Liliom*
Gorky, *The Lower Depths*
Shaw, *Candida*
Romains, *Doctor Knock*
O'Neill, *The Emperor Jones*
Pirandello, *Six Characters in Search of an Author*

DRAMATIC THEORY

GENERAL

Clark, B. H. (ed.) *European Theories of the Drama*
A general and indispensable anthology of criticism from Aristotle to this century.

Nicoll, A. *The Theory of the Drama* (1931)
A revision of *An Introduction to Dramatic Theory*. A sound and scholarly introduction.

PLAYWRITING

Archer, W. *Play-Making* (1912)
Does not deal with modern experiments, but for traditional technique is the best work in a poorly represented field.

Baker, J. P. *Dramatic Technique* (1919)

Lawson, J. H. *Theory and Technique of Playwriting* (1936)
Stimulating, but controversial and difficult.

GENERAL REFERENCES

Sobel, B. (ed.) *Theatre Handbook and Digest of Plays* (1940)
A useful though far from complete reference for facts; biased and undependable for theory.

The Theater

Allen, J. T. *Stage Antiquities of the Greeks and Romans*

Cheney, S. *The Theatre* (1935)
A good one-volume survey; readable; excellent illustrations.

Dean, A. *Fundamentals of Play Directing* (1941)

Dolman, J. *The Art of Play Production* (1928)

Freedley, G., and Reeves, J. A. *A History of the Theatre* (1941)
Too crammed with facts about both theater and drama to be easy reading, but a useful reference.

Histories of the Drama

Stuart, D. C. *The Development of Dramatic Art* (1928)
Scholarly; emphasizes the relation of the theater to the drama.

Gassner, J. *Masters of the Drama* (1940)
Critically interesting and readable.

General Bibliographies

in books listed above

Clark, *European Theories of the Drama*
Bibliographies with each historic group of selections.

Dolman, *Play Production*
Nine pages, well selected for students of play production.

Freedley and Reeves, *History of the Theatre*
A total of 433 items.

Gassner, *Masters of the Drama*
Twenty-five pages.

Nicoll, *Theory of the Drama*
Twelve pages of "suggestions" for reading.

Sobel, *Theatre Handbook*

Thirty pages, compiled by George Freedley, of works in English published during the last quarter century.

IN SEPARATE VOLUMES

Baker, Blanch M. *Dramatic Bibliography* (1933)

"An annotated list of books on the history and criticism of the drama and stage and on the allied arts of the theatre."

Faxon, F. W. *Dramatic Index for Periodicals*

From 1909. Supplements the *Reader's Guide*. "Covering articles and illustrations concerning the stage and its players in the periodicals of America and England; with a record of books on the drama and of texts of plays." Issued separately and as Part II of Annual Magazine Subject-Index.

Gilder, Rosamond. *A Theatre Library* (1932)

"A bibliography of 100 books relating to the theatre."

Index

(See also lists of plays and books in the Appendix, pp. 398–402)